TX
911
L47
2015

Levander, Caroline
Field, 1964-
Hotel life

DISCARD

SEP 0 6 2016

D0712157

Hotel
Life

Hotel Life

The Story of a Place Where Anything Can Happen

Caroline Field Levander & Matthew Pratt Guterl

The University of North Carolina Press CHAPEL HILL

This book was published with the assistance of the
Thornton H. Brooks Fund
of the University of North Carolina Press.

© 2015 The University of North Carolina Press
All rights reserved
Set in Garamond Premier Pro by codeMantra, Inc.
Manufactured in the United States of America
The paper in this book meets the guidelines for permanence and durability
of the Committee on Production Guidelines for Book Longevity of the Council
on Library Resources. The University of North Carolina Press has been a
member of the Green Press Initiative since 2003.

Jacket illustration: Peacock Alley in the historic Willard Hotel,
Washington, D.C. (Photographs in the Carol M. Highsmith Archive, Prints and
Photographs Division, Library of Congress)

Library of Congress Cataloging-in-Publication Data
Levander, Caroline Field
Hotel life : the story of a place where anything can happen /
Caroline Field Levander and Matthew Pratt Guterl.
pages cm
Includes bibliographical references and index.
ISBN 978-1-4696-2112-8 (cloth : alk. paper)
ISBN 978-1-4696-2113-5 (ebook)
1. Hospitality industry. 2. Hotels.
3. Travelers. I. Guterl, Matthew Pratt II. Title.
TX911.L47 2015
647.94—dc23
2014031684

MIX
Paper from
responsible sources
FSC
www.fsc.org   FSC® C013483

For our families

And especially for Torrey,
who loved nothing more
than to have a hotel bed all to himself

And for Tom and Jeanne Pratt,
who would have thought this book
was a hoot

I have kept a hotel room in every town I've ever lived in. . . . I go into the room and I feel as if all my beliefs are suspended. Nothing holds me to anything . . . And I'll remember how beautiful, how pliable language is. . . . I remember that and I start to write.

—Maya Angelou, *Paris Review*, 1990

The [hotel] room is what I need, what I've been imagining for the past two days—a place with much passing and no record. . . . Coming to the motel is a way to trick myself out of anonymity, to urge my identity to rise like cream to the top again.

—Tess Gallagher, *A Concert of Tenses*, 1987

People ask where the "hotel" title/idea came from. . . . The title "hotel" is mainly inspired by the idea of the temporary. . . . We stay in hotels for brief periods of time. They are places where we live but that are not our homes.

—Moby, *Journal*, April 7, 2005

Contents

Illustrations

Acknowledgments

Hotel Life began as an act of friendship.

Over a cup of coffee at the Hotel Zaza's famed Monarch restaurant on one of Matt's research trips to Houston, we asked: Wouldn't it be fun to write a book together? The answer was immediate and unequivocal. The next question was, initially, a bit more difficult to answer: What should we take as our subject? As we looked around the restaurant's lush environs and gazed into the hotel's flamboyant reception area, as we watched the swirling orchestration of staff, the arrangement of space, and started to talk about the building and its complex social life, we began to find our answer. Roughly four years and a thousand emails later, here is the book: proof, if we all needed it, that good friendship can be the wellspring of new ideas.

Other kinds of friendship sustained the effort. Colleagues wondered what we were doing—a literary critic and a historian, writing a book about something that seemed peripheral to our more conventionally disciplined research programs. Co-writing an entire book seemed risky as well—not the norm, particularly as we wrote the entire manuscript a thousand miles apart and split up our fieldwork. We never stayed in the same hotel, but we'd share notes from the bar in a midtown boutique, or a photo taken in the back kitchen of a palatial conference site. Friends joked that we were taking our respective families on "research" trips to some of the most interesting archives of all time. And, of course, family members and loved ones were amused, intrigued, and always ready to be our "scouts" on the ground at every hotel to receive them.

A number of people read the manuscript—in part or in whole—and helped us to develop ideas. Consistently these readers enthused over our effort to establish a certain seamlessness of voice, remarking that they appreciated those stretches where they couldn't tell where one author began and the other left off. We took this as steady encouragement that our project was working. Scott Herring, Denise Cruz, and Katie Lofton read chapters, talked through sections, and prompted us to refine our original conceptions. On the road and moving from one state to another, Khalil Muhammad sent relevant link after link. In Bloomington, Carol

Glaze and Paula Cotner booked rooms, lobbied for financial support, and got behind the idea fast. Because our ambition from the start was to write a book that would intrigue a general, informed audience—those who stay in hotels frequently on their travels through the world's urban spaces, and those who work in them as well—we asked for a lot of help along the way. Nancy Carlson was key to getting us into the Hotel Anatole's back of house, Michele Vobach facilitated an interview with Caroline Rose Hunt, and a range of interested interlocutors and partners in crime including Michael Maltzan, Kevin Kirby, Nicole Waligora-Davis, Jeffrey Schnapp, Tim Dean, Kelly Reynolds, Julie Fette, Dave Jacqua, John Drewer, and Leigh Frillici provided incredibly creative feedback about the project at various stages of conceptualization and execution. Gayatri Patnaik repeatedly gave us good, solid advice. To them all we are deeply grateful.

We owe much, as well, to UNC Press. Mark Simpson-Vos loved this project from the first moment he heard about it, but also let us take it in a direction of our choosing. Anonymous reviewers for the press were constructively critical and enthusiastic—so much so that their words sustained us late in the game.

And at every hotel, guests and staff tolerated our weird fieldwork. Asking to see the laundry room. Hoodwinking the hotel manager and begging for a peek at the pastry kitchen. Ordering a drink at the bar, and taking notes on the field of play. Surveying the room-cleaning cart. We benefited, at every road stop and every detour, from the willingness of service staff, managers, and design experts to speak with candor—and often with great emotion—about the institution that defines their lives, that opens some doors and closes others. We each lingered a bit too long and watched a little too closely, and we hope that the result is as interesting—and as illuminating—for the reader as it was for the authors.

Hotel Life

INTRODUCTION

People stay at a hotel for many reasons. Ask, and you might be told, "I was on the road, and I needed a place to sleep." This is a pragmatist's answer, focusing on the usefulness and utilitarian value of the hotel. But people stay at hotels for other reasons, too. They recognize that there is usually more to be gained by renting a room than just a good night's sleep—that there are a variety of less tangible and often unspoken needs, wants, hopes, and desires that a hotel stay might be able to provide. And whether that additional value can be measured or not, they want it. Whether it is real or not, they expect it.

As the epigraphs of this book suggest, for the poet Maya Angelou the hotel offers release from the everyday and exhilarating connection to creative language; for Tess Gallagher, the hotel's anonymity is itself a provocation, its indistinguishable rooms a challenge for their temporary inhabitants to rediscover a long-forgotten originality and clarity of purpose; and for the recording artist Moby, it is a rich analogy for the impermanence of relationships and life in general, an ultimate referent that is deeply generative of creative musical expression. But, of course, these are only a sampling of the seemingly infinite array of expectations that travelers bring to the hotel in modern times.

This book is about what, beyond sleep and shelter for the traveler, the hotel offers and why, particularly over the past century, people seek it out with increasing frequency and urgency.

Hotel Life is, at its core, an excavation of the shifting hopes, dreams, and desires that go along with the plastic key card in every room rate and package deal. As Norman Hayner observed almost eighty years ago, hotel life is a transient life—it is characterized, on the one hand, by mobility and detachment and, on the other hand, by freedom and release from restraint. The hotel concentrates and packages these differing aspects of "modern life as a whole" to those seeking temporary shelter within the

In this multipanel cartoon from the magazine *Puck*, which appeared in 1901, the hotel "Walledoff"—a play on the Waldorf Astoria—is reimagined as a social machine, transforming a collection of backcountry rubes into members of high society. The transformation, *Puck* assures its readers, who are in on the joke, is rooted in a fundamental error, as the sojourning, fish-out-of-water country folk continually misread each encounter. Nevertheless, the machine does its work, and they emerge, at the end of their stay, significantly more polished and presentable than before. Thus does the hotel make it possible for anyone and everything to be remade. The hotel makes this tiny social revolution possible, but it also makes a hundred other parallel transformations possible, too. (Theatrical Poster Collection, Prints and Photographs Division, Library of Congress, Washington, D.C.)

hotel's welcoming arms, and it has done so with increasing imagination, ubiquity, and comprehensiveness over the second half of the twentieth century.[1] Both Rebecca Onion and Molly Berger point out that the nineteenth-century hotel previewed "something profoundly modern" for guests, offering temporary shelter from "the harshness of modern life" and foreshadowing the numerous contemporary privatized public spaces (like theme parks, cruise ships, shopping malls, and resorts) that have come to define urban modernity.[2] Indeed, modern life at the beginning of the twenty-first century is, at times, so seamlessly integrated with hotel life as to make distinctions between the two difficult to trace and disentangle. And so, the story that we tell in the following pages of *Hotel Life* is, inevitably, a story about the making, refining, and managing of this modern self.

Hotel Life shows how and why the hotel cuts to the core of what it means to be human in modern times. Widely ranging across a dynamic array of archives, materials, and cultural forms, the following pages sketch a particular history for the hotel in the modern era—a history in which the increasingly prevalent and familiar institution of the hotel comes to play, much like its seeming opposites the prison or asylum or the home or the school, a powerful role in the constitution of the modern self. Here, we are providing an alternative history and a cultural genealogy of sorts, a history conceptually driven and therefore a history that engages with a differently envisioned archive—an archive of source material encompassing a wide range of visual and textual forms—for it is through this unorthodox mix of various kinds of materials that we can begin to delineate the ways in which the hotel, not merely as bricks and mortar or physical site but as imaginative location and shelter, comes to enable the creation, design, and curation of the modern self over time. And so, because the hotel provides creative inspiration for musicians, poets, and fiction writers like Moby, Gallagher, and Angelou, it leaves behind a dynamic and diverse evidentiary trail that takes us well beyond the usual source material. The hotel, then, is something of an imaginative challenge because it—the structure, the idea, and the traces of both—is always transforming, shifting, and mobile.

The French word "hotel" did not come into general usage until the nineteenth century, beginning with the opening in 1827 of Boston's Tremont Hotel—the world's largest with its resplendent 170 rooms—but this new feature of the urban landscape quickly differentiated itself from other modern institutions like the prison or hospital or even the home. If, as Hayner provocatively points out, the "best American prisons with their short length of stay, wholesome food, recreational programs and radio in every cell" might at first glance resemble the plethora of second-class hotels springing up in major urban areas to house transient populations, the crucial differentiating factor is guests' freedom to check out whenever they wish—to remain transient and mobile as inclination and necessity might dictate (47). This "chance at hypermobility," Onion rightly observes, proved as powerfully alluring to hotel guests as the hotel's modern fixtures. Popular renderings of the Tremont Hotel emphasized this key feature of the new institution—showing its role as a hub for citizens constantly on the move by placing newly arriving guests, whether they approached by coach, car, or on foot, into dynamic exchange with those satisfied guests who were just checking out.[3]

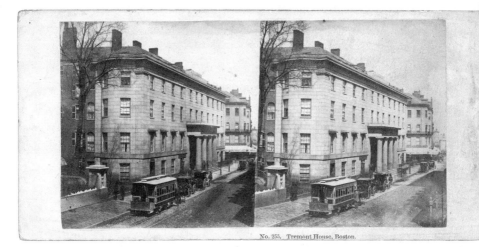

No. 253. Tremont House, Boston.

The Tremont Hotel around 1865, with a line of carriages for people coming and going, precursors to the modern taxi stand. (John P. Soule; Robert N. Dennis Collection of Stereoscopic Views, Miriam and Ira D. Wallach Division of Art, Prints and Photographs, New York Public Library, Astor, Lenox and Tilden Foundations)

This very factor also differentiates the hotel from the prison's seeming opposite—a home life that is, as Hayner observes, commonly associated with "hearth and fireside, wife and children, rather than with movement, bright lights and a detached existence" (50). Sinclair Lewis pinpoints the imaginative release from home that the hotel provides individuals who check in precisely because they want to "get away from feeling at home"—because they are "earnestly sick of wives, yelping children, balky furnaces, household bills, and getting the lawn mowed."[4] For an increasing number of twentieth-century individuals, the hotel became a permanent escape from the home, and both men and women chose to take up permanent residence in hotels, seeing the hotel as an enticing alternative to mind-deadening, time-consuming chores and obligations, thereby providing freedom to live as they chose. Even for those taking up only temporary residence in hotels, the innovations to modern life pioneered by hotels—from bathtubs to modern heating arrangements, to comfortable beds—became desired features in travelers' permanent abodes. As a result, homes came to function, feel, and look more like hotels, even as hotels, conversely, offered family members temporary escape from a home space that could all too easily feel like a prison.

Given the dynamic, mutually informing tensions between hotel life and the life enabled by these other modern institutions, the aim of *Hotel*

Life is not simply to analyze the hotel rather than the prison or home as a physical and cultural location. More pointedly, the following pages assess how the hotel helps to constitute a modern and highly mobile self, a self that is fashioned through movement, escape, and temporary respite in alternative shelter instead of the stasis of the prison, the asylum, or even the home. Because the hotel, as Hayner observes, represents in concentrated form "modern life as a whole," a central component of the hotel's power as a modern institution is its ability to "create" or "manufacture" things as different as empire and affect (182). Yet, even at the hotel's most muscular, such power is never absolute.

In the course of writing the following pages, we have been asked repeatedly whether the hotel is ultimately a site of freedom or coercion— whether, in the final analysis, the hotel, in all its myriad forms, is inevitably part of capitalism's well-oiled machine or a site of resistance to the ubiquitous press of globalization. To understand the complex and multiform work of the hotel in contemporary American culture, however, requires that we ultimately resist this understandable opposition. As the following pages make clear, the hotel and the various kinds of life it enables create uncomfortable, inadvertent complicities and local acts of resistance, both of which are an inevitable part of modern life. The hotel is never just one thing. It is always a site of power and resistance, authority and self-fashioning, dominance and subversion.

Hotel Life calls attention to the powerful role of late capitalism in the life that the modern hotel enables, but the pages ahead simultaneously emphasize key lessons learned from performance studies—that the stakes of revolutions are not always determined by architects and builders and owners and that resistance does not have to take the form of a massive subversion of capital in order for it to matter, historically or philosophically. We position the hotel as a dynamic form of global capitalism in order to offer an account of a modern space that has been created with the capacity to remake us in an uneasy era of biopolitical self-management. But we do not reduce the hotel to an all-determining structure. We seek, among other things, to remap the biopolitics of modern space through careful consideration of the lived experiences the hotel offers, frustrates, and enables. And we look for subtle indications of the hotel's failure to control or constrain individual self-making. While hotels might facilitate release from the discontents of late capitalism, they, nonetheless, remain part and parcel of a largely unrepentant liberal capitalist system. Hotels, though, are not passive sites but bring a power of their own to the resident experience, real or imagined. A central goal of *Hotel Life*, then, is to encourage readers to debate the work of the hotel in modern life, to frame that debate broadly, rather than narrowly, and to include contradictory social, emotional, and psychological investments in the hotel. In what follows we ask everyone to revisit the experience of familiar spaces, to reconsider the systems and structures behind the creation of these spaces, and to reflect on the actions of self-creation that are staged within these spaces—often against the odds.

For anyone interested in the globalized world of the present, the stakes of *Hotel Life* should be abundantly clear: as worldwide movements and circulations increasingly become common, and as notions of the self shift to an internationalist mode, the institutional armature enabling and frustrating fully realized iterations of this self change, too. While the hotel is a fixed structure, made of brick and concrete and steel and rooted, literally, into the bedrock of a specific site, the life it supports and enables—across the full socioeconomic spectrum—is defined by transience and dislocation. For Foucault, such constraining institutions give rise to the carceral state, the medical authority, and the rational subject. But the hotel, we suggest, is an institution that utilizes space to amplify and refine an explicitly mobile, cosmopolitan self—a self that imagines the hotel as a site for fantastic, ever-shifting expressions of living and dying, fortune and failure, beginnings and endings—in short, of a life bigger, bolder, wilder, cleaner, and more therapeutic than "real life." In an age of giant conglomerates, massive box stores, elaborate transit systems, and global communications networks, the hotel has been engineered as the antiprison, a rewarding site "away from home," an alternate domestic universe, and an adult play space. That engineering feat, we submit, has consequences.

Histories

The hotel life we focus on is a contemporary thing, partially a product of a history that, by and large, falls outside of the direct purview of this book even as it shapes our critique. But if the hotel is now a malleable thing—an iconic symbol of modernity's seemingly infinite plasticity and eagerness to please—this functionality developed over time and place. The German philosopher Immanuel Kant, writing in the midst of the Enlightenment, contended that a "*right to visit* . . . belong[ed] to all human beings" and, therefore, that hospitality was a necessary element enabling "distant parts of the world" to enter "peaceably into relations with each other."[5] Kant's vision of a mobile modern society—a society in which peace is attainable through the introduction into close-knit and static communities of travelers, strangers, and world wanderers and the temporary integration of such unmoored individuals into these communities through centers of hospitality—coincided with the development of the modern hotel.

While the hotel, as we know it, sprang up in urban centers across the world in direct response to the mobility and transience coming to define modern life, its emergence, as A. K. Sandoval-Strausz has observed, coincided particularly forcefully with American beliefs about liberal democracy and the consent of the governed. Not only did an officer of the new federal government order the construction of the nation's first hotel project along the banks of the Potomac in preparation for the new U.S. capital, but hotel building was integral to effective U.S. governance because of the extreme need for travel accommodation across an increasingly vast national landscape. George Washington's inauguration in New York City and subsequent travels through the nation's major cities generated community embarrassment about the limits of local taverns and inns to accommodate the new head of state, and Washington often found himself housed in private homes that were temporarily repurposed as hotels for the duration of his stay.

But if the new government-in-the-wilderness's need for temporary housing adequate to meet the needs of an immensely popular first president and his entourage was greater than that of more-established and well-populated nations, the conceptual transformations the hotel underwent in the process of meeting this need were startlingly dramatic. Indeed, this unlikely coupling of U.S. democracy and hospitality has been widely attributed with the invention of what Sandoval-Strausz describes as "the architectural and social form that became the international standard for sheltering travelers."[6] By the 1820s, when hotels were understood as an index of community vitality and economic robustness, one social commentator observed that "a good hotel means a prosperous town, and a public-spirited town would have a good hotel."[7] Built lavishly with the financial backing of each city's most affluent families, the City Hotel in Baltimore (1826), the National Hotel in Washington, D.C. (1827), the Tremont Hotel in Boston (1827), and the United States Hotel in Philadelphia (1828) signaled that the hotel was an economically viable concern in American cities. The quick uptake of this kind of hotel in smaller cities and towns springing up as settlers moved west became a key feature of U.S. economic and commercial development.

Within these luxurious venues, popularly referred to as "palaces of the public," the kind of public that convened to enjoy the hotel's bars, restaurants, lobbies, and meeting spaces captured the attention of foreign visitors, most notably for the hotel's radical social democracy—for its range across all social classes from the richest and most well bred to the speculator and adventurer. The class variability and promiscuous sociability that bubbled up in the alternative public space created by the hotel were widely commented on in local publications as well—the range of customers including all members of modern society, regardless of rank, gender, age, or profession. As a writer for the *New York Mirror* observed in 1836, hotel public spaces were a magnet for all kinds of social interactions between different sectors of the public—"the beau, the belle, the merchant and the scholar, the poet, the editor, the Wall-Street broker, ladies to meet their lovers, and tradesmen" looking to finalize a deal.[8]

But hotels not only provided discrete public spaces that brought unlikely partners into contact at their particular location; they also formed a multisite network connecting people across multiple cities and locations. The first book on hotel management published in the United States—*Hotel Keepers, Head Waiters, and Housekeepers' Guide* (1848)—recognized this very fact and made specific recommendations on how to ensure that each hotel became a successful part of the larger public whole of which it was a member. Author Tunnis G. Campbell insisted that hotel owners and proprietors needed to travel through the country, meet other hotelkeepers, tour hotels in other cities, and learn major travel routes—in short, understand their individual property's location in a larger mobile public network—in order to successfully serve customers who travel from city to city for work, leisure, or both and reside in hotels along the way.

Even as the hotels springing up across the country offered dynamic meeting grounds for an American public, they also worked to refine and segregate the public spaces they offered, creating private reserves for the elite or for those with the same religious or racial affiliations. In its imperial guise, the hotel became all too often the advance guard of colonialist privilege rather than the hospitable peace-building haven that Kant envisioned at the dawn of modernity, carefully parsing privilege instead of extending social justice across national divides. Astronomical prices often reinforced social and economic privilege for a new class of global cosmopolitan elites who traveled from place to place, calling one elite hotel after another home as they consecutively whiled away weeks or even months moving from the Italian coast, to the French Riviera, to the world's most glamorous urban centers. Insulating their privilege regardless of where they traveled, the luxury hotel created a network of elite outposts for the world's most entitled populace.

It is no surprise, then, that mid-twentieth-century civil rights activists targeted the hotel as a particularly fraught site of racial exclusion, protesting against hotels' well-established policies of racial discrimination by carrying signs that demanded "Room at the inn for weary (white) travelers."[9] Aligning race-based refusal of services to the Christian master narrative of the hotel's founding failure to shelter the Messiah, these protesters were responding to a century-long struggle that featured the hotel as a prime site of racial contestation—a struggle that began with Senator Charles Sumner's Civil Rights Act of 1875.

First introduced into the Senate in 1870, this bill initially stipulated that all citizens would be entitled to equal treatment in a broad range of public places, but the hotel quickly became the lightening rod for Sumner's defense of and others' resistance to the bill. Trading on the well-established common law of innkeepers that stipulated that hoteliers could deny service to no one with the ability to pay, Sumner advocated for the bill by stating explicitly that inns and hotels were the legal prototypes from which general principles must be drawn: "As the inn cannot close its doors . . . to any paying traveler, decent in condition, so must it be with the theater and other places of public amusement."[10] Foes of Sumner's bill likewise invoked the hotel, claiming that it was not a prototypical public venue but a blend of public and private concerns—not only a public facility operated according to laws but also a private space controlled by its owner. Here the hotel's intricate and evolving blend of public and private arenas, services, and opportunities was brought into play to resist social transformation. As Congressman Durham of Kentucky put it, it makes no more sense for the government to dictate who can and should enter a hotel than to dictate "who shall enter a man's private house."[11]

When the Civil Rights Act of 1875 did become law by a vote of 35–18 in the Senate and 118–94 in the House, the hotel immediately became the battleground on which the racial transformation of public and private life occurred. Black citizens in Richmond entered the Exchange Hotel asking for service, and a black minister requested a room in the Bingham

House in Philadelphia, sitting in the lobby when he was refused service and collecting evidence on all subsequent white guests who were admitted to the hotel that night—evidence he delivered the next morning to the local U.S. attorney. Unable to confront the change, some hotels in Virginia closed their premises the day after the bill passed, while others repurposed themselves, closing and then reopening as private boardinghouses. Whether or not hotels stayed open, redefined themselves, or became sites of local resistance and rebellion, they were operationally ground zero for political protest and upheaval.

But just as soon as the open lobby was shuttered in segregated hotels, alternate hotels emerged to meet the needs of black travelers and foreign guests. The institutional need, we might say, was too great to be denied. Most famous of these open spaces was the Hotel Theresa, located at the busy, public soapbox corner of 7th Avenue and 125th Street in Harlem, just down the block from the Apollo Theater. Built in 1913 and desegregated as the neighborhood switched over to an African American population, the Theresa was known as "the Waldorf of Harlem."[12] Wealthy guests, unwilling to take the back entrance and stay in a Jim Crow room elsewhere, or hoping to capture the magic of the uptown nightlife, stayed at the Theresa. And they did so until the global edifice of segregation was dismantled, and the real Waldorf—roughly sixty blocks south—became available. By the 1970s, the legendary Hotel Theresa had become an office building, its social function replaced, if imperfectly, by the thousands of other city hotels that now welcomed black guests.[13] Today, it stands as a public landmark in New York City and houses programs and offices attached to nearby Teachers College, Columbia University.

The story of the Theresa reminds us that, over the past two centuries, the great, enduring, weird, and rich institution of the hotel has been the bellwether of social and political transformation, such as desegregation, but it has also been the backdrop and staging ground for a series of discrete yet highly charged political interactions and negotiations. As quasi-public space, the hotel is an alternative to other, more private—and therefore, less accessible—places. One thinks of Malcolm X and Fidel Castro, enjoying "Harlem hospitality" at the Theresa. Or Josephine Baker at the Los Angeles Biltmore, accosted at breakfast by a white patron from the South, having him arrested and practically chasing the police to the courthouse to press charges. Or of the Chelsea, once a hotbed of countercultural ferment, and then a site of union protest against

James Farmer of
CORE in 1965,
speaking on civil
rights, with the
Hotel Theresa
as a backdrop.
(Photo by Stanley
Wolfson; Prints
and Photographs
Division, Library
of Congress,
Washington, D.C.)

unfair working conditions. There is the Algonquin, establishing the vivid wit of New York City and defining the hotel as a creative hotspot. And then there is UNITE HERE, mobilizing service workers within the Global Hyatt chain across borders and empires; the same Hyatt chain, now with protests against the CEO's support of a ban on gay marriage in California; civil rights picket lines, with placards asking for equal access to the "public" accommodations; the Berkeley riots of the 1960s, bringing together antiwar, feminist, and black power constituencies in front of the Sheraton Palace; the burning of the Bull's Head hotel on the first day of the New York City draft riots of 1863; the drafting of the earliest versions of the U.N. Declaration of Human Rights at the Fairmont in San Francisco in the summer of 1945. In these cases, and myriad others, the hotel's enduring popularity as an important crossroads has made it a highly conducive, logical, and often inevitable setting for protest, for awakening, for historic drama.

The institution that emerged from this two-hundred-year history—from the founding of the republic through the desegregation of the hospitality industry and the globalization of consumer capitalism—is the object of our attention in the chapters that follow. Cosmopolitan and seemingly desegregated, the modern hotel that is our subject now purports to be well beyond the national interest, even when it clearly is not. These days, for instance, we do not tend to talk about the service industry, and about hotels in particular, the way we talk about the fate of manufacturing. The hotel, unlike the auto plant, does not seem to foretell the nation's fate. Likewise, these days, the guest is all too often presumed to be homogeneous and raceless. No one talks about a "white only" or "black only" hotel any longer, even if wealth and access are highly racially determined, and even if, beyond "the guest," racial hierarchies are still at work within the hotel's walls. These histories still matter, though they are deliberately obscured, much like any evidence of prior guests' presences is quickly wiped clean from the hotel rooms that the modern guest occupies. The hotel wants us to forget its implicated past.

Writing an analysis of hotel life means, therefore, that we aim to *see* the hotel as more than context, as more than historical backdrop and artifact. It means that we also approach the hotel as the pitch-perfect expression of the dreams and aspirations that can create social change and political risk-taking but are not completely reducible to them, and such an analysis of hotel life highlights the role that the so-called American dream in particular—expressed in an unrepentant liberal capitalist context—plays in the imaginary that the hotel enables and sustains. With a permanent and real upper class set above the rest of the world, elite hotels provide an opportunity for the sort of fawning attentions that differentiate those people who "matter"—the truly rich and influential—from those who do not. In an age of declining wages and abundant credit, middling hotels provide temporary upward mobility, a chance to buy your way into a cleaner environment, a more therapeutic relation, or a racier sex life. For poor people, hotels offer the bare minimum required to survive, which is just enough to contain them, far from the bourgeois crowds of the public square. Presenting itself as a postnational, postracial institution, and infinitely more concerned, at the top end, with luxury, the new hotel—the hotel of the present—foregrounds economic class and social stratification in very particular ways, sometimes mirroring "the American dream," and sometimes cutting against the grain of American culture, and against our general refusal to consider the political economy and institutional perpetuation of wealth and privilege. But at every single step, it reveals nothing so clearly as the desiring, wanting human self.

Once we step back from the history of specific hotels as well as from the history of the hotel's more general development and emergence on the modern scene—replete with its requisite entrepreneurial ambition, new business models, and consumer demand—we are able to see that the hotel's institutional function as an oft-changing backdrop is a powerfully productive constant upon which much of its imaginative power depends for those seekers walking through lobby doors. When we say, here, that the hotel is only partially a product of a history that goes beyond our interests, we mean, then, that the story of one hotel or another, or the story of hotels and social inequality, are merely illustrative examples of the abstract thing itself. This dimension of the hotel and the various kinds of life it enables and frustrates is our focus in the following pages.

Space

To anyone who has ever watched movies like *Pretty Woman* or *Maid in Manhattan*, there is nothing surprising in the fact that hotels and the kinds of flexible spaces they offer guests and workers can effect transformations that are life changing—transformations, for example, of sex workers and domestics into ladies who lunch. No one can be shocked that, in the particular kind of space the hotel creates, there is sex work along with domestic work, or that the staff manages this work, formally or informally, legally or illegally—not when the Hollywood conception of "romance" includes Edward Lewis's weeklong engagement with Vivian Ward, a hard-luck call girl brought to the Regent Beverly Wilshire and given a makeover by the hotel's concierge, or when, in a gauzier version, a sexy maid gets "remade" into the literal image of the affluent woman patron whose room she cleans and whose wealthy suitor she steals. Popular culture is saturated with "proof" that hotels are places where boys can go wild, where rules governing sex, class, and labor can be broken and temporarily remade. And it is filled, too, with images of personal transformation, so that every "hooker with a heart of gold" or underpaid domestic sees, within its interior labyrinth and her movement through its inner cavities, a narrowing route to a better life. These parallel searches for something more, we believe, deserve serious and imaginative scrutiny.

The particular kinds of space that the hotel creates and makes available are the subject of special attention in what follows. To take seriously Henri Lefebvre's observation that capitalism has survived and flourished over the past century largely through the production of modern space—through a radical reconceptualization of urban and rural, public and private, loci of human encounter and exchange—is, of necessity, to see the hotel as an essential incubator of capital's foundational social apparatus. Yet, in the rich analyses of urban space that have proliferated in the past few decades by those working across architecture, social and political theory, sociology, philosophy, literary theory, and urbanism, the hotel has remained oddly just out of view—obscured within the larger networks of modern meaning making that we have developed to understand the current human condition.[14]

And this may be, in part, because of all modern spaces, the hotel is one of the most malleable. This very malleability makes the hotel at once a destination point for the world's transient peoples and a largely invisible and undertheorized dimension of modern life. Its easily repurposed meeting rooms that transform from convention breakout spaces to wedding reception venues in the blink of an eye reinforce on an architectural register what the hotel imaginatively provides the diverse array of guests, workers, managers, security detail, and interested passersby who turn to the hotel to find solace, opportunity, refuge, enticement, and distraction, among many other things. It can be a palace, a home, an outpost, a refuge, a grim factory, a den of iniquity, a veritable slave pen, and sometimes all of these things at once. It can be heaven or hell, home or away, a constraining institution or an emancipatory site, a beginning or an ending. Eugene O'Neill's famous final utterance—"born in a hotel room, and God damn it, die in a hotel room"—recognizes the hotel's ability to move seamlessly from birthing room to hospice. No other institution in the modern world presents itself as the solution to so many of life's different problems. No other institution so perfectly represents the political economy of a twenty-first-century modernity marked by an unbridgeable gulf between rich and poor, by the brief, wish-fulfillment ethos of postmodern capitalism, and by the simple need to house the very rich and the very poor as they move around the globe, chasing profit and survival. As such, the hotel becomes an imaginative place where "anything can happen" and where people's stories unfold with marked urgency and meaning. And it is this fact, in turn, that makes the story of hotel life one particularly worth telling.

If a stay in the hotel is comparatively brief and presumably voluntary, and its impact supposedly fleeting, it is no less true that, like prisons and clinics, hotels narrate a change, or an aspiration. They are, too, sites of permanent privilege and power, sites of ritual relations and wildly unpredictable encounters, staging grounds for the enactment of race, class, and gender, and regulated transfer stations for human traffic and capital movement. The guest comes and goes, and something happens during the stay. That thing—that something that happens—is at the heart of the institutional purpose of the contemporary hotel. In the coming and the going to a single fixed site, there is the hope of transformation of some kind. We intend, here, to expose the deeper meanings of this hope to the light of day and, in so doing, to induce the reader to take the pulse and feel the heartbeat of hotel life.

As *Hotel Life* illustrates, regardless of what its environment enables, the hotel, more than anything else, is a particularly powerful modern institution precisely because it offers latent possibility in material form. It is, first and foremost, an institution of improvement, personal transformation, and reform. A symphony of brick, glass, steel, and concrete, the building can rearrange public and private space, fostering new, stylized rituals of encounter and exchange, isolation and exposure. A way station for strangers passing through some city or town, the hotel can be a substitute for the home, guarding against the knock at the door, and sequestering the tired, foreign face in search of a warm bed. The hotel is a potential therapeutic space, offering up attentive service, from the practiced friendly smile at the counter, the slickly helpful bellhop, the mute busy-ness of the cleaning staff during the day, to the mints, the high-thread-count sheets, the soft bed, the folded toilet paper, the stacks of perfect, fluffy towels, the immaculately clean presentation of every detail. Hotels are also sometimes residential and sometimes commercial zones, where every private space comes with the chance of "add-ons," and where every stroll through the lobby brings with it an opportunity to buy a coffee or some tourist swag.

Within this structure of shifting possibilities, the hotel guest can seemingly become anything, too. The body and mind can be restored, repaired, and put back in order, improved and enhanced beyond what is normal. The sexual self can be released or buttoned-up. Racial fantasies can be temporarily hardened or obliterated. An ordinary person can, for a limited time, become a king or a queen. A welfare recipient can have a modicum of domesticity. A weary traveler can find shelter from the rain and snow, and rest at the end of a day of rapid movement. These are the sorts of tantalizing improvements offered by the hotel, and implicitly or explicitly sought by the guest.

But these changes—when they occur—are temporary, and their affect is aspirational. Whatever happens in a hotel, whatever might change, the cultural logic of the institution dictates that it usually does not survive the guest's departure. Massage therapies fade. A good night's rest is spoiled upon return home. The porn-watching business traveler becomes a church deacon on the weekend. The altered private world constructed behind closed doors can all too easily be dismantled in our wake, even as the linens are dispatched to the laundry, as if each room were a stage for a very unique performance by a traveling troupe of actors.

The celebrated conception of a structure without a single core, one that pretends to create the condition for change within itself, masks, in the end, the deeper perpetuation of privilege and its opposite outside. In the age of rewards programs and group discounts, no hotel seems out of reach. For the rich, hotel life is aristocratic in conception, full of servants and valets dashing through passages meant to keep the staff hidden from view. It confirms wealth. For middling sorts, the hotel is, first and foremost, a safe, clean, reliable depot for the body, an investment in sleep and safety, full of teasing reminders of the assumed life of the rich. Fresh cookies when you come "home," and a hot breakfast in the morning. For the working poor, the hotel is a jobsite, first and foremost. For the women who dominate the cleaning staffs, it is a predatory danger zone, bringing them in brief, too intimate contact with the often fabricated, perverse social worlds of "the guest." For the true poor, for immigrants and those anxiously hoping for a step up, the hotel can be a literal slave pen, a desperate structure pretending to offer domesticity but delivering its opposite. Sites of class fantasy and transgression, hotels are locations where social authority—broadly and narrowly defined—becomes truly legible, where some humans become newly visible and others become utterly invisible, if not lost.[15]

And so, the hotel as modern social institution expresses a wide range of social needs and desires, establishing serenity where once there was chaos and vice versa, but it also functions as a privileged site of exchange and connection, a switching point for cultures and peoples, and thus a particularly fertile production locus for the modern self. *Hotel Life* shows the hotel to be a place of privilege and power, a site of ritual relations and wildly unpredictable encounters, a pageant ground for the enactment of race, class, and gender, and a regulated transfer station for human traffic and capital movement. *Hotel Life* is not, therefore, a typical history of the hotel as a capitalist enterprise, with a focus on successful innovation and major transformations. The following pages are not merely interested in the rise of new business models, in the expansion of hotel chains globally, nationally, and locally, or in the establishment of the hotel as one feature of a vast corporate portfolio. There is, we admit, much to be written about the expansion of chain hotels and guest rewards programs, and the techniques of salesmanship and capitalist seduction that distinguish the high-end hotel from its shabbier cousins. And some of that material drifts to the surface, but it is not the chief aim of *Hotel Life*. *Hotel Life* is not, again, a history of the hospitality industry, but neither is it a whistleblowing exposé of the hotel's corrupt inner workings in the vein of Jacob Tomsky's recent and vastly entertaining *Heads in Beds*.[16]

Our bigger purpose, instead, is to describe the social and political function of the hotel in modern culture, to emphasize the many overlapping and contradictory ways that the hotel—as a structure built of steel and concrete, as a diverse clutch of experiences, and as a layered cultural metaphor—captures and defines the experiences of modernity, of globalization, of class, sex, race, and gender. To define the details of that portrait, we explore four core concepts that give "hotel life" shape and meaning in modern times—space, time, scale, and affect—and we do so by working thematically through some of the illustrative features that define each. For example, the first section attends to the particular kinds of space that hotel life creates, and it does so by starting with the confusing, rolling divides between public and private space that are built into the very logic of the hotel's imaginative and structural fabric. This section then turns to the dynamic relations between sex, patriarchy, and private space that the hotel occasions. The second section turns to the hotel's temporal dimensions—to how the hotel operates as a place of new beginnings and final endings—and it does so by way of approaching the hotel as a quasi clinic, a place providing therapy and a rest cure, a temporary respite from the grind of the everyday. At the other end of the spectrum is the hotel as final interment and resting place—old age home, mortuary, and impromptu cemetery that people in desperate circumstances choose or involuntarily find as a final way out of the worlds that trouble them. The third section attends to the scalar features of hotel life. Here we analyze the very particular ways that the hotel parses space along socioeconomic lines, charting the class dynamics of the hotel within the rise of global capitalism. With an analysis of the resort hotel, on the one hand, and the single-room occupancy hotel, on the other, this section highlights the double gesture by which the hotel enables a fantasy of luxury living where almost everyone can play at wealth, on the one hand, and, on the other hand, reinforces barriers between rich and poor with particular force and meaning. The fourth and final section turns to the particular kinds of feeling and affect that the hotel explicitly cultivates in its occupants—to how the hotel functions as purveyor of both fortune and failure—as a locus of seemingly radical socioeconomic alternatives at the same time that, with a flip of a switch, it can usher guests into a diasporic space—a hellish ecosystem from which there seems to be no escape. These four core elements of hotel life are, collectively, more than the sum of their parts. Space, time, scale, and affect are the primal glue out of which hotel life emerges as a cornerstone of modern self-making. They are the four ingredients that make up modernity's stew.

Throughout these disparate sections, we attend to episodes in the larger story that is the modern-day hotel, and our goal is to suggestively heighten the awareness of hotel guests, workers, and visitors to the complex and multifaceted network of desires and traditions that they are walking into when they walk through the hotel lobby's front door. To that end, *Hotel Life* focuses on particular kinds of hotels—the spa hotel, the resort hotel, the single-room occupancy hotel, for example—and particular narratives enabled within these venues, on hotels that offer housing to the very rich and mobile and on hotels that "serve" the globally poor and destitute, their movements dictated by capitalism's whims. We could just as easily have picked an entirely different set of organizing rubrics—the hotel by the hour or the hospital hotel, for example. But once we come to see the hotel as operating along a continuum of choices and life pathways, once we stress desire and aspiration, the particular nodes along that continuum are less critical in and of themselves than is their function as apertures through which we can suddenly see the larger operational role of the hotel in contemporary society. We offer here a shimmering portrait of the hotel as pure quicksilver in a landscape of want and need.

Because hotels refuse the neat segmentation of experience, some themes surface and resurface throughout this book. The single-room occupancy hotel (SRO), for example, so seemingly far removed from the four- and five-star luxury hotel at first glance, coexists in uneasy relation to it, the overarching tension between home and homelessness being a main driver in the class fantasies let loose by the hotel's revolving door. As a result, the SRO makes guest appearances in multiple chapters as an important reminder of the larger context and backdrop against which hotel lives inevitably unfold. The therapeutic function of the hotel is not the sole prerogative of those hotels that self-brand as offering resort or spa services, and so the various fantasies associated with rejuvenation, rebirth, and second chances are featured, in one way or another, in most of the book's chapters. Sex, as well as the bad boy antics that it addresses, is not safely relegated to the second chapter but resurfaces across the hotel's full range of representations and experiences, dovetailing with all the kinds of desire in which the hotel trades.

Our purview is generally those hotels that are located or have their headquarters within North America, though we recognize that the hotel is a global formation. One chapter does focus specifically on the transnational fantasies implicit in the aptly named "all-inclusive" resorts that are so generously sprinkled along the Mexican Riviera and the Caribbean. In those examples, the hotel is selling the very fact and fantasy of border crossing as a key part of what is included in its package—the desire to take part in global capital and the global North's domination of its southern neighbors. But these geographic distinctions do not hold for various reasons, ranging from the global reach of many hotel chains at all price points and luxury levels to the inevitably international clientele of even those hotels that we most associate with all things "American." Whether in airports, casinos, urban centers, business districts, or recreation areas like Disney World or Lake Tahoe, hotels draw workers and guests irrespective of national affiliation or the ability to pay. As factories that produce human leisure, hotels require a work force of predominantly low-wage workers who come the world over for the chance to better their conditions. Much like Starbucks and McDonalds, mega–hotel chains like Marriott and Hilton market a temporary home away from home that asserts homogeneity and familiarity of experience, regardless of location. A key fantasy—and aspect of the business model—here is precisely the hotel's ability to trump its regional location, irrespective of where it happens to be in the world, and to offer the guest an experience interchangeable with any other hotel in its chain.

The hotel, as we approach it in *Hotel Life*, exceeds the neat containers provided by extant archives—be they housed in libraries in the form of books on hotel history or architecture, in the records of Hilton Hotel chain's corporate office, or within the pages of popular prose and film. *Hotel Life* therefore cuts across these discrete archives, blending their isolated findings into an integrated whole in order to capture the hotel as it exists in the larger textual and narrative record. In other words, just as the hotel's spaces are mobile, transient, and constantly being repurposed and reenvisioned, so too is the material from which *Hotel Life* draws a hybrid blend of different disciplinary approaches, mediums, and narrative forms. Despite efforts to establish brand loyalty and name recognition, the hotel is always an ever-shifting abstraction, and so too is the archival material that provides a fuller, richer picture of its significance to the modern self's making and remaking.

Precisely the hybridity of this archive and the abstractions of the structure make the hotel so powerful for its frequenters, and so each chapter ranges broadly across the archival record, blending popular representations of the hotel as it is depicted in visual culture, media, and print culture, in advertisement and firsthand memoirs, in journalism and in fiction.[17] The goal in each chapter is to create a "migrant archive" of sorts—to summon into view through a disparate array of materials the inchoate power of the hotel to generate new spaces to suit an evolving self characterized and constituted by various kinds of socioeconomic, sexual, and class experimentation.

Because "hotel life" is fully intertwined with the discourses and experiences of sexuality and gender, race and empire, cosmopolitanism and parochialism, the book's analysis of primary material is shaped by emergent literatures on space, power, and landscape, on "the commons," on segregation, and on the circuits and switching points that occupy the attention of transnational American studies. If the hotel is a repeatedly read text, serving as a familiar backdrop against which modern life is narrated and described in film, press, narrative, and visual records, it is all too easily missed—seen as disposable, hollow—or goes unnoticed, and the complex dramas of self and subjectivity that it enables are too often seen as a consequence of the guest, not the institution. When we forget the institution that makes such realities imaginable and then possible, we are capitulating to the sleight of hand that keeps the hotel just out of the spotlight—we are surrendering to the seductive, and often worrisome, story of infinite self-making that, as we will see in the following chapters, is part and parcel of the hotel's allure as modern institution.

Space

1

PUBLIC

═══════

Grand Hotel, a 1932 film about the daily excitements of the world's most exquisite and cosmopolitan home-away-from-home, begins with an overhead shot of a telephone switchboard. Because of the overlapping babble, it is impossible to hear anything in particular, but it is clear that robust human interactions, both near and from afar, are flourishing. The camera turns to a sequence of phone banks, in which several of the principal characters are talking to friends and family far away, questing for information about loved ones, or confessing their heartfelt desires. "All the best people are here," confides one elderly man, determined to spend his final, dying days in posh luxury. And he seems to be right, for within the Grand Hotel there are barons and businessmen, show-girls and secretaries. While Johann Strauss's "Beautiful Blue Danube" plays in the background, we see the romantic bustle of the lobby, first from the doors, then, from far above, a swirling, orchestrated dance set against a checkerboard mosaic floor, and finally from the proletarian perspective of the central concierge table, where the bellhops cheer each other on and wait for their turn to manage the ebb and flow of guests and visitors. Here, in a single scene, the hotel looks like a series of inti-mate, overlapping worlds, brought together in one great public space, a parallel to the deck of a cruise ship or the waiting room of a train station.

Is this a public space, full of chance encounters and unexpected cross-overs? Or is it a series of discrete domesticities? *Grand Hotel*—and the hotel more generally, as this chapter argues—is both, and this medley of seemingly opposed spaces and spheres is a key feature of the hotel's endur-ing allure in modern culture. The constant balancing between exposure and concealment—between public and private spheres—is the daily work of modern life in an urban setting. Indeed, how a society divides its space

A still of the kalei-
doscopic lobby
of the Grand
Hotel, viewed
from above,
from the 1932
film of the same
name, directed
by Edmund
Goulding. (From
the authors'
collection)

into public and private spheres and how this division controls individuals'
movement from one place to another have become, in Lefebvre's wake,
subjects of critical attention in the fields of architectural theory, political
philosophy, and urban studies. If the public-private distinction has been a
key organizing principle shaping the physical spaces of cities and the social
lives of citizens, it is nonetheless the case that relations between public
and private spheres have changed over the course of history, with the rise
of urban society. The intimate space of the home has evolved to embrace
new lifestyles and greater integration of intimate arrangements into the
logic of the city's public spaces as loci of sociability and intermingling.

Yet, if the division of space and society into public and private spheres
regulates individuals' behavior and orientation in the world, transitions
between public and private, as Christopher Alexander has observed in his
landmark *A Pattern Language: Towns, Buildings, Construction*, are never
seamless, simple, or linear.[1] Urban space is characterized by stuttered

SPACE

and staggered gradations between public and private spheres, with walkways, arcades, and various other architectural features creating gradients of intimacy within public spaces. People need these gradients of setting, Alexander contends, to mark differing degrees of intimacy in the fluid cacophony of urban space—to differentiate the most intimate spaces of our built environment (spaces like the bathroom and bedroom) from the more public spaces of the market or municipal building. Not surprisingly, intimacy gradients are built into the architectural logic of the hotel with particular force and meaning, given the hotel's role, on the one hand, as provider of shelter and intimate sleeping space and, on the other hand, as provider of company—of stories, adventures, and encounters that remind the traveler who stays the night in a strange place that he or she is still a member of the human community and therefore in need of company.

In this iteration, the hotel is a hybrid space somewhere between the private arena of the home and the public place of the market, but constantly referencing and offering blended iterations of both spheres to its occupants. Thus the hotel functions much like a highly transient neighborhood with shifting public and private spaces that harbor, for the course of an evening, a self-selecting group of people who choose to inhabit a cohesive physical location. Despite its notable absence from urban studies and critical analyses of private and public spheres, the hotel highlights the fact that public and private spaces exist on an ever-shifting continuum in the modern city, even as it contains in concentrated form the full range of porous possibility that the two spheres provide modern urban space. Public spaces within the hotel, such as the restaurant, bar, and reception area, serve a variety of purposes for those who inhabit them, as do the hotel's most private spaces—spaces like bedroom and bathroom. Indeed, it is precisely through sustained attention to the tangible materiality of architectural space created by bricks and mortar—as opposed to conceptually rich but physically immaterial linguistic or philosophical spaces—that, as Elizabeth Grosz observes, we can come fully into our own as modern subjects.[2] This promise of de-fragmentation, of being a "whole person," holds infinite allure for those who walk through the hotel lobby's front door.

Servility

With its large, malleable public spaces of ballrooms, lobbies, and conference rooms, the hotel is a highly mutable space of modernity; it both offers and ultimately is the "junkspace" that architect-theorist Rem Koolhaas, in a 2002 essay in *Obsolescence*, has identified as an inevitable byproduct of modernity, replete with its accelerating challenges to the political stability of the human subject. Constantly being unmade and remade, the hotel-as-junkspace produces in those walking through its quasi-public/private, multipurpose, and repurpose-driven areas a kind of subjective vertigo much like that captured by the opening scene of *Grand Hotel*—making us uncertain of where we are, obscuring where we want to go, and undoing where we thought we were. Hotel-as-junkspace asks those who enter its domain, in short, the most fundamentally political of all questions: Who do we think we are and who do we want to be. Precisely for this reason, among others, Fredric Jameson, in his 1991 polemic, *Postmodernism, or the Cultural Logic of Late Capitalism*, turned to the hotel and, more particularly, to the Los Angeles Westin Bonaventure as a prime example of the kind of "total space" and "complete world" promised by what he terms "hyperspace"— those urban spaces springing up in the interstices of stabilized domains that facilitate new collective practices and new modes of moving and congregating.[3]

The following pages focus on these more overtly public spaces and functions of the hotel and the opportunities they afford occupants to envision and reenvision themselves, while the next chapter turns its attention explicitly to the hotel's more private domains and the very personal activities they enable. Read together, these opening chapters move the reader through the hotel's intimacy gradients in order to lend shape and texture to the permeable space that is the hotel—to show the fluidity and interplay of public and private worlds ongoing within its walls. This chapter moves through the hotel lobby to the less readily visible public domains of service and business operations in order to consider how these worlds blend in powerfully generative ways for a wide range of occupants, some of whom stay for a night and some of whom end up staying for decades. Within the highly mutable architectural space provided by the hotel, public and private spheres are in constant dialogue—the hotel's public spaces serving to create distinction in an impersonal and transient world and its private spaces becoming staging grounds for the most intimate dimensions of the modern self. Through engagement with all of these varied spaces, inhabitants test out different and new iterations of self—iterations that can simultaneously offer powerful new ways of being in the world and pungent reminders of the constant threats that modernity poses to individuals.

Thus, when *Grand Hotel*'s Dr. Otternschlag sits at the bar and asks himself "What do you do in the Grand Hotel?—in a hotel in which "a hundred doors lead to one hall" and "no one knows anything about the person next to them"—his answer that you "eat, sleep, loaf around, flirt around, dance a little," makes implicit sense. In such a world public and private spheres blend, offering an alluring array of fantasies about self-making and distraction. This fantasy world, which Henry James and more recently Cornel West term "hotel civilization," is a world in which comfort, convenience, and contentment wipe out the harsher realities of life, be they pain, misery, or racism.[4] Thus the film's most famous line—Greta Garbo's "I want to be alone"—signals the seamless power and ubiquity of the sanctified privacy and protections the hotel offers those cloistered within its walls.

Indeed, the film industry's quick uptake of this concept—its use of the phrase "Grand Hotel theme" to refer to any movie that tracks the activities of people in large and busy places who may not know each other but whose lives overlap signals the film's (and, more fundamentally, the hotel's) foundational importance to how contemporary culture understands and represents alternative public and private worlds. By virtue of their industry designation, "Grand hotel" movies—no matter their setting—overlay the hotel's unique ability to summon into being a rich array of gradations between public and private worlds and to architect these gradients of intimacy into the lived experience of hotel guests. *Grand Hotel*'s 2007 selection for preservation in the Library of Congress's National Film Registry as culturally, historically, and aesthetically significant indicates how powerful and enduring its vision of the hotel as the place where these public and private lives are at once carefully protected and yet intermingled has been over the past eighty years.[5] The public and private environments that the hotel offers help guests and managers curate visitors' experiences, keeping them apart and bringing them together, and they are engineered to do both without calling attention to either task.

The hotel life envisioned in *Grand Hotel* and reproduced ad infinitum for a modern public is about producing a kind of wish fulfillment through which the building and all of its smaller intimacies change, at a moment's notice, to suit the needs of the guest. The institution's infinite capacity to serve as a rented replacement space for anything is a reflection of the demise of those spatial possibilities beyond the generic bricks and mortar of the local airport Courtyard by Marriott or outside of the sculpted European facade of the Plaza. Partly because of its genuine revolutionary potential—on powerful display, for example, in the so-called Arab spring of 2011—true public space now seems heavily constrained or controlled, and surrogate spaces must be found and, by and large, contracted. Domestic private space is also imagined to be under assault, but a hotel provides hundreds of perfectly sealed-off private preserves, and its attentive staff guarantees (or professes to guarantee) discretion and privacy. So these alternative privates and publics, built within the hotel on purpose and with intimacy gradients that carefully curate movement between spheres, emerge as a substitute for what we imagine to be the unsatisfactory domesticities of the home front and the dwindling public spaces of the traditional cityscape. The hotel's ability to offer guests and workers an alternative private or public arena (or both, as needed) is thus a perfect symptom of this neoliberal epoch, with its seemingly innocuous transfer of responsibility from agencies as different as the state or the family to the corporation.

The hotel that we are describing evolved over time to its present architectural and functional role and only gradually came to be such a powerful provider of the seductive blend of public and private spheres that it is today. We can begin to understand the hotel's gradual evolution to its present social form by considering Italian architect and surveyor Giambattista Nolli's famous mid-eighteenth-century map of Rome. The meticulously executed twelve engraved copper plates represented in microscopic detail the approximately eight square miles of this ultimately modern city, and the Nolli map continues today to be one of the best resources for understanding Rome, used by architects, surveyors, and demographers. Nolli used scientific surveying, careful base drawings, and precise architectural scale achieved through magnetic and astronomical compass use to create a breathtakingly complete and minute picture of the Roman city. But the true innovation of the Nolli map lies in the architect's creation of a way to measure urban density by designating public space in white and buildings in black, and so the Nolli map continues to be widely accepted in urban design as a way to show public space in urban settings.

Within the context of the Nolli map, hotels over time became increasingly represented by white areas within the dark outlines of the private building, their lobbies in particular offering literal light spots of public encounter and interchange as the city became increasingly dense. La Pianta Grande di Roma ("the great plan of Rome") may be one of the most revealing and artistically designed urban plans of all time, but its attention to the flexible and evolving iterations of blended public and private space, particularly within the context of such venues as public houses and hotels, is, for our purposes, its most powerful achievement. If the Nolli map captured the eighteenth-century hotel's evolving ability to offer those who flocked to it alternatives and innovations to public and private space, contemporary hotels stand as the "home away from home," the public square, the marketplace, the crossroads, and the old neighborhood, now owned and operated by Marriott.

When we consider *Grand Hotel*'s kaleidoscopic opening sequence, we see the venerable hotel lobby, long a site of social mixing, as the slowly evolving quintessence of this marriage of public function and private space. We recognize, for example, not only that this lobby evolves from the Roman city's public venues as they are captured by Nolli's map but that it is the logical next iteration of the nineteenth-century U.S. public sphere—a place in which the hotel and its venerable lobby loomed large. In the 1870s, President Ulysses S. Grant, a lover of fine cigars and brandy, embraced the neoclassical foyer of the Willard Hotel in Washington, D.C., as an escape from the oppressive formality of the White House, but found himself besieged by a swirl of "damned lobbyists," thereby coining the political phrase that would continue to signal the hotel's foundational role in the public domain.

But if, in Grant's day, the entrance hall of the hotel was once merely a neutral meeting ground for self-interested parties, in the age of the service economy it has become far more than that. As Siegfried Kracauer observed in his now iconic "The Hotel Lobby," a person can, all too easily, "vanish into an undetermined void" while sitting in a hotel lobby, and this is because the hotel lobby offers a sort of groundless distance from the everyday that can be exploited by those who linger on the lobby sofas and overstuffed chairs.[6] Recently returned to prominence by architects, businesspeople, and hoteliers, it might well be one of the most overdetermined and overtheorized spaces in the modern world. We see this most clearly in the endless repetition of ranked lists—"Coolest Hotel Lobbies" and "15 Hottest Hotel Lobbies"—that marks the space as an object of interest, if not fascination, for the general traveler. "The lobby

is the first chapter in the story of your experience at the hotel," suggests design ingénue, Kelly Wearstler, thinking more broadly; "everything happens there. You arrive, you meet, you leave all through the lobby. It's one of the souls of the hotel."[7] Once a retreat from work, it now sets the tone for a series of escapist and therapeutic interactions.

For contemporary architect, Michael Maltzan, the hotel lobby— unlike other public venues such as the beach, the shopping mall, the movie theater, the auditorium, or the amusement park, all of which direct occupants' attention to a particular object of shared attention whether it is the surf, stores, movies, or rides—offers arguably the best venue for interactive public encounter. The lobby, therefore, is one of

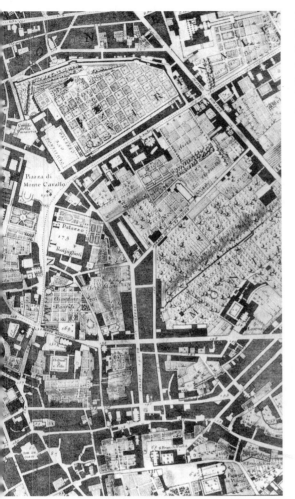

Detail from "La nuova topografia," by Giambattista Nolli. (Earth Sciences and Map Library, University of California, Berkeley)

the last public spaces geared toward interaction and connection. Other public spaces foster a certain parallelism, encouraging visitors to become an audience witnessing a spectacle, arranging side-by-side seating around the open water, the shimmering film, or the excitement of the ride. A public park might well be a meeting ground, or be occupied by groups with competing interests, but it is designed to foster a solipsistic experience, not a productive mixing of the classes.

At the very street-side front of the hotel, the lobby persists as a common meeting ground for guests and staff, for those new to the hotel and those on their way out, for anyone and everyone who stands on the threshold of the institution, staring into its depths and considering engagement of some kind. But it is also a social site, defined by music, seating, trim detail, and lighting. It is meant to make connections happen, to stage a social mixture. When Dave Horton, head of the Hilton Hotels & Resorts "global brand," set out to reimagine the aesthetic of the venerable chain, he began with the lobby.[8] Discouraged by the emphasis on "transitional space all about checking in and going to your room," Horton and his design team focused on their McLean, Virginia, hotel and installed an "18 hour bar" that could also serve as a breakfast café, or a wine-tasting station, filling the redecorated space with a range of chairs and tables, new art, and bigger flat screen televisions. Instead of a common aesthetic, they created a diversity of social scenes—a trio of couches clustered tightly around a coffee table, or a pair of armchairs nestled intimately together. The goal was to create a plurality of community spaces serving a range of communities and guests, all a part of the global brand and each about comfort and style. This cosmopolitan crossroads—like the street-side edge of the urban skyscraper—is ringed by coffee shops and newsstands, sandwich shops and even clothiers, notations of the guest's arrival and settlement not in a strange and frightening place but a place defined by its thoughtfulness and its exquisite servility.

This version of the lobby does not happen by accident. It is made or designed. In the early 2000s, JW Marriott, working with the design firm IDEO, set out to remake its high-end lobbies. IDEO, one of the world's most famous design firms, describes itself as "human-centered" and "design-based," with an emphasis on scientific study and data mapping. Working closely with the industrial furniture company, Steelcase, IDEO set out to develop what it called "The Great Room Lobby" concept. Like a team of anthropologists, IDEO "shadowed and observed guests and employees" and "identified" the "key touch points in the guest journey." It produced a geography of the ideal entrance hall, filled with overlapping zones of contact—the "Individual Zone," the "Relaxing Work Zone," the "Social Business Zone." Glass walls and varied seating allowed the guests to feel as if they were defining the borders of each zone. Background music was "developed" for this Great Room Lobby, and "special air scents" were deployed. The result, one Steelcase working paper suggested, echoing the thinking of Koolhaas, "was a third place, a space between home and work, where people feel comfortable and open to work, play, and relax." "The lobby," the paper concluded, was "the symbol of [a] new flexibility. A series of well-linked public spaces, the flow from one to the other happen[ing] naturally when people need large spaces. The different seating areas, the restaurant, the sight lines and paths all connect with other transitional spaces," including, of course, "the Starbucks around the curve."[9] For IDEO, for JW Marriott, and for Steelcase, the goal was not merely to make the perfect space for cross-connections; the goal was also to hide that making so that it appeared effortless and natural—so that the intimacy gradient of the hotel's most public lobby space was at once unavoidable and unobserved by hotel guests.

The hotel lobby, IDEO noted, was a managed "third space," distinct from home and work, a bigger, bolder, more prescriptive version of the local pub, or the public library, or the coffee shop around the corner. But it was also like a factory floor, the central production site of the "hospitality industry," where its best and most durable product—hospitality itself—was activated to bring together strangers and friends interested in networking and constructive community building, but not kin and co-workers. As Bryant Simon has so smartly shown, some such spaces can be class bound, emphasizing the virtues of a specific clientele and excluding—through force, if necessary—those who might not have been overtly denied access to a bar or a library.[10] Intrigued by the decline of wide-open green space and the unruly street corner, Simon singled out Starbucks as a perfect example of a third space that is, in the end, more privately run than publicly owned, more managed than truly free, but he could as well have pointed to the hotel lobby as a more durable, ubiquitous expression of the same phenomenon—a phenomenon depicted by the Nolli map more than two centuries earlier.

But if the hotel's front of store offers seemingly infinite possibilities for social interaction and public encounter, the back of store—the hotel's room service and restaurant kitchens, laundry rooms, dishwashing rooms, pastry kitchens, silver service rooms, banquet kitchens, and banquet setup and table storage rooms—provide an equally malleable place of social encounter, formation, and remaking. As massive as its hotel lobby, meeting areas, and shops, the famous Dallas Hotel Anatole's service areas, for example, do not only serve as the invisible engine driving the smooth workings of the hotel's public areas but function as a series of discrete public arenas in their own right. Much like a small city, the distinct service venues that keep the 1,606 room hotel and its banquet rooms, award-winning restaurants, and room service humming are, on the one hand, self-contained and, on the other, interlocking and mutually aware. At the helm of all the Anatole's public areas is Walter

One of the many multipurpose meeting spaces, dining halls, and conference rooms at the astonishingly vast Hotel Anatole in Dallas, Texas. The Anatole's promotional paratext perfectly captures what is a standard feature of such images: their extraordinary emptiness. Vast rooms devoid of people—or with just one or two guests—appear everywhere. Such images suggest a structure poised to act, prepared to be awakened, but, until the guest arrives, dormant and prepared. (www.hiltonanatolehotel.com; accessed May 27, 2014)

Maloy—the general manager and maître-d' of the Anatole's service and lobby operations. As link between lobby and service areas, Maloy, like any effective manager, oversees the interface between the highly visible lobby and the invisible service arenas.

The manager's job, among other things, is to ensure that one public arena remains unnoticed and largely invisible to the other—that the thousand-plate luncheon banquet is set up without noise or incident while guests mill about and make business contacts before honoring recipients of a Dallas not-for-profit service award or some other critically important affair. The phalanx of workers who silently man the setup and breakdown of the hundreds of round tables floats through banquet room and service areas with the precision of structural engineers, its object to remain as unobserved as possible by the luncheon guests whose eyes are riveted by large screen TVs that project the awardee table and the series of speakers behind its podium to all guests.

Here public community is formed around the shared act of eating a lunch that honors prominent residents and the shared activity of watching larger than life projections of the select few who honor them, but another public community is formed around those who, like a special forces team, convene to troubleshoot a particular iteration of the hotel's public life. With up to ninety workers in the main kitchen alone, at least five pastry chefs at work in the pastry kitchen not to mention the bakers, a laundry-room team of north of a dozen, as well as the large crews that move tables, man the dishwasher, and cook in the banquet kitchens, the larger hotel's back-of-store world is a densely populated one indeed. Street cleaners of the sort that can be found brushing residential city streets are driven by workers who move their machines between the various rooms and hallways, keeping the heavily trafficked areas clean of debris, much like a public works commission. The head chef presides over the various kitchens, conferring with special projects chefs and the coordinators and expediters that make sure that everything runs on time.

In a hotel of the Anatole's scale, the armies that move into a banquet room for prep are more anonymous and corporate than in a three-hundred- to five-hundred-room hotel, operating much like a city as opposed to a small town. To find oneself working in a hotel of the Anatole's size after working in a smaller hotel, according to Maloy, is much like finding oneself transported to New York City after growing up in Altoona, walking down streets surrounded by strangers who don't greet you by name and having chance encounters with random passersby. It is, in short, to find yourself suddenly in a public sphere that is anonymous and alienating but that can offer the opportunity for new connections, friendships, and associations.

But, regardless of the scale, the seemingly infinitely mobile public and private spheres that these workers create among themselves ultimately work within the logic of the hotel's greater goal, forming a tightly knit infrastructure to support the sumptuous lobbies that invite guests to linger and mingle. The emphasis on comfort and familiarity reveals the hotelier's desire to create a home-away-from home out of purest quicksilver. Just beyond the front door of the hotel, cavernous spaces, twisting hallways, and the series of cordoned-off work rooms collectively form the connective tissue—and constitute the DNA—of an inchoate public sphere waiting for definition. Vast spaces can be "multipurposed," enclosing a wedding one night and then redecorated and redeployed to stage a political fundraiser the next. Temporary walls can be moved, taken down, and installed; chairs and tables can be added and subtracted. In portmanteau fashion, the hotel brings these reinvented privates and publics into new, intertwined relation, as a single commodity available to all in one format, but individually tailored, too. This plasticity of space brings new possibilities and forms of modern life, both

The Mansion on Turtle Creek. (http://www.rosewoodhotels.com/en/mansion-on-turtle-creek-dallas/gallery; accessed May 27, 2014)

freeing and constraining, into temporary view for occupants. "I want to be alone," says Garbo. And the hotel springs into action. Just as it would for a hundred other requests for intimacy or publicity, for connection or isolation.

Intimacies

The hotel's unique ability to provide a graded blend of spaces that collectively provides a mobile, mutable, and yet deeply familiar "home away from home" in which new forms of modern life become possible makes it irresistibly compelling not only for those who check in but also for business owners, CEOs, and managers. Consider, for example, Caroline Rose Hunt, stay-at-home mom turned premier hotelier after the age of fifty and one of the most successful businesswomen of the late twentieth century. The founder of the Rosewood Property Company, Hunt summed up her hotel philosophy and motto explicitly as that of providing "a home away from home" to all guests. The first hotel that Hunt opened—the Mansion on Turtle Creek—was originally a private home to the King family before it lost its fortune in 1935 and sold the home to oilman Toddie Lee Wynne, who turned the mansion into the headquarters for his American Liberty Oil Company.

If the history of Hunt's first hotel site is one that captures the hotels' migration from private to public space, its development into a hotel reflects the constant movement between public and private that is the hotel's particular métier. After purchasing the site in 1979, her transformation of it into a hotel was one that carefully emphasized the mansion's private origins and history—in other words, her business plan was one that aimed at turning the home-become-business into a business-turned-home. The idea of turning the site into a hotel was, appropriately, provided to her by the house's first owner, and Mrs. Hunt's first act as hotelier was to put a statue of horses at the Mansion's entrance in honor of the former owner's love for riding. The whole idea was to make it feel like a home, Hunt stressed, and so the $21 million renovation kept the home's veranda, library, and living room but transformed them into part of the hotel's dining room and turned the fur and silver vault into the wine cellar. When the Mansion at Turtle Creek opened in 1981 the magnitude of the Hunt business plan was immediately apparent in its much sought after Five Diamond AAA rating and Mobil Travel Guide Five Star designation. As a powerful proof of concept, this first hotel—opulent, exquisite, sumptuous, but available for renting—became the prototype and model for all future Rosewood hotels, including Los Angeles' Bel Air and Santa Fe's Inn of the Anasazi, as well as hotels in Saudi Arabia, Dubai, Abu Dhabi, England, the Bahamas, and British Columbia.

Hunt not only masterminded the transformation of the private home turned business into a worldwide hotel empire that sells the idea of the hotel as the ideal home away from home—the home that you wish you lived in year-round but need to travel to return to—but, in addition, her emergence as a business leader in the hotel industry radically altered the public and private dimensions of her own life. As she recalled in our interview, "The hotel business changed my life dramatically and it was a change I liked." Before she went into hotels, she described herself as "an at home person" who "didn't go out at night, and was very involved in church and the kids' schools." But with the Mansion at Turtle Creek, all that changed, and she "suddenly became a public figure." One of her first responses to this move from private to public arena was to hire a public relations person who told her that she was "going to develop a brand" and that she was the perfect embodiment—the "perfect personality"— for the Rosewood brand. Part mother, part grand dowager and hostess, part astute businesswoman, Mrs. Hunt has presided over the Rosewood Hotel and Resort empire for the past forty years with a combination of maternal wisdom and incisive street smarts about what makes people tick. As she cannily observed when asked about Rosewood's success, "People want personal attention and comfort," they want a restaurant that serves local cuisine of a caliber such that they do not have to leave the hotel in search of dinner, and most of all, when people check in, they like to be greeted by name, because "everybody loves the sound of their own name."

Yet Hunt's personal transformation from private into public person not only was the result of the launch of her famous luxury hotel chain; it was, in fact, enabled and facilitated by her own change of residence from private home to hotel. Since 1987, Hunt has lived in one of her hotels— the only permanent resident in Dallas's Crescent. A few families set up short-term house in various penthouse suites, one family renting the whole seventh floor so that its dogs could each have a separate bedroom during the year that it renovated its Frank Lloyd Wright house. But Hunt is the only resident of any real duration—over thirty years being long-term by any estimation. She described this move into the hotel as spontaneous, unequivocal, and the result of her daughter renting a room for her in the Crescent. Newly divorced and tired after a long day in town, Hunt decided to stay there one week, and she "never went home," or, rather, she created a new kind of home for herself out of the rented space in which she had initially sought temporary shelter. Using the motto she coined to describe Rosewood hotels, Hunt says of her hotel home, "it's my home away from home . . . I guess it is my home." The very things that sold her on it as a home are, of course, the things that turn guests into repeat customers: the service, proximity, convenience, and the fact that "they all treat me like I'm the queen."

Collapsing the space between a hotel and a home as Hunt does— turning home into business and business into home—makes explicit the underlying complementarity between public and private arenas that the hotel enables and the ways that this complementarity can and does enable new modes of existence for a wide range of individuals. To stay in a hotel permanently—to call it home—asserts the blended nature of public and private spheres in the modern epoch and the ways this blend enables new forms of living, even to those resistant to this fact. When English novelist Will Self, writing for the *New York Times Style Magazine*, stayed in the London W Hotel to investigate the claim that "metropolitan hotels are now the favored working, socializing, and culture-consuming loci of the mediatized professional," he found the experience of staying there—in a hotel in his home city—to be unnerving and deeply threatening to his preconceived ideas about self, space, and human capability.[11] Even as luxury hotels like the Four Seasons were building mixed-use facilities—half permanent luxury residences and half hotel—Self's visceral belief that people are just not *supposed* to live permanently in a hotel, just as they are not *supposed* to stay in the hotel down the block from their home, reflects long-held but outmoded ideas about how space is parsed in an urban setting and how it can impact and alter dwellers. Self's perspective about space upholds the sanctity of public and private arenas—the distance between home and work—only by overlooking the hotel's long-standing function as deeply evocative ideation space and home to a vast array of transient modern subjects at every end of the social spectrum, from the affluent to those down on their luck and unemployed. Indeed, the hotel's ability to provide sustained, reliable long-term shelter is testament to its capacity to meet the full spectrum of human needs for privacy and companionship, for every bodily need and craving, and to do so for those at every stage of life and location on the socioeconomic scale.

Utopias

The hotel's ability to foster trust and nurture people who are otherwise temporarily homeless and dependent has been a long-standing feature of the modern landscape, and this functionality makes the hotel an irresistible magnet for those across the entire socioeconomic spectrum. Kay Thompson famously captured the hotel's imaginative allure for the vulnerable wealthy in her 1955 fabulously popular Eloise stories, and the resulting marketing of these stories as a distinguishing feature of the hotel she—and her creator—called home attests to the hotel's ability to incubate new kinds of identity and self-making even for those guests who seem to have it all. A ward of New York City's Plaza Hotel, the six-year-old Eloise roams the hallways of one of the world's finest hotels, her mother perennially absent. Without the protecting spaces provided by the hotel's public and private venues, Eloise would be alone in a dangerous and unprotecting world, but in the generative habitus of the hotel she invents a world rich with play at self-making. If her room is depicted as messy and boring, filled with toys and books, each a discarded substitute for the missing affections of her mother, it is still filled with sunshine and with "Nanny," her aged British minder. Leaving the suite, Eloise endlessly wanders the floors of the hotel, plays with guests and the staff, and explores, through the hotel, how to exist as a solitary self in a larger world. Long a favorite of young girls, Thompson's *Eloise* demystifies the labyrinth of the hotel and suggests, instead, that the indomitable spirit of one particular six-year-old can triumphantly make a happy home even in the least sincerely domestic spaces of the world, and even in the absence of her mother.

The Plaza, as Thompson describes it through Eloise, is a home, a family, and a neighborhood—a microcosm of the larger world that Eloise will ultimately inhabit when an adult and thus a testing ground for a modern subject in formation. But Eloise has help with her self-fashioning—the hotel offers a series of surrogates and stand-in communities that enable and enliven her progress. She and Nanny routinely enjoy room service, and never cook for themselves. During the day, when Nanny is apparently otherwise occupied, Eloise tours the entire hotel. She attends weddings. She plays with the busboys. She boasts that she has been to "56 affairs including Halloween." She is the unofficial charge of legions of stewards, bellhops, concierges, and guests. Instead of the proverbial neighborhood block, she has an endless supply of hallways, each door a gateway to another temporary "home" at the hotel. When young Eloise playfully scoots down the hall, rapping a stick against the woodwork or stomping her roller skates, a row of doors opens, and the proto-neighborhood awakens to watch, to instruct, to "parent" collectively. We see a man with a mixed-drink and striped pants, a comely woman behind him, and another man, wearing a bathrobe, shaving cream still on his face, and a third man, fastidiously dressed for business, with a small dog. Behind closed doors, the Plaza is full of discrete domestic spheres. Once the doors open—in this case, to make it possible to attend to a playful young girl—an alternative public emerges, a neighborhood constructed not through sidewalks and the front stoop, but through the privately owned and temporarily contracted corridors, lobbies, and elevators of the hotel.

This homelike community of nurturing transients and the kind of self-making they encourage in the story's child heroine are both what inspire the book's authors and what the Plaza Hotel's subsequent marketing plans exploited mercilessly. Thompson and her illustrator, Hilary Knight "holed up at the Plaza" in 1955 where they described their collaboration as one in which they "wrote, edited, laughed, outlined, cut, pasted, laughed again, read out loud, laughed, and suddenly had a book."[12] Immersed in the world that is the Plaza Hotel, Thompson literally mimicked the words and intonations of a little girl wandering the hotel halls until she perfected her story. Forty years later the hotel was designated a literary landmark—the official "Home of Eloise"—which enabled the hotel to develop a marketing strategy that fully exploited the seductive allure of the hotel's surprisingly nurturing intimacy gradients and the opportunities they promised to provide guests to reimagine themselves. The literary landmark plaque that still graces the Plaza's entrance declares that "Kay Thompson lived at the Plaza while writing Eloise," and it is her own firm position within the comforting arms of the hotel that enabled her to bring "this fictitious charmer to life" with such effectiveness and to sketch with unerring accuracy and power how "a six year old who lived on the top floor of the hotel" might consequently see the world anew.[13] A painting of Eloise by the illustrator was immediately hung in the hotel lobby after the book's initial publication and quickly became a pilgrimage site for mothers and their young girls, Princess Grace reputedly being dismayed at the painting's temporary absence when she toured the hotel with her young children.

But it was with Donald Trump's purchase of the hotel in the 1980s that the story of the hotel's attempts to cash in on the Eloise narrative became something of a cliffhanger. Trump hired the original illustrator, Hilary Knight, to design a children's suite based on the Eloise drawings and thus to create a kind of three-dimensional literary arena where guests could inhabit and potentially reenact the hotel's healing habitus. But it was Trump's refusal to provide Kay Thompson continued rent-free shelter within the hotel—something the previous owner had done for years—that provoked her to block Trump's plans to use Eloise to promote the hotel and so the work was not completed. Though the hotel had an Eloise Room where visitors could sit and imagine themselves in the story and an ice cream parlor named after the character, it was only after Thompson's death that the Plaza fully monetized the text, building it robustly into the hotel's marketing as well as architectural plans. In late 2009, the Eloise marketing campaign caught national attention, with stories on *Good Morning, America* and headlines in the national press about the hotel's new Eloise store and special packages like the Eloise Pajama Party Brunch, The Essential Eloise Birthday Party, and the Most Wonderful Platinum Eloise Party, in honor of her fifty-year birthday. Executives traded in the incipient logic of homelike privacy that Thompson's stories depicted as a hotel trademark by saying that after all these years "Eloise deserved a home."[14] Executive vice president of retail admitted to having "high hopes for Eloise": "She's such a character and a personality, a lot like the Plaza," that the Eloise store, she predicted, would give the publicly traded American Girl stores a run for their money. These days, Eloise is a brand, with her own flag—a gesture to the stateless geopolitics of the Plaza's interior —hanging over the main entrance to the hotel.

The highly malleable alternative public and private spaces that the hotel can seemingly will into being with the flip of a door lock and turn of a knob are not solely the stuff of fiction and affluence, the fantasy world and exclusive privilege of poor little rich girls who become irresistibly charming while roaming through four-star hotels. Nor are these self-making spaces available only to those elite consumers who engage in the literary voyeurism that the Plaza subsequently marketed so ruthlessly. Rather, this often overlooked element of the hotel's allure and promise cuts to the very heart of how modern architects envision multiunit temporary housing for that sector of society as far removed from Eloise as possible—the urban homeless whose various drug addictions, mental illnesses, and physical disabilities defy any existing public and private spaces city or federal agencies have historically been able to dream up to provide sanctuary and temporary shelter.

Take, for example, the multistage project that Maltzan has undertaken for the Skid Row Housing Trust. The Carver and Rainbow short-term residential complexes are different from traditional single-room-occupancy hotels, which pluck those who relentlessly occupy public spaces under freeways and in subway stations and relocate them in private domestic locations out of the public's view. Rather than offering a series of private rooms for each guest that are connected by long hallways and that work solely to seal individuals off from each other, Maltzan's design begins by asking how the homeless construct public and private spaces for themselves. Putting up walls around themselves to try to create a feeling of safety—be the walls cardboard or psychological—is one of the first things people living on the streets tend to do, and so Rainbow and Carver provide those reassuring walls but also offer alternative social spaces and community-creating possibilities for the buildings' traumatized guests.[15]

Rainbow and Carver stimulate spontaneous community interactions by revising a standard architectural concept of the traditional hotel— the double-loaded doors that grace long and narrow hotel hallways. By trading this dual entry model that prioritizes individual private spaces

SPACE

Michael Maltzan's New Carver Apartments—the reimagining of the single-room occupancy hotel as adjustable and improvisational domestic space. Here, a view of the rooftop seating area, with a view of the city, a reform of what is possible, aesthetically, for the very poor. (Robert Nickelsberg/Getty Image News)

and minimizes opportunity for alternative kinds of public formation to occur for a single-loaded doorway concept, Rainbow and Carver balance private and public worlds, even as they create imaginative opportunities for guests to experiment with healing kinds of social encounter. The individual room doors are on the outer-facing interior walls of these cylindrical buildings, and the circular interior wall offers guests views into the buildings' center and the multipurpose spaces that are at their heart. The buildings' central courtyards are home to a host of community activities ranging from laundry to community kitchen space to outdoor gathering areas and a multipurpose space for yoga classes and a host of club activities requested by inhabitants of the eighty-seven- and ninety-seven-unit buildings. In other words, alternative public spaces are the core element of these cylindrical housing units, offering inhabitants opportunities to reintegrate themselves into both public and private arenas and to experiment with creating public communities of their making and choice.

Occupying the same stretch of the I-10 freeway as affluent hotels like the Radisson that caters to the University of Southern California crowd, the Carver works with rather than against its urban environment, its curved facade mirroring the curve of the freeway on-ramp and offering guests intermittent views of the freeway from long horizontal laundry room windows, while sheltering them from the harsher realities the guests are all too familiar with—domestic lives rendered relentlessly public, private ablutions captured in the headlights of passing cars. Unlike the guests that stay a night or two at the Radisson before returning to homes within high-rises, suburban neighborhoods, or gated communities, those at the Carver experience a different kind of transitory occupancy. Without a home base safely separated from on-ramps, public parks, and deserted parking lots, these inhabitants carry their private worlds and worldly goods with them on their backs and in their minds when they check in. Rather than seeking a temporary escape from the constraints of home life and an oasis from crying children and the demands of a dog in need of a walk, these guests are challenged and encouraged by the Carver to unpack their emotional bags, to settle into a built environment that attempts to serve as a healing palliative to the chaotic destabilization of public and private that is the lived reality of the homeless, and gradually to reenvision their place in the world.

The vision is a utopian one for sure—at first glance and in Maltzan's description of the project, as far removed from Foucault's "Panopticon" with its disciplinary regimes of regeneration as one might get. Of course, the Skid Row Housing Trust requires payment despite its nonprofit status. The 1,500 men, women, and children who stay in its facilities, many of them for up to one year, don't stay for free. Like any hotel guest, they pay. The temporary shelter provided for a diverse range of inhabitants, including the disabled, geriatric, veterans, counselors, artists, gardeners, young adults, transgender men and women, and the clergy, is envisioned as offering the amenities of a traditional hotel without the anonymity so desired and prized by visitors to the Plaza. While those strangers who open their hotel doors when Eloise knocks find passing diversion in the homeless child's face that greets them, the residents at the Carter know too well the more alienating kinds of encounter that urban homeless can expect from strangers. And so, when they do enter Rainbow or Carver, they become, according to Skid Row, willing members of a vibrant community "united by their experience of overcoming homelessness," even if that experience ends up being temporary and transitory.[16]

HOWEVER AND WHEREVER it appears, the crossroads purpose of the hotel ends, definitively and universally, at the threshold of the private sanctum. There, visitors and guests, dowagers and little girls, confront the formidable gateway to the domestic. More specifically, they stand before a door that is made of sterner stuff than your garden-variety interior door. Indeed, the modern hotel room door is a singular reflection of the institution's complex combination of public and private functions. It features no sidelights, no frosted glass windows, and no indication that anyone is home, or awake, or moving about. It is an impossible barrier, peppered with locks and chains on the inside, and marked only by a number, identifying the space inside, and a peephole, which allows the guest to surreptitiously view the community hallway. Such a door is necessary, in the end, to reassure guests that they are safely tucked away within an otherwise public structure, and that, for the contracted length of time, the room belongs entirely to them, to be shaped or remade to match their wishes and desires. When a door and a doorway might otherwise draw the eye into another room and suggest what lies beyond the threshold, the boring blank, heavy, soundproof, and fireproof hotel room door, in the end, is a signal of the machine's commitment to truly private space, so long as the bill is paid up. What happens behind that door is, truly, nobody's business.

2

PRIVATE

On a brisk October night, actor Charlie Sheen was arrested in the Plaza Hotel, having caused roughly $7,000 of damage, and having constrained, threatened, and otherwise terrified Capri Anderson, a porn star and his paid escort for the evening. Sheen had taken the twenty-two-year-old Anderson, contracted through an agent in Los Angeles, to dinner with his ex-wife, Denise Richards. As the adult film auteur later related on the morning talk shows, the evening deteriorated rapidly over drinks, racial slurs, and physical violence. After Sheen and Anderson returned to the hotel, the critical transaction—sex-for-money—was eclipsed by a whirlwind of destruction. Ultimately, the police were called. Ever the "bad boy," Sheen greeted the arriving authorities at the door naked, complaining that someone had stolen his wallet. Anderson, for her part in this drama, never got paid.[1]

Sheen's rampage repeats the live cliché of men behaving badly, perhaps inevitably, in hotels—in large part because of the particular kind of privacy in which the hotel trades. Indeed, amid all of the writings and rewritings of this torrid and familiar story, one essential, enduring fact remains: it is an apparent certainty of modern life that many men, if left to their own devices, will tend to sexual exploit in hotels. There is something about the particular kind of privacy that the hotel offers that encourages this sexual fantasy making become reality. It is to this indisputable fact of hotel life that Alain de Botton refers, when he observes the "metaphysical importance of hotels" to stimulating erotic desire in the modern psychosexual self.[2] But if this self-making, on one level, seems to cut against the grain of contemporary cultural norms, its ubiquity immediately suggests just the opposite—that going "out of sexual bounds" within hotel walls is very much a norm of the commodity culture that the hotel sells, as much a part of its promise to guests as free Wi-Fi and breakfast buffet.

If the preceding chapter explored hotels' various gradations of intimacy circuiting out from the distinctive kinds of public spaces the hotel affords, the following pages take up the question of what happens behind closed doors—in other words, these pages explore what happens to the modern subject when we venture into the private spaces that the hotel creates and makes available to guests. A short, encyclopedic essay—ranging in scale from the transgressions of Eliot Spitzer to those of Tailhook—would make for depressing, predictable reading. Within the hard terrain of the hotel, it seems, a certain genre of man is loosed from domestic restraints, and dangerously released into the only social institution in the world that promises (if you seek such a promise) to feed you, get you drunk, introduce you to strangers, shield you (if possible) from the eyes of the police, emancipate you (if you want it) from the rules of your ordinary life, and wake you up to start it all over again. No wonder, then, that such cruel hijinks inevitably ensue.

We aim, here in this section, to explain the social functions of the perversely gendered, interior private spaces of the hotel. *Hotel Life* in general and this first section in particular argues that the hotel's various public and private spaces work, not merely in sequence or as complements but, importantly, in jarring, discordant, grinding fashion. The welcoming, cosmopolitan logics of the lobby are not merely a part of the seduction, later consummated in the bedroom-for-rent; they also stand in surreal relation to the dangerous, hierarchical, sexualized domestic worlds—each an idiosyncratic expression of the guest—on the deep, deep inside. The mythology of the hotel might, then, promise "great sex" within the inner sanctums marked as black on the Nolli map, but what it delivers is something very different. Space, as it is created and articulated by the modern hotel, enables experiments in modern subjectivity that can, all too easily, move individuals from the privacy of the bedroom to the front page of the *New York Times*, and the hotel's seemingly infinite capacity to enable vertiginous movement across intimacy gradients and liminal spaces makes the hotel such a regular and enduring stage in the play of modern life. The acts that unfold on this stage, when they seem to be at their most private, constantly flirt with radical publicity, and the dynamic sexual "resistance" that guests feel as a result of this friction is the secret and most powerful driver of their larger-scale conformity to the very norms against which they push, with the hotel's help.

This particular part of the hotel story is so pervasive, we think, because, looking around, one might well think that the modern luxury hotel is built for sex as much as sleep. Heavy doors, thick walls, and privacy curtains envelop the room in secrecy and silence. An attentive staff is committed to keeping secrets and privacy. But, still, the sound of sex drifts, occasionally, into your room and into the more public venues of hallway and elevator waiting area, carried through the walls by ventilation shafts, like background music in an elevator. Oversized beds with soft linens are the focal center point, dominating most rooms, and leaving precious little room for doing anything that does not involve lying down. A well-appointed, chilled bar is at your disposal. Showers are built for two. And a wide screen television is positioned just in front of the bed. You might see some of these same features in the garden-variety roadside hotel, but only if those places attempt to mimic the feel and function of the most elite spaces: the spa hotels, the getaway hotels, and the historically prominent retreats of the rich and famous, or those who wish to imagine themselves, if briefly, as such.

When historian A. K. Sandoval-Strausz, in *Hotel: An American History* (2007), tracks this theme of sexual experimentation, risk taking, and misbehavior backward into the nineteenth century, he notes that "some people went to hotels for the wrong reasons." In this telling, hoteliers and innkeepers were engaged in a constant struggle to control and purify the experience of an overnight stay, a struggle that pitted them against a veritable horde of "adulterers, seducers, and prostitutes," "burglars and confidence men."[3] In an act of moral stewardship, late nineteenth-century reformers began to place Bibles in hotel rooms, in the hopes that the mere presence of the good book might inspire, in a moment of great temptation, a patron to stay on the straight and narrow path to grace. This tradition—of viewing the hotel as a den of iniquity, challenging the strength of weary and weakened travelers—continues to the present. "We urge you to do away with pornography in your hotels," two religious leaders recently wrote, in an open letter to a handful of hotel chains, "because it is morally wrong to seek to profit from the suffering, degradation, or corruption of others. You are placing temptation in their path—temptation for the sake of profit."[4]

In contrast, we read the articulation of this struggle as a clever bit of public relations, a papering over of the fundamental contradiction of the spatial politics of intimate space-for-rent. Offering porn to the guest is merely an indication of the bigger issues, because sex is built into the architecture of the modern hotel right alongside and often in dynamic tension with domesticity, intimacy, and privacy. Elite sites like the Plaza—"new hotels," as architectural critic David Collins named them in 2001—imagine the bedroom as "the most private and intimate area of the hotel," or as "the destination beyond the destination," so that every point of contact from the street inward flows into the interior sanctum and the bed.[5] When we focus here on "men behaving badly," it is only because these too public disruptions illuminate what has previously been hidden, and what is always understood to be a part of the enterprise. Had Sheen simply retreated to his room with his hired consort and conducted his business with reasonable discretion, he would have been accepting the soft logic of the hotel, in which "reasonable discretion" excuses all manner of sins, and in which the pleasure of sex in a fancy bed is the object being sold. Having eschewed such a course, Sheen's tabloid wildness still served to remind people—if they needed such a reminder—that the hotel and the particular kind of privacy it affords is also a site of seeming liberation and reckless abandon, even if this temporary abandon ultimately enables regimes of state and self-regulation. When Sheen went wild in the hotel, it simply meant that, contra public moral outrage, he was in the right place for all the right reasons.

The hotel room is thus a production site—one of many—for the modern sexual self. And hotels work, generally, to create and confirm contemporary notions of sex and sexuality, and to make possible, at the same time, a planned, if carefully delimited, escape from the normal rules, especially, but not only, for men. There are, then, no "misdeeds" in a hotel room; no one really behaves badly there, and this tends to be the case because of the fluidity and seeming infinite flexibility that, as we saw in the preceding chapter, is literally built into the hotel's architectural and social logic. Indeed, by confining an escort to the bathroom, tearing his room apart, and losing his wallet, his clothing, and his cool, Sheen was merely doing what came, as the institution stressed, naturally—surfing just a bit too easily across the intimacy gradients that are the hotel's stock-in-trade. Pleasure is partly a production of space, and nothing is *naturally* sexy.

But nothing is naturally private either, and the seemingly illicit sex that the hotel's private spaces enable inevitably shapes public and political debate at the level of the state. Not only does the individual citizen, like Sheen, run the risk of making headlines from behind closed hotel room doors, but as was all too apparent in the details of the 2012 Secret

Service scandal in Cartagena, Colombia, national politics and credibility can be called into immediate question when the sex happening within private hotel room chambers seeps out into public view.

In the spring of 2012, a dispute between an agent and a local call girl over the cost of a sex act already performed, a private argument between individuals, spilled out into the public areas of the Hotel Caribe, and drew the local police, the security staff of the institution, and national military personnel into a densely knotted international tangle. "Boys Gone Wild," the headlines read, suggesting that the problem was rooted in men, in masculinity, and in patriarchy. An accompanying chorus of outrage from Republicans and Democrats alike stressed the potential, in such a moment, for a breach of national security, a serious charge, given that this was a team preparing in advance for the arrival of President Obama, then on a Latin American tour. Like many Latin American hotels, the Hotel Caribe had rules and regulations governing the proper work and conduct of professional sex workers. The woman in question—a twenty-four year-old escort, accustomed to a high wage, "not a prostitute," the *New York Times* insisted earnestly—had spent the night with the man. In the morning, as is the custom of the hotel, she was awakened by staff, and reminded that she needed to leave by 6:30 A.M., so that the guest could have his life restored to some semblance of order. Offered a pittance for her labor instead of her usual fee, she was, as she later described it to the *Times*, bullied into the hallway, belittled and reduced to tears, and locked out of the room. A fellow sex worker, also subject to the morning curfew rules, tried to help her leave. A local policeman got involved and went back to the room with her to ensure that she was paid fairly and that the verbal contract agreed to the night before was honored. Hotel security arrived to broker a compromise fee. Then, with little fanfare, the young woman was walked out of the hotel, put into a taxicab, and sent home.

Many professed to be shocked, and the incident called into temporary question the reliability not only of the individuals involved but, more generally, of the U.S. government protections abroad. As the scandal unfolded, the hotel loomed as a key background player in the drama. Recognizing an opportunity—and more honest than most in its assessment of the affair—tiny Spirit Airlines released a new advertisement, offering "More BANG for your BUCK" to travelers eager for the supposedly unparalleled thrill of sex with a prostitute in a hotel bed. The ad featured four buxom women in pink bikinis in the lower background, their hands on their hips, coy and welcoming smiles on their faces. On the right side, oversized, was a man with sunglasses and an earpiece—a simulated Secret Service agent—with his finger over his lips, indicating silence and secrecy. Come to the Hotel Caribe, the ad seemed to say, where anything goes, and where the price of "anything"—from the airfare, to the accommodations, to various illicit add-ons—is low, low, low. From national headlines to public advertising, the Secret Service scandal migrated across public discourse communities, alternately eliciting national panic and lurid pleasure precisely because of what the hotel's private domains reveal about the erotic workings of state organizations as well as individual citizens.[6]

We focus here on the specifics of sex to make the broader point that, despite persistent efforts to cleanse or purify the public image of the hotel—ranging from the moral reforms of the nineteenth century, like the curative placement of Bibles in bedroom side tables, to the more recent elimination of porn from the room pay-per-view menu—these spaces are engineered to make "something wild" happen behind the proverbial closed door, to encourage those who pay for temporary cover in the hotel's alternative public and private spaces to make full use of the spatial opportunities the hotel offers for self-making, experimentation, and renewal. Whether representatives of the state or private citizens, the hotel's private spaces enable what appear to be alternate worlds of erotic longing and renewal. And so to talk more about sex, as Alain de Botton suggests, must inevitably entail engaging with the hotel and the intimacy gradients that are built into its deep social logic. Indeed, the most significant thing that takes place within these massive institutions, and within the rented spaces of every suite or room, is the intimate, occasionally pleasurable, and always logical consequence of the structure itself, and of the many meanings we attach to it.

Markets

One could write a book, or a series of books, on all of the representations of sex in modern hotel rooms, representations that range (in spirit and in politics) from *Pretty Woman* (1990) to *Dirty Pretty Things* (2002). We are not simply talking about books that detail how hotels feature sexual representation—how flamboyantly decorated hotels like the Texas Zaza chain, for example, use raunchy photographs to direct guests both to their rooms and to the range of possible erotic activities in which they might engage once inside. Nor are we talking about the lore that can develop around certain hotels like the Chelsea—a mythos that helps to credential these hotels as historically significant sites of sexual escapade and destination in their own right. Some hotels, like the Library Hotel, of course, make explicit the link between the hotel room, sex, and the book. Its Dewey Decimal System organization has helped to make its exotic literature room the privileged location for the "Erotica Package" that the Library Hotel sells—its Kama Sutra Essential Love Package including books like *The Kama Sutra* and *The Art of Arousal* as well as erotic videos and champagne. Even these brief examples suggest the myriad ways that textuality and sexuality converge in the hotel with particular force and meaning.[7]

But the story of how the hotel sells sexual experimentation as a key component of self-discovery does not end there. Books not only document the link between sex and the hotel and the various kinds of personal awakenings that result—some go further, fetishizing the hotel as a privileged space for sexual encounter and, consequently, are written with the specific aim of encouraging, even seducing, readers into becoming active participants rather than passive observers of the hotel's sexual antics. These stories about the hotel describe it as nothing less than a sexual maker space in which individuals test out and design different sexual experiences for themselves that ultimately enable new ways of being in the world once guests move beyond the hotel's front door.

Rachel Kramer Bussel's *Do Not Disturb: Hotel Sex Stories* (2009), for example, instructs readers of this multiauthored collection of short stories to read "in situ"—to pick up the book while "lounging in a hotel lobby" or while "making so much noise in your hotel room bed that someone calls security." If Bussel finds hotel rooms in and of themselves sexy—"Hotel rooms are, in a word, hot" she begins by observing—her aim is to use books to make hotels' public as well as private domains even steamier destinations.[8] Here, reading is a kind of affective foreplay—a promiscuous, semipublic activity that suggests, through the heightened arousal of the reader, the fireworks that can go off behind closed hotel doors. If reading, within the context of the hotel, is imagined here as a promiscuous activity that fully implicates all the readers' senses and erotic longings, authorship can also capture and reflect the unique sexual energies pulsating through the hotel's public spaces—its bar, lobbies, and reception area.

Once we turn to crowd-sourced websites like The Hotel Sex Guide, we can see how the hotel functions as habitus and laboratory encouraging past, present, and future guests—wherever they happen to be— to collaborate in the sexual discovery that is the hotel's stock-in-trade.

Providing information about specific hotels in various cities that "tantalize your senses, light your fire and heat up those hotel sheets,"⁹ The Hotel Sex Guide asks its visitors to consider sharing "a sexy hotel experience" of their own and, in so doing, imagines hotel sex as an inevitably shared imaginative activity. Much as TripAdvisor or Wikipedia taps the collective wisdom of thousands of users, so too is The Guide looking for "writers, readers, and lovers from around the world to contribute" or coauthor this text about "the sexy trip down love's highway" that the hotel offers its visitors. From Craigslist announcements of upcoming hotel stays posted by individuals seeking sex with strangers to hotels that market themselves as "gay friendly" and "gay hotels," hotel same-sex activity has become a recognizable subgenre of sex sought and has been advertised to travelers as a key feature of the hotel as erotic utopia, playground, and radical experimental environment. Regardless of orientation, the sexual risk taking, adventure, and discovery that the hotel's private spaces support push its conceptual gradations of intimacy well beyond the hotel's walls—thereby solidifying the hotel's place in the cultural imaginary as a powerful incubator for the psychosexual self and a privileged site for radical experimentation and adventure.

The therapeutic benefits of reading, writing, and loving one's way through the world's major hotel sites are described in detail in such relatively esoteric publications as *Men's Health*, suggesting the larger cultural norms that the hotel's deep privacy ultimately serves. Its instructional treatise, "Get a Room: How to Make Hotel Sex Even More Wild," encourages readers to exploit the exhibitionist elements of the hotel room—its big windows facing other buildings and the requisite possibility of being seen in the act of sex offer, according to the authors, real health benefits—simultaneously increasing the voyeuristic pleasure and therefore the aerobic intensity of the sexual workout.¹⁰ Whether focusing explicitly on the bed or on the hotel room's connections to the outside world, the rich range of texts devoted to sex and the hotel focus on the erotics implicit in the hotel's capacity to bridge and blend public and private domains, and precisely this capacity causes them to concur that sex is distinctly sexier once you check in and before you check out. Of course, this sexual energy, heightened by the hotel's innermost recesses, also works temporarily to disrupt and more generally to uphold business as usual once guests' stays are over and the suitcases are unpacked.

The ubiquity of these representations establishes the expectation of sex in the most refined hotels, and allows a wide swath of people to see solicitations for sex everywhere in locations marked as cosmopolitan. They foster complementary conceptualizations of the hotel as a restorative, heterotopic space and as an ungoverned, deeply sexualized playground. They help one to see the smiling couple, ordering up champagne and strawberries, pouring the baths salts, and getting lost in a romantic weekend. But they also cognitively associate the hotel with boundary-breaking erotic antics of breathtaking proportions—allowing us to envision, without difficulty, Viagra-enhanced geriatric politicians spontaneously leaping out of showers and into the arms of supposedly willing domestics or sexually insatiable nearly-over-the-hill playboys being enthusiastically serviced by nubile porn stars.

But the hotel room is not merely a passive structure, onto which we project fantasy. Sex is a silent feature of the advertising strategy for nearly every hotel chain. Less than ten years ago, *Time* reported that the average time spent viewing an adult film in a hotel room was just over twelve minutes, a rather suggestive detail. When the *Time* article came out, roughly half of the guests staying in major chain hotels were purchasing adult material through various on-demand systems, accounting for the great bulk of profit that flowed from in-room purchases. In a thousand deliberate ways, the hotel makes the privacy—and sexualized privacy—of guests not only possible but seemingly inevitable.

Hotel rooms are not only a privileged venue for the consumption of pornography but are also a primary staging ground for pornographic production, choreography, and narrative making. Tapping into the hotel's robust set of associations with sexual experimentation and fantasy production, pornography, not surprisingly, finds a happy home within the confines of the hotel room. Aesthetically, hotel rooms offer a common terrain, not merely a collection of neutral colors and familiar material features, but also an arrangement of things—beds, tables, lights, mirrors—that should be familiar to just about everyone. The hotel room's anonymity and seemingly infinite capacity for replication become the canvas upon which viewers can tease out their own psychosexual fantasies, loosely collaborating with those on screen. As a standard setting of porn scenes—both gay and straight, amateur and professional—the hotel room, therefore, provides guests a particularly fantasy-rich venue for the watching of pornography—a setting in which boundaries between hotel guests and the pornography they watch recursively blur and blend, adding to the voyeuristic allure of hotel porn.

The "Corfu Suite" at the Blacks Hotel, London, named the Sexiest Bedroom of 2013 by Mr. and Mrs. Smith, internet travel agents who annually "hunt down" the most romantic, rentable intimate spaces, and who, with a wink and a nod, "give them a thorough going over." The Corfu Suite, for them, is a "gorgeously gauzy, bright-white bolthole," the sort of quasi-pornographic space "soft-focused memories are made in." (Publicity photo: http://www.blakeshotels.com/sexiest-bedroom; accessed June 4, 2014. Text of the award notice: http://blog.mrandmrssmith.com/2013/12/the-smith-awards-top-10-sexiest-hotel-bedrooms/#_ga=1.161005502.2055445512.1401929948; accessed June 4, 2013)

Yet this pervasiveness of porn, much like the ubiquity of sex, is not a fully visible, well-articulated feature of hotel advertisement. It remains private—much like the hotel room itself, largely hidden from view. Robert Kumpel, touring San Diego in 2002 for the *San Diego Reader*, found pornography available in every single local hotel, from SROs to the very best, but could not find a hotel manager who was willing to talk about it candidly. Perusing the pay-per-view menu at one, he chose the option marked "Red Hot"—the movies were clustered, it seems, by intensity. In the morning, he was surprised to see that the bill only indicated a thirteen-dollar charge for "Movies/Internet/Games." All of this, journalist Timothy Egan, writing in the *New York Times* in 2000, suggested, flowed from the new technologies "that make pornography easier to order into the home than pizza." Though they preferred not to be named, major corporations, Egan continued, were now "stakeholders in the proliferation of adult content into every private space, from the bedroom to the cubicle to the hotel suite."[11]

Hotels, of course, cannot market themselves publicly as places where every room is its own den of iniquity, where boys can be boys, under the supervision of solicitous staff, and where hotel security keeps the cops away. The Marriott chain, hoping to build good public relations as a family friendly venue, announced in the late 2000s that it was removing adult material from the plans for all of its new buildings. Demand for pay-per-view movies had, quite suddenly, decreased. And Marriott, like other chains, was moving quickly to recapture lost profit potential, largely by charging fees for Wi-Fi. The *Daily Mail* blamed the iPad and suggested that business travelers were now more likely to bring their illicit entertainment with them or access it through third-party streaming sites online. This, then, was not a reform but a revolution, and less a matter of taste than a reflection that laptops, tablets, and smartphones had become ubiquitous, making it easier and easier to access adult material within the prescribed safe zone of the hotel room. Better profits—and better PR—would come from providing access to the internet, and letting the guests choose to find their way to whatever was on their mind.

The particular kind of privacy the hotel room offers its guests makes it not only a privileged site for the viewing as well as filming of pornographic material—rather, it can all too easily and quickly become a dynamic venue for on-site enactments of sexual boundary crossing. We can see the ease and facility with which the hotel room enables seemingly impromptu expressions of sexual aggression and excess all too frequently in contemporary culture. For example, one May night in the spring of 2011, less than a year after Charlie Sheen's presumably thrilling night, an immigrant chambermaid from Guinea, working at the high-end luxury Sofitel in Manhattan, entered the suite occupied by a certain head of the International Monetary Fund and likely candidate for the presidency of France, none other than Dominique Strauss-Kahn, one of the most powerful men in the world, a grizzled veteran of continental and global politics. In the unexpected, jarring encounter that followed, the prescribed distance between her and DSK—between the world's elite cosmopolitan class and the world's downtrodden global migrant class—dramatically and violently collapsed. A few hours later, he was hauled off an Air France flight, arrested by the New York Police Department, and accused of rape.

If the "pornification" of the hotel room is an elaboration of the already troubling conventions of the patriarchal world, the space that the hotel offers its guests is key to understanding this fact of sex, the hotel, and the modern self. This aspect of the story—the spatial dimensions of this story of sexual self-making and unmaking—both fascinated and yet consistently eluded those who reported on the episode. Despite the iconic familiarity of this story, the actual physical scene of the event remained strangely elusive and hard for readers of the story to visualize—it remained so ill-defined, in fact, that a July 8, 2011, article in the *New York Times* ("What Happened in Room 2806") helpfully supplied visuals of the scene to try to "crack" the case. A map of the twenty-eighth floor of the hotel was prominently displayed on the page, and we were asked, detective style, to follow John Eligon's three theories of that night's events—theories that, in the fashion of a modern-day Miss Marple or Hercule Poirot, the author drew directly from the evidence lurking in the blueprint of the hotel and the relations of the twenty-eighth floor's public spaces to the room of the crime scene.[12]

With the diagram of the hotel interior in front of us, we could suddenly begin to see how things might have unfolded—how the gradients of intimacy that the hotel offers its guests might have been leapt with a single bound by individuals on their way somewhere else and how the hotel room could be transformed, in a heartbeat, into a dangerous laboratory for sexual self-making activities that wreak real damage. Keycard records showed how rapidly the chambermaid moved across the floor, that her work was frenetically paced and constant. The question of whether she entered and cleaned an adjoining room suddenly assumed prominence in determining culpability. The time frame of her movements—late morning and midday—corresponded to the moment at which most travelers were out of their rooms, when the hidden agents of the service economy emerge like nameless automatons to tidy up the rooms and tighten up the bed sheets. And there, in the middle of the twenty-eighth floor, was the service lobby, wherein these typically invisible attendants stored their supplies, stacked their clean towels, and kept their perfumed soaps and shampoos.

These visual aids may help us graph the events, but they do not answer the question of why the hotel itself remains so elusive and yet looms so prominently in this modern psychodrama. What is it about hotel life that makes it such a ripe field for scandal and internationally riveting professional unmaking? These are the questions that were not asked despite the wearying plethora of articles and reportage on the

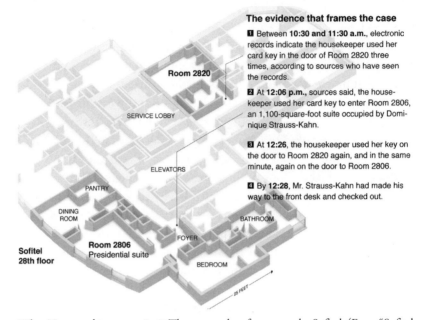

The evidence that frames the case

1 Between **10:30 and 11:30 a.m.**, electronic records indicate the housekeeper used her card key in the door of Room 2820 three times, according to sources who have seen the records.

2 At **12:06 p.m.**, sources said, the housekeeper used her card key to enter Room 2806, an 1,100-square-foot suite occupied by Dominique Strauss-Kahn.

3 At **12:26**, the housekeeper used her key on the door to Room 2820 again, and in the same minute, again on the door to Room 2806.

4 By **12:28**, Mr. Strauss-Kahn had made his way to the front desk and checked out.

Room 2820

SERVICE LOBBY

ELEVATORS

PANTRY

DINING ROOM

BATHROOM

FOYER

Sofitel 28th floor

Room 2806 Presidential suite

BEDROOM

25 FEET

What Happened in room 2806? The geography of power at the Sofitel. (From "Sofitel 28th Floor: The Evidence that Frames the Case," *New York Times*, July 8, 2011)

event, but these are the questions that cut to the very heart of the thrall and fascination that the event itself had cast over worldwide audiences.

In fact, the hotel's repeated appearance as understudy and best supporting actor in such riveting and protracted media dramas suggests that the hotel—replete with its private spaces, public venues, and gradients of intimacy that create dynamic hybrid spatial blends—is centrally important in the sexual self-making and unmaking enabled by modern culture. The alleged rape of the chambermaid by the head of the IMF—an event so melodramatic, so metaphorical, and so clichéd that it might have been an episode of *Law and Order*—could have happened only in a hotel and, more particularly, in those spaces of the hotel (somewhere after the hallway and between the bathroom and bedroom) that elude easy or fixed representation—those spaces across which the highly mobile bodies of workers and guests move with ease and facility.

Domesticities

The private domain of the hotel room is not the exclusive purview for men's sexual exploits, despite all the press coverage attesting to that fact.

The unique kind of privacy offered by the hotel room can and does become the habitus for a diverse and rich array of experiments that women travelers and guests undertake in the process of gaining sexual knowledge, regeneration, and forms of "healing" that can, at times, resist and, at other times, reinforce the circumstances they seek to remake.

We can track this history with the rise of the sexual revolution in the 1960s and with Curt Donovan's 1965 novel *Hotel Widow*. Clarise, the "hotel widow" of his book's title, is an object of desire for the cosmopolitan executives and businessmen and servants who sweep into her orbit. As the lurid cover of the book suggested, she is the sort of woman who—once emancipated from her loveless marriage—chooses to entertain older men wearing steel-gray suits and bearing cocktails, all while wearing a two-piece bathing suit and admiring herself in the mirror. A shallow temptress and sexually liberated new woman, she is also a perverse ideal: a woman whose willpower and sexual appetites are dangerously strong, and who settles at the nexus of male travel precisely because it affords her a rotating stable of lovers. "She ran men's lives with the power of a witch," the pulp text enticingly suggests to its presumptive male readership, "and she was a witch—a blue eyed, beautiful one."[13]

Hotel Widow revels in the lowest form female objectification, but it also generates a corrective to the overwrought and timeworn story of male wanderlust and female domesticity. The official narrative suggests that women in the hotel are in full retreat, reduced to a role as the passive subjects of male desire and sexual self-making. There is, though, more to this story and to how the kind of privacy the hotel room offers enables women's sexual experimentation. Take the more recent example that Lisa Zeidner provides in Claire Newbold, the protagonist of her 1999 novel *Layover*, and nothing less than a modern-day Erica Jong. Sexually betrayed by her husband and suffering the tragic loss of her only child, Claire Newbold cuts loose from a house and home she can no longer endure, and she turns to the hotels in which she has stayed while traveling for work to engage in an epic series of hotel trysts across the United States. These "layovers" are vengeful, but also redemptive. They are simultaneously the acts of a wounded soul and a gradual healing for what ails Claire. "On the lam from tragedy, grateful to humbly enter and exit" the hotel rooms that she once paid for but now sneaks into covertly, Claire begins to rid herself of the "extraneous" things that get in the way of her experiencing the "core self" that she believes should remain—"the self [that] would feel vulnerable" and carry a "sensation of rawness" in the wake of her husband's sexual rejection and her son's death.

As the *New York Times* reviewer suggests, it is only on the surface that Claire's voyage through the hotels of America "is a simple sexual one."[14] On a deeper level, this is a story about a self in desperate need—a self that admits "I was no longer, in some sense, even a woman" (17). This self in need of sexual wholeness starts a computer file on all of the hotels she knows intimately, replete with information on how to crack their security barriers and code key access devices—in short, with the information that will enable her to illicitly leap across the intimacy gradients she so enjoyed upholding as a paying guest and to covertly enter the most private terrains the hotel offers in an effort to resist the social forces that have become unendurable. These leaps of sexual faith—with sons and then their fathers—gradually enable Newbold to desire her husband again—to "want to have the kind of sex one can have, with one's husband, only in hotels."[15] Thus, while the illicit sex she has in the hotel rooms in which she covertly squats offers Newbold temporary freedom from a life that has become empty, these escapades ultimately work to reengage her as wife to her once wayward husband—as a woman who wants to have hotel sex with her husband rather than with strangers.

As a facilitator of real and virtual intimacies, the hotel and its most private chambers do a certain kind of sex work for those on the move and in search of solace, seduction, and secrecy. A brothel for some and a suburban home for others, it is a refuge from patriarchy *and* a male-centered structure, all at once. It makes Charlie Sheen's antics possible, but it also facilitates transgressive feminine performance and female sexuality, like Newbold's leap of despair into the emotionally empty room in search of the sexual thing that will make her self whole again. Capable of sanitizing one room and adding illicit, lurid zest to another, offering women a space of their own but encouraging boys to be boys, the hotel is a third domain of sorts, an imaginative construct as well as a built environment where public and private worlds blur in ways both unexpected and heavily scripted. In so doing, it ultimately promises to vivify all worlds, but such a heavily wrought oasis inevitably generates collateral damage.

The hotel's role in women's sexual experimentation and healing is not confined to the world of fiction—it is front-page news and the stuff of real-life reporting, with stories by jilted spouses like Denise Richards peppering the covers of *US Weekly* magazine, among others. The July

SPACE

The Standard Hotel, viewed from New York City's High Line trail, where guest rooms are routinely ranked among the "sexiest" in the world because of the illicit promise of public exposure. (Photo by Matthew Pratt Guterl)

26, 2011, cover story titled "Denise Richards Finally Opens Up about Charlie Sheen's Hotel Meltdown," as well as her 2011 autobiography, *The Real Girl Next Door*, are both animated by the self-declared desire to tell her side of the story after protracted silence.[16] The hotel episode is one from which Richards distances herself, declaring that she left Charlie and his companion in the lobby and before they entered the hotel's most private arena. Attuned by years of marriage to the signs of brewing sexual volatility of her now ex-mate, Richards knows how to navigate the hotel's fluid public and private arenas in order to keep herself out of the line of fire. Precisely because she has been so well educated by her "home training" with Charlie, she knows all too well what awaits in the hotel room and wants to tell her readers her side of the story. If Richards has the dubious distinction of being the worst Bond girl of all time, as *US Weekly* reminds its readers, she is nonetheless breaking new ground navigating the cognitive dissonance created by the hotel for those family members who remain on the other side of the hotel door and its "do not disturb" sign. When asked what she tells her young daughter about her father's hotel activities and how she integrates this version of patriarchy into her daughter's education about domestic life, Richards says there is no ready-made language to integrate the hotel story into that of the nuclear family's bildungsroman, but that she is developing one as she goes.

As we have seen in the preceding pages, that language is already there, waiting for her to take it up within the hotel's most intimate chambers. Richards assertively offers up her own version of the hotel room as comparatively prim and proper, as a space where good parenting takes place. At the Plaza, she books her family into the "Eloise Suite" that, as we saw in the first chapter, depicts so powerfully for readers and visitors to the Plaza Hotel the life of a spirited young girl who lives in the same hotel. Rather than condemn hotels generally, Richards makes a distinction between the various temporal, spatial, and moral authorities in operation within the Plaza. In her suite, control and "home training" rule the day. In her room, the aesthetic is child-friendly. Richards even sleeps in the "parent's room" attached to her suite, a sign that the network of spaces she has chosen to rent have been designed to foster appropriate supervision even as they enable the play of children. She clarifies that a nanny watched the children while she ate with Sheen and "some friends," lest the reader think she'd brought the children with her. And she quickly dismisses the women at Sheen's dinner table at Daniel—women like

Capri Anderson—as "prostitutes" and "hookers." Her account of the dinner is detached, as if she were an old-school anthropologist watching a primitive mating ritual and not a participant-observer, not a part of the story itself. Back at the Plaza and down the hall, in the midst of Sheen's explosive uprising, something else prevails in the Eloise Suite, where the furniture is pink and frilly and girly, and where "good" motherhood is made possible. Richards's narrative is the counterpoint to Sheen's, but both inevitably reveal the function of the hotel and the private spaces their guests call temporary home.[17]

These expressions—in newsprint, the novel, the popular press, and the historical record—of women's gravitation to the hotel in search of sexual activity push against the vortex of domestic monogamy differently but as determinately as does Charlie Harper in *Two and Half Men*. They collectively stress the hotel's private spaces as sites for sexual opportunity, narrative, and story making for both sexes, regardless of object choice. Richards's retreat to the safety of the hotel room as her own domestic construct is, then, not just an escape from the wildness of Sheen, but also an effort to tap into the alternate possibilities of the building and its cultural capital, creating a safe harbor for the family amid the "havoc" that such a building can and, so often, does wreak. Richards's creation of the domestic sublime in a hotel is accompanied, always, by her paratext as a sex object and celebrity. But—in her autobiography and elsewhere—she raises and elides that paratext, emphasizing, for an audience of millions, her motherhood, her humanity, and her quixotic desire for privacy. In 2011, in the midst of her public relations tour for the book, she adopted a child and named her Eloise, a poignant reminder of the power of the hotel to shape the domestic, often in unexpected ways.[18]

As it turns out, though, there are a lot of things that can happen in these highly mutable, constantly repurposing hotel private spaces: illicit and secretive, intimate things, like extramarital sex, paid sex labor, class-conscious rape, or the consumption of pornography; but also productive things, like business meetings, and literary salons, and professional conferences, and policy decisions; or dangerous things, like binge drinking, or suicide, or murder; or unexpected things, troublesome things, weird things, pleasurable things, things to worry about, and things to marvel at—things that make and break careers in a single night and things that promise redemption and second chances. It is worth lingering over the significance of sex in the private spaces of the hotel, not

The street front of the Plaza Hotel, facing Grand Army Plaza, featuring the "Eloise" flag, which hangs between the United States flag and the banner for the Plaza's interior shopscape. (Brechtbug/Flickr)

because it is titillating, and not, again, because the sex is so good, but, rather, because these things—these titillations and expectations—are troubling evidence of the successful public work of the hotel, proof of the broadcast mythology of the hotel as a great, discreet staging ground for everything from a romantic getaway to the rape of a chambermaid.

If this part of the story is pervasive, it has also been dramatically underreported, unspoken, and obscured. The work of the hotel in the modern self's psychosexual journey generally goes unremarked, as does its capacity to generate an erotic environment—both built and imagined—for its guests. There are exceptions, of course, like Sheen's wild night, or the DSK scandal at the Sofitel, and, when they happen, they carry the psychic weight of all the stories that are not told—they unleash firestorms of retribution and fascination. They are told and retold with insatiable relish precisely because they give, for a moment that readers want to last as long as possible, a hint of the shape and texture of this other side of the modern luxury hotel's sexual story. These illicit stories gain luster and allure from the sexual boundary crossing that is the hotel's (not so) secret stock-in-trade, but, more fundamentally, they awaken the insatiable appetites of modern audiences because they speak to our desire for the kind of space, both real and imagined, that the hotel offers—the kind of space that enables guests to go off the grid. It is not just that the hotel offers us the chance to do things naughty enough to warrant a cover-up—that "what happens here stays here" kind of promise. More fundamentally, it is that the hotel offers up a uniquely modern kind of space, an uneven, unfair adult playground of sorts that guests encounter and help to create when they check in. The resulting sensationalized stories that the hotel periodically coughs up let us know that "what happens in the hotel" is because of the hotel and the constantly changing, ever malleable blend of public and private spaces it offers us.

Time

3

BEGINNINGS

A young, weary white man, carrying his dry cleaning on a city street at night, is openly mocked by a trio of young rap impresarios. Dejectedly, with his shirt collar loosened and his shoulders slumped, he stands still, the subject of a steady torrent of ridicule and abuse. But then, miraculously, he straightens up, throws his shoulders back, passing off his dry cleaning, and belts out a rich, responsorial rhyme. Throughout his charged counterpoetic, his black critics sit in total shock. They look like witnesses to a miracle. "I'll bet you're all wondering why my rhyme is so tight," our prototypical white investment banker concludes, even as his rap falls back into the normal cadence of speech: "I did stay in a Holiday Inn Express last night."

The modern business hotel, as this interlude suggests, is such a powerfully regenerative space that it can give the white body the gift of black song. At a time of declining wages, rising unemployment, and an increasingly hostile workplace that requires its laborers to make ever more sacrifices to their quality of home life in order to remain employed, the hotel becomes a refueling station of a particular sort. Offering the anxious laborer a temporary respite from the very market that requires that he move from client to client and city to city with ever-greater frequency, the hotel becomes both a hiatus and a haven—a space in which the market-weary laborer can seek solace, comfort, and new beginnings while on the road doing global capitalism's work. With affordably cozy comforts, it can repair the tired physique, offering an internal space of respite and regeneration. "Stay smart," runs the advertising campaign of the Holiday Inn Express chain, a slogan meant to capture the market for pennywise shoppers, needing a place to stay, wanting a space that attends to the body and the soul, but desiring, as well, a steal. But while value might be one factor, the overall emphasis here is not on pinching pennies but on a transcendent recovery of the spirit worn down by the daily grind—on new beginnings and a fresh start for the bedraggled and world weary, even if that new start ultimately enables the weary traveler to continue to function as a capable soldier in capitalism's global army on the move. The rather successful marketing scheme of the Holiday Inn Express chain rests on a liberal expansion of the right to high-thread-count sheets and name-brand aromatherapy shampoos, a right that privileges the pleasurable experience over the threadbare virtues of economy and thrift and that promises infinitely portable renewal—a renewal that seems to offer respite but is ultimately part and parcel of the market phenomena that exhaust and dis-spirit the modern self.

In this instantiation, the hotel as purveyor of the therapeutic wraps the constantly mobile traveler in a space resembling a cocoon, gesturing inward and encouraging a gestation that promises nothing less than a second coming and new life—a rebirth and reawakening into one's true and authentic self. The hotel parses space differently, as we saw in the last section, enabling iterations of the self that blend public and private arenas, encouraging modes of socialization that are essentially hybrid, and creating gradations of intimacy that alter the sexual expressions of self-hood, as we saw in the preceding chapter. But once we attend to the role of the therapeutic in the hotel's arsenal of enticements—once we look specifically at the kinds of implicit therapy and renewal that the spa hotel makes palpable and unavoidable—we come to see how the hotel functions not only as a kind of seductive portal or doorway into new modes of self-making but also as a kind of doorstop or holding pen, encouraging the disoriented, anxious, and perpetual traveler through space to take advantage of a momentary respite from the pressures of global capital—a much needed time out from thousands of air miles logged, car rental queues, and GPS automated voice instructions. In other words, once we attend to the spa hotel—its history, evolution, and ongoing appeal in contemporary culture—we come to see highlighted the hotel as both conduit and passageway through which the modern self moves but desires to linger on the way to a new life. That this new life is a shimmering promise ultimately ephemeral and transitory is part of its seductive appeal and a key feature of the psychological work it does for those selves pressed into capitalism's service.

A fantasy habitus encouraging individuals to stay put and dwell in a moment of renewal and new beginning rather than move on, the spa hotel and the therapy that is its stock-in-trade at first glance seem to defy the mandate of the modernly mobile self. This very allure, as we will see, has made the spa hotel a more rather than less dominant feature of the hospitality trade over the past two hundred years—a commodity of increasing value to those who wander the earth in search of homes not troubled by mortgage balloons, negative equity, fear of foreclosure, proximity to superfund sites, or urban violence. In a world that demands the self to be ever more mobile and that encroaches in creatively brutal ways on the sanctity of the endangered homes that laborers travel so far and wide to protect, the spa hotel provides psychic sustenance to a psychically starving self—it offers nothing less than the opportunity to feel renewal, a life rendered temporarily new and fresh once again because momentarily unencumbered by care.

The spa hotel does nothing less than promise to dial back the clock for people whose lives seem to be moving too quickly forward and to the grave—for people who feel and look older than their years and thus are in desperate search of lost youth and hope when the future looks bleak. And this promise of renewal inevitably assumes a temporal dimension. The hotel, when approached with an eye to temporality, suddenly promises to be a fountain of youth—to offer life-giving properties to those exhausted and prematurely aged by the press of modernity at a time when the mandate to remain perpetually youthful has never been stronger. The hotel, in sum, both occasions and promises to solve the ravages of time all too evident on the brows of travel-weary laborers of global capital.

How did we come to see hotels as therapeutic spaces, or as sites of bodily and soulful renewal, replete with life-giving properties of repair and restoration? How, in turn, did we come to see access to the hotel-as-spa as a right of the traveler? There is, of course, no obvious home for the therapeutic. At first blush, the hotel is an entirely functional institution, a sort of sanitary warehouse for strange bodies on the move and out of place, or a temporary meeting space for groups too informal to own a more permanent site somewhere else. But, looking backward, one needs only to think of structures of refuge and sanctuary along the pilgrim's trail, or of the oasis, providing shelter from the heat of the trade routes and offering up vital sustenance, to see a long-standing connection between such spaces and the representation of both physical and spiritual recovery. It was not uncommon to have a hotel, or a boardinghouse, or a way station of some kind next to a religious shrine, functioning as a complement to the destination. Indeed, for a long time, the sites of refuge and spiritual communion have been proximate, intertwined, and mutually reinforcing. Given, on the one hand, the accelerating demand that global capital makes of the world's workers to be mobile—to move ever more frequently through space in pursuit of clients, customers, and new business—and, on the other hand, the accelerating economic inaccessibility of institutions of succor, help, and support—institutions like the hospital, the asylum, and even the prison—it is no real surprise that the therapeutic function of the hotel has become more evident and appealing over the past two hundred years and that the healing and time-reversing properties of the hotel seem endowed with the ability to confer new life.

What makes the hotel a powerful locus of life-restoring properties is its connectedness to sites of medical intervention and surgical correction—its interconnectedness with life-giving institutions like the hospital. While Theresa Brown observes rightly that "hospitals aren't hotels," it is still true that their increasing focus on patients' level of consumer satisfaction and the patient as consumer closes the distance between patient and guest—between meaningful and long-term corrective surgical intervention, which Brown observes is surprisingly difficult to assess, and temporary, restorative treatment focused on the relieving of pain, the palliative alleviation of distress, and the short-term benefits that accrue to a stay.[1]

In fact, the rise of the hospital-hotel as a hybrid institution over the past century makes palpable and evident their overlapping missions. Hospital hotels have sprung up to fill a growing need not only for family members to be close to those who are hospitalized but to expedite the fluid transformation of guest into patient and patient into guest. As early as 1926, *Time* observed the cultural significance of the "hospital-hotel" when $4 million was allocated to build a "hospital and hotel building" in Manhattan—what would be called Doctor's Hospital on the Upper East Side. According to the author, the announcement caused a stir among newspaper columnists who found "irresistible" "the vision of a high jinx victim being trundled from his bedroom to the convenient emergency ward."[2] While news of the hybrid building generated much "wit-stirring material," by the 1920s the inability of hospitals to provide sufficiently sumptuous accommodation and therapeutic intervention was a well-known fact—only 19 percent of beds in Manhattan hospitals, for example, were in private rooms, while the demand for such private care and shelter was easily double that. In such a climate, the hotel filled a need particularly for the wealthy, and the hotel's role in such an endeavor was clear to all. The *New York Telegram* headline "New Hospital to Be Run Like a Luxurious Hotel (April 25, 1929) only made explicit what had been a well-known fact for decades—those in search of therapy, succor, and pampering along with their medical procedures needed to turn to the hospital hotel rather than the hospital.[3]

Like the hospital, the spa is another institution whose promise of physical renewal is integrally tied to its partnership with the hotel. Just as the hospital hotel emerged in response to a felt need, so too did the spa hotel respond to individuals' increasing demand for a life-giving oasis that promised a softer healing. Over the course of the nineteenth and twentieth centuries, with increasing rates of global travel and worldwide competition between massive corporate conglomerations for consumer dollars, the spa became a natural function of the hotel itself, and a destination in its own right. One can mark critical moments on this timeline rather easily: the mid-nineteenth-century invention of the private resort—of the hot springs and artesian waters variety—offered access to a burgeoning middle class and drew tourists to the newly settled landscapes of the American heartland, far from the supposed dangers of cities. The geographically remote spa hotel occupies one end of the historical spectrum, marking the spa hotel's emergence on the cultural scene to offer relief to those overtaxed with the labors of an industrializing nineteenth-century market. At the other end of this temporal spectrum is the rise in the late twentieth century of the work-hotel-spa complex, strategically located proximate to white-collar urban workspaces and conceived as a way of offering temporarily overwrought masters of the corporate universe quick and immediate (if dramatically abbreviated) respite from the pressures of global capital. These two iterations of the spa hotel are removed from each other by over a century, but collectively they chart the evolving shape and texture of human need for the succor, renewal, and new beginnings that the spa promises, even as they suggest the increasing urgency of that need in the face of global capital's rise. In short, they suggest that one key promise the hotel can and does make to guests is the intangible but irresistible promise to give new starts and reverse the effects of brutalizing time.

Origins

We can see the origins and emergence of the spa hotel on the American scene in Indiana's famous French Lick Hotel, which opened in 1845 as a hokey frontier spa and by the end of the century featured aristocratic landscapes, handcrafted mosaic floors, locally bottled mineral water, and a railroad stop. Linked in the twentieth century to the political ambitions of Indianapolis mayor Thomas Taggert, the French Lick Hotel now features multiple golf courses and functions as a retreat for the regional and national elite and a second home to the Democratic Party. At the height of its fame, the rehabilitative ethos of the French Lick Hotel was always about the little touches that accompanied access to the life-giving mineral springs. Famously, the hotel was the "birthplace" of tomato juice, offered as a "healthy" component of a balanced diet. The in-house restaurant was famous, though, for dessert, and chiefly because it arrived balanced on the heads of the exclusively African American waitstaff, all while the happy tune "As the Saints Go Marching In" was played. A vital part of the physical repair, then, was the presentation and enjoyment of the ubiquitous servile class, from porters and bellboys carrying luggage to your room, to attendants in the baths, to the delivery of silver trays of caramel ice cream, mascarpone, and coconut custard pie, smiling and laughing as proof of their contentment. "I walk and drink water and take baths—that is all I do," one woman wrote to her confidant, "Hazel," on the back of a postcard in 1906. But the atmospherics of the French Lick site were such that she, and all of those who visited, did all of these things while enveloped within a web of other, equally meaningful instruments of recovery—among them, the happy black waiter, the gold-leaf details in the lobby, and the tomato juice.[4]

The lifespan of the French Lick Hotel was linked to the uniqueness of the life-giving and youth-restoring mineral springs in the region. And once the therapeutic functions of those springs became portable—once mineral water, mud baths, and hot-stone massages could be offered anywhere—it was easier to begin the process of repair and restoration locally, without traveling to the remote French Lick. As the hotel-as-spa expanded and opened closer to exhausted laborers' workspaces, many of the massive spa resorts of the nineteenth century fell into ruin, their promise of geographic escape as an essential element of renewal fatally compromised. By the mid-twentieth century, parts of the West Baden Springs Hotel—a nearby twin of the French Lick Hotel—had been turned into a Jesuit seminary, fulfilling a social function in which geographic isolation was actually essential. By the late twentieth century, the structure had partially collapsed, leading to its designation as a national landmark, and the commencement of efforts to restore it.

The Atrium at the West Baden Springs Hotel, photographed in 1903. Note how philosopher Jeremy Bentham's Panopticon—the central tower in the middle of a prison, hiding the gaze of the warden, which is directed outward toward the cells on the periphery—is, here, reversed, with the ramparts and rooms facing inward, not toward authority, but, instead, toward the common, multipurpose, "public" space of the atrium. (Prints and Photographs Division, Library of Congress, Washington, D.C.)

Now, the French Lick Hotel and the West Baden Hotel, restored to some semblance of their original magnificence, are joined as a single resort. Prospective guests can choose from a drop-down menu of dazzlingly specific therapies and assemble packages that promise a return to physical grace. But while the "healing waters" of the "Pluto Mineral Spring" are still a seductive feature of the place, the real draw is the massive gambling casino that opened in 2006. The newly reconceived complex thus functions as a place where the already rich have myriad satisfying opportunities to display their "excess" capital and where those less fortunate have the chance to leave with their pocketbooks miraculously replenished.

As iconic nineteenth-century spa hotels like the French Lick evolved into other public forms of leisure, new spa hotel complexes cropped up in urban centers like Dallas, Chicago, and New York and specifically aimed to provide immediate—even lunchtime—relief to the corporate elite. Dallas's Crescent is a prime example of this luxurious hybrid urban space, announcing itself as "the centerpiece" of the Dallas business district and boasting a complex of three almost-twenty-story office buildings contiguous to a luxury hotel and spa. The spa is as commodious and opulent as the business and hotel portions of the Crescent urban experience, occupying twenty-two thousand square feet and offering seventy-seven treatments and services explicitly aimed to increase not only the "mental acuity" but also the health, strength, and youthful appearance of those who live and work at the Crescent, as well as those leisured family members of visiting corporate elites.[5] In the design of the Crescent, we can see the broad and deep uptake among twentieth-century urban planners and real estate developers of the spa as oasis and regenerative locus for the market.

This new, now naturalized and nationalized function of the hotel-as-spa draws us, unnervingly, in two directions at once. On one side, there is the startling embrace of detailed sumptuousness and the wholesale acceptance of the elite spa hotel as a restorative temporary habitus for business travelers. Previously fearful of the public perception of their interior extravagance, or perhaps just shy about advertising their endorsement of class privilege, these rarified spaces now enthusiastically embrace their exclusivity and unapologetically name themselves as "spas" and "resorts."[6] On the other side, in an age of stagnant wages and expansive credit for most everyone else, there is the drive to democratize luxury itself and to push downward at least some of the sensory accoutrements of the elite spa. This impulse is best exemplified by Holiday Inn Express, but also captured in the creation of slightly more refined "niche" hotels, like Courtyard by Marriott, and in the international expansion of major chains and hotel networks, like the Starwood group. Even in lean times, midrange hotels seem determined to ape the gilded opulence of the class preserves of the very wealthy.

These two different directions, though, suggest a common point of origin. When we say, echoing Foucault, that the hotel is like a clinic, we mean it literally, because these spaces now offer themselves as technologies of restoration and renewal. Every detail is meant to convey a great calmness and reassuring class position, from the hushed tones of the uniformed staff to the afternoon turndown. But by emphasizing that inner repair depends on the scientific attention to the needs of the body, and in defining those needs with heavily weighted therapeutic language, the ethos of the hotel-as-spa even more directly parallels the clinic. The entering body is diseased and is diagnostically cycled through an exercise regimen, cleaned and perfumed, given a soft and warm place to sleep, and then, rehabilitated, it is released back into the wild. The day after the release is transformative, and different. This, it seems, is as true for a guest at the Holiday Inn Express—where aromatherapy shampoos, "sleep-number beds," and massage showerheads approximate the embodied clinical functions of the elite hotels—as it is for a visitor to the Houstonian. Whether these clinical touches are embedded in the architecture or embodied by staff experts, they are conceived by a broader cultural interest in the care and maintenance of the damaged physique.

But the hotel also echoes the old language of fantasy, defined by Foucault as a casualty of the "birth" of the modern clinical gaze. The notion of therapy in play here goes deeper than technical repair, marked by sensual oils and buff personal attendants. And the clinical feature of the hotel is not dispassionate or removed. It is an active, all-encompassing thing, manifested through no single agent, and appearing across the entire spectrum of experience. The restorative nature of hotel life can be heard in the sound of water flowing from gentle fountains in the lobby, felt in the soft sheets of the bed, seen in the mountains of folded white towels in the bathroom, worn in the robes and slippers provided by staff, and tasted in the small chocolate on the pillow. Each minute and every second of time spent in the hotel—from the Plaza to the Holiday Inn Express—is meant to be balm for the "road warriors," healing the cracked feet and tired shoulders of sojourners far from home in order to ready them for another day pressed into the service of global capital. But there is little difference, really, between Foucault's eighteenth-century healer, Pomme, "who treated and cured a hysteric by making her take baths" and who witnessed the passing of the hysteria through urination,[7] and the purifying airs of the contemporary sauna.

The persistence of the hotel-as-spa fantasy is an inevitable consequence of the failure of the hospital to resolve or successfully address the most regular and bothersome physical symptoms of modern life. In an era when medical privileges are being cut, copayments denied, and the hospital therefore recedes as a viable habitus of healing for many, the spa hotel takes its place with a vengeance. For a fraction of the cost of one night's stay in a hospital, the spa hotel guest has temporary access to

A promotional image, emphasizing solitude and repair—and not the commonplace, shared experience of your typical hotel pool—from the Lake Austin Spa Resort. (http://lakeaustin.com/gallery-1/spa; accessed May 28, 2014)

the healing waters, restorative balms, and soothing touches of soft clinicians and hotel workers. Averaging more than $1,700 a day in 2012, the hospital is now out of sight as anything other than a place of last resort for most Americans, even those with health insurance, and so we turn to the spa hotel as substitute and surrogate.[8] Clinic and shrine, rich with medical knowledge and spiritualist fantasy, the hotel is old and new all at once.

The foremost object of institutional interest here is "the guest," a voluntarily admitted body, contracting for a private service that aims to reset life's clock and the steady march of time to death. Brochures, advertisements, and websites speak in concrete and sometimes loving terms about the rich benefits of being a "guest" of the hotel. Assigned to a much-revered body nestled in the bosom of a vast and attentive structure, guest status is given and purchased, active and passive. The concept of the guest is at the very heart of the hotel-as-spa: he or she is asked to submit to the clinical scrutiny of the hotel, exposing inner wounds, even as he or she requests, if not demands, the figment of real and meaningful healing. At times swaddled like an infant in salt wraps, pampered like a young spoiled child, and provided with womblike environments that seem almost embryonic, the spa hotel guest is returned to life's beginning in an effort to dial back time.

Futures

The contemporary hotel-as-spa—where the guest willingly is constituted—is nowhere more evident than in such places as Canyon Ranch, which (much like the French Lick Hotel before it) announces itself as not just "a place" but as "a state of mind and a way of life," or the

Lake Austin Resort and Spa, which blends the "luxury of a world-class spa with the warmth of a best friend's lake house" to make it the number-one destination spa in North America. Despite hybrid urban complexes like the Crescent, the contemporary spa hotel—derived from such class antecedents as the French Lick—continues to flourish and caters to a mixed but predominantly female clientele unconstrained by the rigors of a nine-to-five workday, thereby offering a heavily gendered kind of hotel as place of remaking. Whereas sex and the hotel, as we suggested, tends to target the male traveler in search of narratives of sexual rejuvenation and experimentation with women travelers having comparatively less run of the sexual house, the spa hotel configured along the lines of a Lake Austin Resort and Spa offers predominantly women guests with time on their hands and literally fat as well as money to burn a similarly seductive opportunity to reverse time—to remake themselves into the fully realized, lithe, and irresistibly winsome younger and more powerful versions of themselves and to wipe away the fatigue lines and cellulite generated by children or age or both. In this particular vision of remaking, the spa hotel promises guests that they will "relax and find greater balance" in life as well as an "unforgettable escape from the everyday." The core mission of the spa hotel is one of empowering people to "live healthier, longer, more joyful lives through fitness, nutrition, stress-management and integrative wellness."[9] Spa hotels occupy a range of positions on the clinical continuum. At one end, Canyon Ranch offers guests a health and healing center replete with sleep apnea clinic, on-site podiatrists, and board-certified physicians, as well as licensed therapists and chiropractors. At the other end, one can hang out with girlfriends and gossip while having facials and mani/pedis and taking classes on "skin." Regardless of the relative degree to which individual spa hotels deploy medical apparatus, intervention, and logics, the hybrid blend of the clinic, the beauty salon, and the ashram that the spa hotel offers ensures that guests will "relax and find greater balance in life—and an unforgettable escape from the everyday."

In fact, one of the things that distinguishes this kind of hotel venue is the "clinic with velvet gloves" feel that it ensures its world-weary clientele of transients will enjoy. In the tradition of the popular nineteenth-century sanatoriums in Arizona and the Adirondacks, these contemporary spa resorts offer guests the run of the house. They replicate a home away from home enhanced by fresh air, new activities, and modern regenerative technologies and practices. Bodies move in spa hotels differently than they do in typical hotels, with greater emphasis on and access to domestic areas like the kitchen and bathroom. There is an iconic "kitchen" where one takes cooking classes from the masters, and the large family-style dining room in which how guests eat is very much based on the logic of the home. Self-serve beverages and desserts in a community refrigerator combine with roundtables set for six or eight to encourage guests to mingle and befriend each other over meals. Guests move fluidly and at will from the kitchen, living room, and dining room to the spa complex or health and healing center, circling through these spaces much as family members do in a home. The emphasis is less on the private hotel room that the guest occupies and more on these shared spaces of regeneration and cleansing. Such fluid gradients of intimacy ensure that these spaces offer a community "home away from home" that feels safe and secure—stable and enduring—in ways that many modern homes do not, even for their upper-middle-class occupants and owners. Untroubled by underwater mortgages, deferred maintenance, and family hostilities, the spa hotel offers common spaces in which intimacy gradients are smoothly functional and unencumbered by the stress of those struggling to hold on to the fraying fabric that is the twenty-first-century domestic cloth.

Guests are free to mingle with strangers and to walk around these shared spaces in a terry cloth robe and often, to stay healthily hydrated, with a personalized, labeled water bottle that is given to each guest at check in and that is oddly reminiscent of a baby bottle. The spa hotel is, in short, the rest cure writ twenty-first century large, where a yoga ball workout is part of the aesthetic of wellness right alongside a bikini wax, weight management class, and minuscule small portions of "healthful" food that guests can eat as long as they like. Spas like Canyon Ranch and Lake Austin, fat farms based on the concept of excess and plenitude, regularly offer guests tiny muffins that are harder than bricks and that are stacked around for guests to eat guiltily as they take such classes as "communicating with your pet," "bead spinning," or "tarot archetypes and reincarnation." Without arguments about whose turn it is to walk the dog, take out the trash, or clean up after dinner, the spa hotel creates domestic spaces that are better than the genuine article could ever be. Thus, on the one hand, they create therapeutic spaces that are wiped clean of hypodermic needles, IV drips, excruciating price point, and the more threatening detritus of the hospital, while, on the other hand, they improve on the home space that so many travelers both struggle to retain and feel ambivalent about occupying. It is no wonder that the spa hotel's life-giving allure has become ubiquitously seductive.

Time as well as space operates differently in the spa hotel, and a key aspect of renewal lies in refuting the workweek-weekend logic of the business traveler. With packages of four nights to ten nights and a reservation policy that disallows fewer than three night stays, these spa hotels insist that the therapeutic transformations they offer trump the imperatives of more traditional labor—that the timeline for the labor of renewal of necessity encroaches on and ultimately defies the labor of the traditional workplace and constitutes a kind of distinctive work in its own right. Spa labor is a hybrid labor—a blend of work and play that alternately entices and exhausts. And the various activities offered by this kind of elite spa experience reflect a therapeutic function in which labor and leisure, exertion and repose are blended so seamlessly as to be indistinguishable. Indeed, this blending is a defining feature of the spa experience.

If its idiom is respite, rest, and inactivity, exercise, in various forms is, nonetheless, at the core of the spa-retreat-hotel regenerative regime. In search of a discipline in which punishment masks itself in the gentle sunrise yoga pose, the "life goals" strategy session with a seasoned personal career coach, and the enforced stasis of bodies on massage tables, in meditation rooms, mud wraps, and hammocks, the bodies that enter the spa hotel do so to expunge toxic substances, radically reduce the amount of physical space they take up (in the form of body weight), radically expand the amount of psychic space they take up (in the form of "me" centered seminars and coaching sessions), repair the accumulated effects of overuse and the chronic wear and tear of the upwardly mobile, and restore the "inner harmony" that is the inevitable casualty of a volatile workplace market.

Exercise, in short, is the promise and the punishment of the spa-hotel-retreat. It takes various forms and operates on a continuum of rigor and duration. At one end of the spa hotel spectrum is nothing more intrusive than a luxurious workout room with yoga balls and various aerobic exercise machines. At the other end are spas like the Lake Austin Resort and Canyon Ranch, which routinely offer a daily exercise itinerary as guests check in that ranges from kayaking to hiking and running to various situationally specific group exercises such as lakeside jujutsu and tantric breathing, taught by specialists culled from local communities. This exercise agenda reassures guests that they are not indulging but rather committing to rigorous self-improvement regimes as they hand over their credit cards, regimes that would impress the likes of Benjamin Franklin and Jonathan Edwards. Indeed, workshops offered to guests with titles like "To Change or Not to Change" and "Peak Performance" are distinctly reminiscent of Franklinian regimes full of transformative promise through rigorous self-examination and list making.

As exercise's evil twin and doppelganger, rest carries an equally significant, and potentially fraught, weight in the spa hotel's wellness arsenal. Rest is organized and choreographed with great care and ranges from formal rest activities like meditation and "just 'be,'" and "don't hold your breath" classes to massages, facials, and aromatherapy. Here "rest" is not sloth, procrastination, or laziness, but an intentional engagement with and control over one's body with the ultimate goal of betterment. Even sleep, the classic rest behavior, falls under the purview of the spa hotel, and not only the attention to sheet thread count, pillow density, and mattress composition but also sleep seminars, coaches, and monitoring ensure that guests rest with the same optimizing force and rigor that they bring to physical exertion. Exercise and rest therefore engage in a delicate dance—a give-and-take throughout the duration of the guest's stay—in which one bleeds into the other and vice versa, but the hybrid medley that they collectively produce is more than the sum of their parts. Through a constant movement between self-improvement and self-indulgence—between rest and activity—the guest who signs over somewhere between four and ten days of life not to mention thousands of dollars develops the iconic spa-induced, life-transforming well-being that is the distinctive and ultimate spa commodity.

The energy that the guest ingests, as well as that which he or she expends, plays a crucial role in this cathartic spa hotel experience and in the promise of bodily renewal and sensory stimulation that it offers guests, and so smelling, talking, chewing, and experimenting with food are focal points of the spa resort stay. Food seminars and cooking classes are common features of the upper-end spa resort and regularly focus on expanding the guest's knowledge of different cuisines, culinary practices, and strategies for maximizing flavor and minimizing health risks. Spa water is abundant and infused with orange peels or cucumber slices to make hydrating (that ever important component of healthful living) a more sensory-intensive experience. But the knife cuts deeper than mere instruction in cooking and eating—food is the seductress and the tantalizing desired and elusive object. It stands in for sex as an object warranting attention, energetic advocacy, and experimentation, and it must be creatively handled—like any delicate, infinitely desired, elusive, and ephemeral lust.

And like sex, food is full of mixed messages at the spa hotel. The minimuffin with butter as midmorning snack, for example, suggests indulgence but within tight restraints, and the "guilt-free" cheesecake reinforces deeply engrained associations between guilt and eating that are all too traditionally gendered. If you are what you eat, then eating differently is self-transforming, and this is the promise the spa hotel offers. Spa menus, developed by award-winning chefs, therefore, list calories, fat grams, and carbs beside every menu choice, and cuisine philosophies routinely announce their rejection of transfats and artificial ingredients. The health benefits of such thoughtful eating practices are immense, but the sensory benefits are not to be minimized. In the hands of experts, the spa hotel promises, eating can offer exotic sensual experiences hitherto unfamiliar to the midwestern beef eater or the fan of the TexMex enchilada. The generalized and supposedly healthy options on the menu are offered as "choices," a description that suggests the freedom to eat as you wish, but the overall emphasis, within the kitchen, is on restraint and limitations, on the limitation of choices.

The prominent place that food occupies in the daily regime and imaginative apparatus of the spa resort stimulates guests' appetites even as it works to channel and suppress these appetites—indeed, one of the spa resort's most seductive assumptions is that guests have uncontrollable desires in need of management. The finicky eater has no place at the table of the spa resort, even as such a guest, repackaged as a discriminating eater, is the spa resort's most-prized product and alumna. Those who naturally prefer carrots to cookies or salad and salmon to fried cheese steaks are not the target spa audience, and preaching to the already converted is not a popular spa pursuit. Managing and refining desire to produce a sense of personal renewal, then, is the subtext extraordinaire of the spa—stimulating hitherto unknown desires of the palate and strategically sublimating others, and it is this pursuit into which all comers enter with varying degrees of abandon.

Water occupies an even more central and complex place in the spa's creative architecture and built environment. Capitalizing on the idea of providing a literal as well as figurative oasis—an amniotic sac of sorts—even the most threadbare, utilitarian spa hotels, of course, identify a swimming pool as a focal point and one of their signature and distinguishing features—Holiday Inn Express, for example, advertising its state-of-the-art pool as the centerpiece of its spa. This attention to the aquatic originates in the spa's outgrowth from and ongoing reference to the hot spring, replete with its mineral-rich water, and to the "taking of the waters" in such historically significant locations as Bath, England. But this universal acclaim for spring water in hotels is nowhere more obvious that in the simple bottle of water, left out for new guests on dressers, or set out for visitors to the on-site spa or gym. Each bottle offers a chance to consume and absorb the magic of the natural spring.

In the desert regions of the United States where elite spa resorts seem to proliferate, water counterintuitively looms large on the spa's regenerative agenda. Its outdoor hot tubs and various water treatments, for example, are the mis-en-scène of such elite spas as Ten Thousand Waves in Santa Fe, New Mexico. Located in a mountainous desert destitute of even the remotest possibility of a single wave not to mention ten thousand of them, this aquatic spa retreat literally offers a proliferation of restorative watering holes in the form of outdoor tubs nestled amid sagebrush, scrub cedars, and aspen for hourly, daily, or evening rental by couples, individuals, or groups. Outdoor tubs are individualized and come replete with ancillary accoutrements such as waterfalls, saunas, and cold dunks, thereby constituting personalized aquatic treatment centers in their own right. Combining spa services that complement water immersion, such as salt glow or herbal body wrap, guests can maximize the restorative impact of this desert hot spring. Of course, the bodies that are brought "back into balance" by such targeted aqua treatment are healed at a high price not only for individuals' pocketbooks but for the earth to which visitors are seeking realignment but from which they are consuming vital and all too limited resources. The lake against which Lake Austin Resort and Spa is perched similarly bears the brunt of the spa as consumer of natural resources with speed boat resort trips offered to resort guests, and with water pumped out of the chronically depleted and overtaxed Edwards Aquifer to fill the spa's renowned Olympic barn pool and its two ancillary swimming pools.

Just as hospital nurses are on call to oversee the patient's successful recovery, so too is there a veritable battalion of body management specialists on site and at the ready to oversee and facilitate clients' rejuvenation. Client care personnel greet guests when they check in and are quickly followed by the facialists, massage therapists, wellness and meditation experts, exercise gurus, and culinary counselors best suited to address the stated recovery regime of new guests. The relation between spa guest and specialist is one of physical as well as emotional intimacy and vulnerability. Partial or full nudity is most often a precondition for treatment; the guest is most often reclining on a massage, facial, or other kind of table; and the sharing of intimate bodily information punctuates the verbal exchange between the two. Unlike the family doctor or hair stylist back home, the spa specialist is destined to remain a stranger, anonymity built into the spa hotel treatment experience. In such a context, guests can alternately be inhibited or emboldened to reveal parts of themselves metaphorically or physically hidden from view in other contexts and environments. The talk that occurs as mud is spread on bodies, exfoliants applied to faces, or massage oils rubbed into aching joints is often intermittent and inconsequential—soothing and unobtrusive, much like the new-age music that is piped into the treatment rooms. With the voices of Yanni or Enya as backup, guest and clinician enter into an unarticulated verbal contract of sorts that reinforces inconsequential intimacy and impersonal interaction as a part of the renewal process.

Outcomes

Because large-scale improvement over time cannot be a ground condition of the exchange, the long-term effectiveness of many of these youth-conferring treatments is not measurable. At its most extreme, the hotel-as-spa always offers repair and new beginnings beyond the immediate and merely physical. Indeed, in promising to permanently change the beat, or return a person to youthful vigor and reset the clock, it can offer a permanent, if unusual cure. When, for instance, the three middle-aged protagonists of the otherwise forgettable film *Hot Tub Time Machine* (2010) return to the hotel lodge at the Kodiak Valley Ski Resort, they do so hoping mainly for a chance to remember, fondly, what it was like to be young. But when they inadvertently trigger a temporal vortex in their suite's hot tub, they are given a chance, quite literally, to remake themselves. And each man, in turn, does so, often without a concern for consequence. One man falls in love—true love, this time, we are assured in the final scenes. Another, wishing for fame, takes the stage and establishes himself as a musical performer. And the final protagonist in this magical realist tale trades on his knowledge of the late twentieth century to become the world's wealthiest and most influential mogul. All of this, we want to believe, is made possible by the worn out hot tub, a cosmic metaphor for the healing power of the hotel-as-spa, and a reflection of the truly radical chances for self-fashioning in the therapeutic spaces of these institutions.

A stay in the spa hotel, then, is a wish for a newer and better life, rooted in the search for a younger, presumably healthier body, mind, and spirit. It is more accessible and affordable—even at its highest price points—than the receding wellness services of the hospital, even as it masquerades as a rare and hard-won commodity. We assume that an overnight stay in any corporate space can be comprehensively restorative—that it can repair and rehabilitate our corporeal selves, and stave off, as Foucault might say, the fact of death. But no such space can offer any permanent fix. We want the therapeutics of such spaces to have a medical and scientific quality, but we just as sincerely want the lavish pampering and abundant comfort rarely associated with the hospital. In the spa hotel we find our own wish fulfilled for a modern institution that both focuses on the discipline and soft punishment of our bodies in the interests of infinite regeneration and renewal and refuses the hard facts of the modern institution of the asylum, detention center, hospital, or prison. We fantasize an institution into being that betters all of us by enabling each of us to pursue a "personal best" in our work, social, and love lives as well in our physical, spiritual, emotional, and psychological lives. This focus on the age-defying self— indeed, this pressing the spa hotel into service of this vision of a perpetually youthful self—is built into the very fabric and texture of the spa hotel, and in this fantasy of a self infinitely able to be restored we find one of the most seductive of the hotel's promises.

As we will see in the next chapter, this is only half of the story. The hotel does not only stave off the "fact of death" through the new beginnings that is the spa hotel's explicit promise, but the hotel is an institution that also facilitates death and endings in ways uniquely its own. As the next chapter details, the hotel offers those who check in a complete arc of opportunities that moves across the full spectrum of life renewal to death—hopeful beginnings to traumatic or regretful endings. Like the hospital, it is a place where life hangs in the balance; where people can go either to live or to die, as well as merely to spend the night. When we approach the hotel with an eye to its temporal dimensions—with an eye toward how it moves people along the life cycle—we see its profound ability to cultivate new hope or stimulate despair in those who check in. We see that for the world-weary traveler the stakes can be very high, indeed. The hotel can offer a life or death experience, as well as everything in between.

4

ENDINGS

If at one end of the life spectrum the hotel provides those who check in powerful, if ephemeral, narratives of healing and renewal, so too does the hotel's pervasive association with death attract those who seek within its walls a final way to check out prematurely from despair, failure, chronic illness, and depression. The kinds of death that the hotel enables prove as compelling, varied, and, at times, irresistible as its life-giving properties. Offering a range of opportunities to kill oneself and others, the hotel is, indisputably, a place to accelerate life's natural clock and to refuse to let nature take its course. So ubiquitous is death in a hotel that it can at times feel staged, a bit melodramatic—the modern subject's final refusal to move another step and ultimate capitulation to the strains of modernity.

Despite the concerted, costly, and at times heroic efforts guests make to reverse time and steal back a crucial year or two by visiting spa hotels that cater to the modern subject's deep commitment to perpetual energy, freshness, and youth, people also gravitate to the hotel when they are officially beaten by life's tough game and have decided it is officially time to fold. Just as the hotel seems to offer temporary resistance to modernity's crushing burden in the form of youth-giving properties, so too does it offer permanent respite for those who no longer have the will to keep playing life's tiring game. The ways in which those who check in looking for untimely endings make their final exits suggest the deep fatigue and despair of those who no longer care to write their own scripts. A fall from the guest suite balcony, or down an elevator shaft, is spectacularly, cinematically terrifying and yet oddly familiar. An unexplained death during sleep is mysterious and potentially murderous, immediately a subject for speculation and intrigue. A fire, sweeping up the stairs or burrowing

Russell Sorgi's 1942 photo for the May 8, 1942, edition of the *Buffalo Courier Express* of a suicide at the Genesee Hotel. A young woman in her thirties, renting an eighth-floor room, had sat on the ledge for nearly twenty minutes, drawing a crowd of two thousand onlookers, the *Courier Express* reported. A cameraman, racing to the scene, got there just as she jumped, and, waiting to take his shot until she had descended to the third floor, caught the image. "Her face," he remembered, had "frozen into a mask of terror."

A still image from the 1951 film *Fourteen Hours*, directed by Henry Hathaway, based on the real-life ordeal—and ultimate suicide—of John William Warde, a twenty-six-year-old man who, after a lengthy ordeal on the seventeenth-floor ledge of the Gotham Hotel, killed himself. Warde was a "man on a ledge," as Joel Sayre called him in the April 16, 1949, *New Yorker* profile of the same name, an example of a phenomenon that is an enduring feature of the hotel as a site for such dramatic endings. (From the authors' collection)

outward through the walls, resurrects images from *The Towering Inferno*. Each death, by virtue of its inherent drama, carries the potential for a permanent scarring of the institution's very structure. But this assumption of melodrama is produced by the hotel itself and is an aftereffect of the corporate conceit that, in life and in death, every guest has a story to tell. A hotel is, we are implicitly told, good for an ending as well as for a new beginning. Surrounded by the plastic, unreal ethos of the hotel, we know, at the very least, that the body will be found, that the corpse will be removed, that the police will come, and that the other guests will serve as funeral witnesses, acknowledging the passing, if briefly.

Yet, despite the assurance of material attention even after death, the hotel also creates the social circumstances in which untimely death—either by accident or with intent—seems more likely. Sterile corridors and antiseptic living spaces, relentlessly cleaned, erase every trace of the guest. The endless repetition of décor and aesthetics, from lobby to elevator to room, undermines the sense that any space is truly special, truly "home," and extinguishes emotional connections. The groomed servility and perpetual cheer of the staff have an air of falsity, of over-the-top stagecraft aimed at our function as "guest" and not our basic humanity. Despite its very best efforts to manifest care and attention, then, the hotel can seem fundamentally insincere. And that insincerity, in turn, can be alienating, even for those who are not already on the edge, terminally ill, or down on their luck. And, for those who are, it can hold a dangerously attractive allure—like a moth attracted by a scorching flame, the guest on the verge of breakdown or teetering dangerously on the precipice between self-protection and self-destruction can seek out the hotel as hostile habitus.

For those in a dark place, the hotel is a place to die, either inadvertently or with forethought. Take the tragic case of an aging superstar, at the tail end of a long, dark slide from grace, who was preparing for the Grammy Awards show. A part of the grand caravan of celebrities arriving in Los Angeles, she checked into a hotel room at the Beverly Hilton. She had been rehearsing for a performance at the event, but her throat was sore and she was tired. She needed the label's financial support for this trip because she was broke, or nearly so, and on the verge of losing everything, yet again. Her body felt older than it might otherwise, because she had been a habitual drug user for decades. She dispatched her assistant to Neiman Marcus—to pick up a few items for a party that evening—and decided to take a bath. She had taken Xanax a few hours earlier, along with a handful of prescription cold medicines and muscle relaxants, but this therapeutic cocktail seemed to not be enough. So, as the water filled the bathtub, the coroner would confirm that she heated some crack cocaine in a spoon and used a makeshift paper pipe to smoke it.

Room 434—the stage for Whitney Houston's tragic death—is in the Wilshire Tower Executive Suites of the whitewashed, midcentury modern Beverly Hilton. Like many other hotels, the Beverly Hilton had been aiming, more and more, at business travelers, and as a consequence room 434 would surely seem surprisingly plain and corporate to anyone who imagines that celebrities enjoy vast, ornate spaces, never seen by the public. Roughly 560 square feet of "spacious comfort" includes a "king size bed and the privacy of a separate sleeping and living or working quarters." There are walls of windows, providing a view of the city skyline, and the usual material necessities—a big plasma screen TV, a Bose "music system," Wi-Fi and Ethernet, cotton robes and sheets, and decorative pillows. There is nothing inherently special about these arrangements, which are reproduced in every suite, in exacting detail, like perfectly duplicated Hollywood sets, each a generic version of the Hollywood hotel, in which a deal goes bad, a romantic tryst ensues, or a promising starlet dies.

When Houston died in room 434, though, she joined a weird pantheon of the globally famous types, troubled souls who met their end in a rented space. John Belushi died in a bungalow at the Chateau Marmont, his body discovered naked, laid out on white bed sheets, by a personal trainer. Janis Joplin, a tortured genius working on a new album, died in room 105 of the Landmark Hotel, after an overdose of heroin. Anna Nicole Smith, accidently mixing the wrong prescription medications, passed away at the Seminole Hard Rock Hotel and Casino. Nancy Spungen, the erstwhile muse of Sid Vicious, met her violent end in room 100 at the Chelsea after a riotous binge. More recently, James Gandolfini, who played Tony Soprano on the hit HBO series, died unexpectedly in room 449 of Rome's Boscolo Exedra Hotel. Winning the dubious distinction of most anguished exit, there is David Carradine, who was found naked and hanging from a rope in his Bangkok hotel while on a film shoot, the apparent victim of accidental asphyxiation resulting from sexual self-bondage gone bad. Hundreds and thousands of singers and songwriters, drummers and bassists, starlets and authors, proverbial shop workers in the entertainment industry, have drowned their sorrows or consumed their pharmaceuticals, and brought about their "accidental" ending.[1] The drug-fueled, celebrity death in the hotel might be a cliché, but it is a living one, rooted in the documentary grit of reality.

These deaths make the body a character in a well-worn plot, in which creativity and self-destruction are linked. The hotel ensures the narrative conventions and makes them public. A death there is a sad thing, invariably an ending of isolation, away from friends and family, and away from doctors and nurses, too. It is also a discoverable event. The regularity of room service and housekeeping, the presence of close neighbors, all ensure that soon, and dramatically, your material remains will be found. And because so many other once-greats have died in the same way, their bodies shockingly found floating in bathtubs, tangled in bedcovers, and sprawled on the floor, there are preset expectations for the story to emerge. In the days before Houston's death, a cache of blog posts, tweets, and status updates worried that the end might be near. Word that she was dead reached the lobby of the hotel just as the press began to gather for the evening's Clive Davis fête. The setting and the timing ensured that words like "tragedy" and the notion of a "great loss" were quickly affixed to the evening news. The evening's gala, staged a few floors below the rapidly unfolding police investigation, was hastily transformed into an affair to remember the extraordinary life. "The show must go on," one of the gala's production staffers insisted, echoing the hoary chestnut of Hollywood.[2]

The self-destructive and untimely death of creative genius run amuck makes explicit and visible what we might all too easily overlook—the hotel's pervasive role as purveyor of untimely, precipitous end-of-life moments, the hotel as final stop on the way to the grave. If the hotel, at one end of the life spectrum, provides a softer, healing palliative of restoration and repair for those in search of new life and beginnings, the hotel, at the other end of the spectrum, steps in again where the hospital leaves off, providing minimal shelter and care at a fraction of the cost of a hospital stay, making it an attractive option for governments and health care providers looking to economize. In an effort to contend with "bed blocking" or the problem posed by the plethora of geriatric and terminally ill patients who occupy hospital beds though they no longer require the hospital's full attention, Britain's government has recently explored adoption of the "Scandinavian model of hospital hotels"— privately run patient hotels situated next to hospitals for easy access to medical treatment when needed.[3] In 2013 alone thirty thousand geriatric British citizens occupied hospital beds because of dementia, infirmity, or general inability to take care of themselves, costing the British government north of 4 million pounds a week. Confronted with a skyrocketing elderly population and an unsustainable care model, Whitehall turned to the hotel as an economical solution to the problem of what to do with the chronically ill and dying, beginning discussion with Travelodge, Marriott, and Hilton.

In this iteration, the hotel's association with death is apparent and unequivocal—it is immediate precursor to the cemetery, the penultimate stop leading inevitably and soon to the mortuary and graveyard. Here the concierge becomes a grim reaper, welcoming apprehensive incoming guests to a world they sought to avoid for as long as possible. To be greeted by name is equivalent to a death sentence and grisly homecoming. As an economical, almost final resting stop for those who do not have economic, familial, social, or class resources that would open up other alternatives, the hotel becomes a kind of ghoulish holding pen for not quite yet dead bodies, locked in a death struggle with their rented sheets. Proponents of the British developing a hospital hotel system in concert with hotel chains like Travelodge claim that it is a way to treat patients "with proper dignity" and "in a manner that is up-to-date with the modern consumer world," rather than the current British practice, which Deputy Director Nick Seddon for the think tank Reform describes as "stuffing people away wherever we can fit them."[4] And yet, despite or possibly because of its consumer trappings, when aligned so explicitly with terminal illness and age, the hotel bed lurches dangerously close to the coffin, and no high-thread-count sheets can hide this fact. Oscar Wilde, who died in room 16 of L'Hotel Paris in 1900 aptly summarized the tense and terse relationship between the dying and the hotel rooms that witness and intangibly contribute to their last struggles when he said, reputedly in his final hours of life: "My wallpaper and I are in a struggle to the death. One or other of us has got to go."[5]

Suicide

If death is an ever-present element of hotel life, suicides reinforce and make explicit this association of the hotel with untimely death, casting a spotlight on the death-dealing dimensions of hotel life. The alignment of the hotel, suicide, and notoriety is not a new phenomenon—the prerogative of the contemporary scene and the glitterati who rivet the attention of *People* magazine readers—but is rather built into the hotel's logic and infrastructure. In the 1870s, the "uncanny" reputation of "The Suicide's Hotel" in Paris, and the repeated propensity for suicides therein, led to its tearing down. The final straw, according to the December 1877 report of the Quaker newspaper, *The Friend*, was the suicide by hanging of the newest owner. Over a hundred years ago, the *New York Times* contemplated the hotel as a privileged habitus of death dealing. A 1910 article on "The Hotel Suicide" observed that going to a conspicuous hotel specifically in order "to take one's life in a public reception room is suggestive of a desire to make one's ending more or less historical."[6] "One hotel manager," historian Paul Erling Groth writes, "explained that after gaslights and gas heaters became standard equipment, suicide in hotel rooms was more common; suicide with gas was easier than using a gun or a razor blade."[7]

In the past century many have continued to make their final resting place in the hotel—to understand the hotel not only as a temporary getaway offering respite from the troubles of the world in the form of bubble baths and romantic room service but as a graveyard of sorts, offering a final resting place and permanent solution to pain, suffering, and burdens too heavy to be endured. "Maybe the anonymity of a hotel room appeals to people in that condition," suggests one character in the Carole Feathering mystery, *The Hanging in the Hotel*; since "suicide is the ultimate act of selfishness," there is not much thought of "the reactions of the staff" for "someone who chooses to end his life in a hotel room."[8] Most recent efforts to make sense of the hotel's role in suicide tend to focus on psychological forces and are the work product of armies of therapists and hotline operators. "Why kill yourself in a hotel?" becomes, through the perverse translation of Google and Yahoo, a critique of those who need an intervention, who are "selfish" or "unwell." The language of evaluation is thick here, precisely because the subject is thought to be so confusing, so serious, so dramatic.

Nowhere is the hotel's function as stage for self-immolation more evident than in that mecca of hotels that define Las Vegas. Dubbed the suicide capital of America, Vegas has the highest visitor suicide rate in the nation, and, not surprisingly, the city's hotels have come under fire for not doing more to prevent guests from killing themselves.[9] Suicides in Vegas hotels occur multiple times a month according to a recent Clark County Coroner's report, whereas only a third that number occur in Atlantic City hotels and none have happened at Disney World hotels. The reasons that guests kill themselves with such frequency in Vegas hotels are as varied as the fantasies that Vegas's famous casino hotels provide—despair over financial losses, frustrated desires for "one more chance," a reversal of fortune at the gambling table, attraction to the anonymity of Vegas culture, or Vegas's famous reputation as a place of no consequences—where what happens in Vegas stays in Vegas. So frequent have hotel suicides become on the Strip that the Vegas Suicide Prevention Center has unsuccessfully lobbied hotels to add a suicide hot line number next to hotel room phones.

Vegas's hotel suicide culture is most notably memorialized by John O'Brien's 1992 novel *Leaving Las Vegas* and his own suicide subsequent to the novel's adaptation into the 1995 film of the same name. The setting for much of the story's action is a Vegas hotel called the Whole Year Inn, which Ben, the story's protagonist, reads as "the hole you're in." Filmed on site in Vegas, the film's low budget forced cameras to shoot in the thick of uncleared streets and in a wide range of hotels that both look and don't look like the Whole Year Inn. From luxurious hotel suites that serve as workplace for Ben's love object, the hooker Sera, to the final seedy hotel room where Ben dies in Sera's arms, the hotel serves as the privileged site and occasion for a wide swath of self-destroying behavior. And so it comes as no surprise that in the hotel both Ben and Sera can get closest to their despair and their hope of salvation.

The Academy Award–winning Mike Figgis film version of the novel, starring Nicolas Cage and Elizabeth Shue as Ben and Sera, visually exploits the hotel as privileged backdrop for self-destruction, lingering at times lusciously on hotel signage, lobby, and hallway as quasi accomplices in the self-staged exits that various characters script. Sera's repeated requests that Ben move out of the Whole Year Inn and into her apartment reflect her firsthand knowledge of the hotel's role as facilitator and occasional agent of untimely self-destruction. In a hotel room Sera finds her pimp in the middle a paranoid premonition and reverie about gangsters coming for him, and as she walks down the hallway from the room, she sees the gun-toting gangsters on their way to kill him in that same room. If her pimp Yuri does not resist his own death in a hotel room, Sera wants to save Ben from the same fate, and so the one thing she asks of him is that he not "rot away in a hotel room" but stay with her. But if Sera seeks to extract Ben from the hotel's soul-deadening influences, she also turns to the hotel as a place of fresh starts—as the best and possibly only place where she and Ben might first make love. Taking a long weekend at her favorite hotel outside the city, Ben and Sera sit by the pool drinking and sharing an intimacy born of true human connection and awakening love. Against the backdrop of the Desert Sun Motel's glaring neon, their bond gains a kind of tragic majesty, exacerbated by Ben's drunken destruction of the pool furniture and their subsequent eviction by the hotel owner.

The film's repeated use of hotels' neon signs as backdrop and framing device—from the glaring hues of Circus Circus to the Silver Dollar— attests to its significance in the dramas of self-destruction that unfold in, against, and around the hotel. Sera is gang raped in an anonymous hotel outside the strip, while Ben finds himself once again in a dingy hotel room after Sera throws him out upon finding him with a hooker in her apartment. Ben's death against the hotel's threadbare sheets is both a defeat and a celebration, for, as the film tells it, he finally makes love to Sera and knows the fulfillment that comes from being accepted unconditionally. Sera gets out of the bed in the hotel room in which her lover has died and moves not to another hotel room but to a therapist's couch, and her ultimate recovery is one that requires that she leave hotels permanently alone. To survive, she must flee the dystopian narrative of the hotel.

If *Leaving Las Vegas* captures the downward spiral of people bent on self-destruction and untimely death, its storyline of hotel suicide is not unique or even unusual, as contemporary accounts of hotel suicides make clear. Take the example of the Heywoods. In early January 2012, on a Tuesday night, a former radio host, Bill Heywood, along with his wife of several decades, Susan, booked a room in the Homewood Suites in Scottsdale, Arizona. On Wednesday morning, a maid discovered their bodies in the room. The local police, called to the scene, subsequently recovered two guns and declared it a joint suicide. Within hours, the story was saturated with high sentiment, as the slow drip of details in the media confirmed a narrative already rehearsed. Heywood's career, it seemed, had been on a downward swing. Susan's health had been deteriorating rapidly. She had cancer, the newspapers revealed, and a recent heart attack had robbed her of some vitality. Family friends confirmed that Bill and Susan could not stand to live without each other, a likely consequence of her rapid physical decline. And their finances, most tragically, had been gutted by the recession, adding a dash of gritty realism to the tale. Bill had left radio, it seemed, to join the booming real estate market, but when boom turned to bust, they lost their magnificent home in the Arizona Biltmore—"A Waldorf Astoria Resort"—to foreclosure. All of these details were truthfully told, presented like expected clues, found right where they should be.

What is most striking about this story is how entirely superfluous—and also central—the hotel is to the actual act. "Superfluous," we say, because suicide by gun is, after all, rather portable. One can enter a restaurant restroom, or return to an apartment, or sit on a park bench in the sunshine. A hotel plays no necessary role. Unless, that is, the goal, beyond bringing an end to oneself, is to wrap your untimely death in a very particular context, a context unique to the hotel.

For a couple on the dreary downslope of life, the Homewood Suites in Scottsdale represents an attempted return to normalcy. "Our accommodations," their promotions suggest, "allow you to feel closer to home whether you're traveling for a few nights, or longer." "Closer to home," in this case, meant nearer to their once luxurious homestead. Metaphorically, the presence of a big, new television, clean towels and sheets, a big bed, a separate bedroom and a small kitchenette must have been, in a way, reassuring, a nostalgic reflection of a lifestyle lost.

But the issue was not merely about a comforting last few hours. It was also about ensuring that, in the aftermath, the act was understood, or read, in romantic, melodramatic terms. A script had to be provided, so the Heywoods left careful instructions for family members at their more modest Kierland condo. And then, in the morning, after spending the night, Bill and Susan left another note on the outside of the hotel room door—the border between the public and private spaces of the institution—for the room service maid, informing her that they had killed themselves within their rented space, and that she should be prepared for what would be found inside. This thoughtful gesture, a warning to staff, was also a storytelling cue; in this suite, it read, you will find star-crossed lovers, entwined in tragic death.

In gravitating to the hotel to stage their final dramatic exits, suiciders not only make explicit their desire to matter in death in ways that might have eluded them in life but also gesture to the hotel's affinity with other modern despair-inducing institutions like the prison, for the prison along with the hotel is a locus for hopelessness and, all too frequently, final endings. Suicides are second only to illness as stated causes of death in U.S. state prisons, accounting for 32.3 percent of all prison deaths, as opposed to 47.6 percent for illness. Homicide, in comparison, counts for only 2.1 percent of deaths, and these hard facts sharply contradict the media's general depiction of prisoners as irrepressibly violent and therefore in need of restraint rather than despairing and in need of suicide prevention.[10] And if it is prisoners' unmitigated contemplation of their hopeless states—the damage unrecoverable, lives permanently wrecked, dreams unfulfilled, and families torn apart—that too often leads them to end it all with bed sheets turned into ropes, these final acts of defiance and desperation within the cells they are compelled to call home are mirrored within hotel rooms that guests purchase for the explicit right to stage their own final acts. In fact, next to the prison, the hotel seems to be a leading institutional locus for self-immolation, leading more than one researcher to undertake sociological studies of the impact of suicides on hotel staff, the need for pre- and post-suicide training of hotel personnel, and the design changes that might prevent suicides.[11]

Murder

But despite their prevalence, hotel deaths are not always self-imposed but very often the direct result of intentional malfeasance: the hotel as crime scene includes perpetrators as well as victims of manslaughter and premeditated murder. Crime scene tape has been a long-standing if quickly hidden feature of the hotel landscape, and hotel murderers run the gamut from guests to workers to owners. In the early nineteenth century, for example, Lavinia Fisher, proprietor of Charleston, South Carolina's Six Mile Wayfarer House liked to offer her guests poisoned tea as a welcome to her home away from home. After the American Civil War, in hardscrabble Osage County, Kansas, the "Bloody Benders" operated an inn, but the transition from killing fields to hotel lobby remained fluid, and the hoteliers repeatedly murdered their visitors, slitting their throats, bashing in their heads, and disposing of the bodies on a patch of ground later rechristened (after the discovery) "Hell's Half-Acre." But the hotel's function as murder site is not solely a nineteenth-century phenomenon. Joe Ball, the twentieth-century owner of the Sociable Inn in Elmendorf, Texas, kept a pit of alligators to entertain tourists but also used it to secretly dispose of the bodies of his tiresome girlfriends. And the link between serial killing and the hotel continues—if in slightly less dramatic, and much less proprietary form—in the more recent "work" of the so-called Craigslist killer, Phillip Markoff, who lured his victims to a string of New England hotels before killing or assaulting them.

But perhaps the most dramatic and sordid case of hotel murder occurred in the shadow of Chicago's 1893 World's Columbian Exposition, the event that Richard Harding Davis described as the greatest event in the country's history since the Civil War[12]—in the hotel that Henry Holmes designed and built explicitly for the purpose of murdering his female guests. Holmes has the dubious distinction of being the first known serial killer in the United States, and while the number of women he murdered remains unknown, many speculate that the number far exceeds one hundred. Known as the Castle by locals, the three-story block-long hotel opened purportedly to house the deluge of visitors who came from far and wide to see the World's Columbian Exposition, but the maze of one hundred windowless and soundproofed rooms along with the labyrinthine corridors and secret passageways, built by a string of architects, ideally served Holmes's diabolical purpose. Hearst newspapers, which serialized the story, paid the imprisoned Holmes handsomely for his confession and the lurid details of his torture and murder of a horrifying string of pretty young women. As a result, the Castle became a sensationalized murder site before it was mysteriously set on fire and burned to the ground in 1895.

The hotel-as-murder-site's capacity to fascinate audiences did not end with the hotel's physical destruction. Books—both fiction and nonfiction—have continued to be written over the past century, documenting and describing the Castle and its diabolical architect-turned-hotel-proprietor. A notable recent example is Erik Larson's *The Devil in the White City* (2003), which hit number one on the *New York Times* best seller list before becoming a finalist for the National Book Award (2003). So compelling has *Devil* been for readers that Leonardo Di Caprio acquired movie rights to the novel in 2010 and has cast himself in the lead role of Dr. Holmes. It is Larson's lurid and detailed description of the hotel of horrors that Holmes builds just blocks from the fairgrounds—a hotel replete with acid vat, dissection table, and crematorium—that has fascinated millions of readers. The title takes its cue from Dr. Holmes's self-description in his 1896 confession that he was "born with the devil in me" and that he "could not help the fact that [he] was a murderer, no more than the poet can help the inspiration to sing."[13]

But it is the novel's descriptions of the hotel that this natural born killer creates to do his work that has captured the attention of readers worldwide. As a stark counterpoint to the building of the Chicago World's Fair that serves as a powerful testimonial to U.S. progress—a veritable white city of buildings designed by the nation's leading architects—Holmes's idiosyncratic design of an architectural space for killing reminds readers of the dark and savage undercurrent that inevitably lurks beneath the nation's celebration of its liberal democratic development. Larson repeatedly exploits this architectural dichotomy, reminding readers that in contrast to the fairgrounds being so carefully constructed to showcase human progress Holmes's hotel "building was dead space, like the corner of a room where the gaslight could not reach." This is in part because Holmes "had not consulted an architect, at least not a competent one"—but the building's "corridors were dark and pocked with too many doors" and "passages veered at odd angles" for other, more sinister reasons as well.[14] A built environment for murder, this World's Fair hotel becomes a killing field to which Holmes lures victims by telling them romantic stories that feature hotels like the luxurious Chicago Palmer House—the wedding gift of the besotted millionaire Potter Palmer to his lovely wife Bertha. But, of course, romantic stories of the hotel quickly turn into horror stories for those women who check in.

Larson's book blends fact and fiction to spin a riveting story of intrigue, horror, and history featuring the hotel, and in so doing it joins the ranks of an extensive genre of writing. As any reader of Agatha Christie knows, a murder in a hotel makes for a good plot in a detective novel. Indeed, such things happen with so much regularity in film and media that they barely register as unusual. The popularity of "murder in a hotel"—a role-playing, performance game, often played within hotels—suggests a prurient interest in experiencing the drama of murder, if at a safe distance. Alluring narratives of cloak-and-dagger espionage—think James Bond and Jason Bourne—depend, invariably, on the hotel to permit and to shroud "righteous" kills within its four walls. The hotel's suggestive self-presentation as a gleaming paradise layered over a sordid den of iniquity makes it possible for murder to be both disruptive and confirming, surprising and entirely expected. This grim reputation also makes it possible—thinking of Norman Bates in Hitchcock's *Psycho*—to imagine the hotel as both a way station for weary travelers and a logical base of operations for serial killers.

And yet the safe distance that "murder in a hotel" games seem to provide for prurient guests to voyeuristically encounter hotel death can and does violently break down, bumping up unexpectedly against dark realities both macabre and bizarre. When guests paying two hundred pounds a head for an evening murder mystery event arrived at the luxurious Down Hall Country House Hotel in Essex, they thought that the crime scene tape and police officers that greeted them were the first act in the evening's murderous play. A few guests commented on the remarkable likeness of the crime scene to a "real" murder scene and yet continued to believe that they were witnessing a staged event, even after being questioned by police and told that the murder mystery evening was canceled because of the mysterious deaths of two guests in the hotel swimming pool. Guests were invited to stay the night at Down Hall Hotel and found themselves witnesses to the unfolding investigation, questioned regarding their whereabouts in relation to the two young guests who were found dead at the bottom of the hotel's luxurious pool.[15]

The particularly intimate relation that the hotel has to untimely death can destabilize the world as hotel guests, workers, and visitors know it in the blink of an eye, turning a game into a macabre reality or transforming a seemingly real event into farce. Indeed, individuals' temporary inability to differentiate "real" from "representational" events characterizes death as it occurs in hotels and works to confound even those most expert and cognizant of death's macabre machinery. In early December 2010, for example, much of the Pittsburgh police department

rushed to the George Washington Hotel, where firefighters had accidently discovered what J. R. Blyth, the chief of police, later called "the
most grisly murder scene in his 35 years of law enforcement." For eight
hours, crime lab technicians and police detectives sifted through thousands of blood spatters and bits of flesh and hair. At some point, though,
investigators realized that the spectacular scene in front of them was
actually a movie set, left untouched in case reshoots were necessary.[16]
The movie that had been filmed in the George Washington was *New
Terminal Hotel*, a direct-to-video revenge story, chronicling the efforts
of a failed screenwriter, living in the proverbial "last chance" hotel, to
understand murder—chiefly by killing just about everyone who comes
to his room. The gore on the set at the George Washington reflected
the endpoint of the film, when the successive waves of slaughter and
dismemberment left the room bathed in crimson. But just as it was easy
to imagine that a hotel in Pittsburgh could stand in for one in LA, it was
simple to enter the room, see the abundant blood spatter, and assume
that it was the real thing.

There is something wild in this idea that a hotel is—after everything
else we have documented here—a place that also draws murderers, or
that seems a good staging ground for the taking of another life. Or two.
Or three. The public nature of the institution is what makes it possible
for strangers to meet. The anonymity of the space and its capacity to
shield the guest from surveillance are what make it possible for some
to think that they might actually get away with it. If the hotel industry refuses to keep statistics on the murders within its boundaries, that
is not merely because such events make for poor publicity; it is also
because the very nature of the hotel is murderous. Or maybe it is just
that the hotel constructs itself as a destination, and death is, of course, a
final endpoint.

Broken Bodies

At its darkest, the hotel defies the rules we impose on death and the
distinctions we make between suicide and murder: the hotel reminds
us that these designations are ultimately irrelevant, a futile and insufficient orderliness we retroactively superimpose to "manage" and catalog death. The profusion of corpses that have long occupied hotel
spaces—their tangled limbs, bodily secretions, and unendurable aromas
seeping into the hotel's most public and private spaces—insists on this

disorderliness, the cipherlike stories their bodies don't quite tell often stymieing the best efforts of officials to decode the final hours of life and "explain" the event.

There are some hotels that have become iconic symbols for this particular narrative chaos—places like Los Angeles' Hotel Cecil, which has been in business since 1927 and has been the chosen site for so much death in the form of murder, suicide, serial killing, and bizarre accidental death that it now has the dubious distinction of becoming a destination site for those overinvested in death. Death seems to permeate the air—and, more particularly, the water supply—at Hotel Cecil, where as recently as February 2013 a Canadian tourist was inexplicably found dead in the hotel's water tank. If this mysterious death was the end of the story, it would be sufficient to distinguish Hotel Cecil in the annals of hotel death, but its long history of suicide, inexplicable death, murder, and death from seemingly natural causes has made Hotel Cecil an attractive home to international serial killers like Jack Unterweger, the convicted Austrian murderer who launched a successful writing career from jail while he did fifteen years for murdering a hooker by strangling her with her brassiere. Once again at large, Unterweger traveled to the United States and stayed at the Hotel Cecil for three weeks, during which time three Los Angeles prostitutes were brutally murdered, in each case with their brassieres turned into nooses. Though never charged in the United States, Unterweger was successfully tried for the LA murders along with eight more murders in Austria and ultimately hung himself with a noose in jail. Hotel Cecil has been home to multiple serial killers, such as Richard Ramirez, who was named the Night Stalker for the brutally violent means he used to kill people and who was taken into custody while resting in his fourteenth-floor hotel room.[17] The association between the hotel as institution and death seems particularly acute and chaotic at the Hotel Cecil, a magnet attracting in irrationally high numbers those accident prone, desiring to die, or with a proclivity for killing others.

Broken inexplicably and beyond repair, individual bodies, like the hotels in which they spend their final hours, create narrative challenges for those tasked with making sense out of the brutal fact of their death and often raise more questions than answers. We can see such a challenge in the bodily remains of fifty-four-year old Richard Descoings, director of the internationally renowned Institut d'Etudes Politiques de Paris, colloquially known as Sciences Po. Descoings's final hours in April

TIME

2012 at New York City's elite Michelangelo Hotel remain shrouded in mystery—the cause of death, agent of death, and ruling of suicide or homicide continuing to baffle crime scene veterans. A highly contentious national figure because of the reforms he was making to French elite education, his friendship with recent French president Nicolas Sarkozy, his views on affirmative action, and his indeterminate sexual life, Descoings was the subject of numerous smear campaigns, one so intense that he was asked in an interview with the left-wing *Liberation* two months before his death if he feared a plot on his life.

On the night before he died, Descoings had been surfing gay hook-up sites on the internet, and his laptop and cell phone were subsequently found thrown from his hotel room window on a landing that extended out from the hotel's third floor. While the room was in disarray, there were no signs of trauma on the body or of a struggle, but there were conclusive signs that more than one person was in the room with the victim immediately before his death and that two men had been frequenting the room in the days immediately preceding his death. Even Descoings's time of death is confusing: hotel staff went to his room to check on him when he failed to show up at Columbia University as planned and reported hearing snoring and a grunt before he continued sleeping, but, when he failed to check out, hotel security found his naked body splayed in the bed, the cause and time of death completely unclear.

Given the recent depression that friends reported, suicide seemed a likely possibility, but given his complicated sexual life—unsubstantiated reports of homosexuality, including a "forced" outing by *Le Monde*, colliding uncomfortably with his married life, perhaps there was a personal angle. And then there were the threats on his life due to the political waves he was making, which made ideologically motivated murder equally logical. The corpse was a cipher, leaving no definitive clues nor generating the singular well-scripted narrative of a Whitney Houston or a Dr. Holmes. Suicide? Murder? Happenstance? What happens when we might never know? The mystery, then, becomes the plotline.

As we wait for clarity, and bear down on the details, the signature gold and red embellishments that let guests know they are safely sequestered within the protecting walls of the Michelangelo's comforting environs seem to momentarily fail. But even as images of the corpse being carted out of the Michelangelo's iconic front door litter the front pages and webpages of contemporary culture, something happens. As his body leaves the Michelangelo, the irresistible promise of new life and the untimely and grisly fact of inevitable and often nonsensical death, the potent cornerstones of the modern hotel and the heavy bookends for this section of *Hotel Life*, loom like metaphorical doormen, watching over the departed and waiting patiently for the next guest to arrive. Order is restored. The hotel resets its clock, committed to enabling precipitous death and supporting perpetual youth for yet another day.

Scale

5

RICH

Hotel life, as the preceding section illustrated, covers the full life cycle—from beginnings to endings and from life to death—leaving no stone unturned, no chapter unwritten in the messy entirety of the individual's time on earth. But the hotel does not only link those who are in motion to the larger circadian rhythms of life and death that are constantly pulsing within the hotel's walls. As we saw, it can and, at times, does encourage guests to gravitate toward both ends of the temporal boundaries within which we live—it encourages those who check in to resist or accelerate the passage of their time on earth. As importantly, the hotel locates those individuals who are constantly in flux and on the move within scales of space, as well as time, that flow well beyond discrete hotel property perimeters or city boundaries. Hotel life, as we approach it in this section, lets people know how much and what kinds of space they can take up in the world. This section, in short, explores how hotel life helps, alternately, to cement the soft bonds of elitist privilege and to affirm the harsh realities of economic disadvantage that bind the world's peoples into transnational alliance, regardless of national, racial, or religious affiliations.

The hotel, as this section suggests, plays a crucial role in architecting the larger geopolitical circuits that give shape, meaning, and texture to global capitalism and to individuals' relationship to it—the hotel, in other words, carefully doles out varied access to space and aligns that access to socioeconomic privilege in ways that more often than not work hand in glove with the various fantasies and ambitions in which global capitalism trades. To be clear, we are not speaking here merely of the relative number of square feet that differentiate the price point of the hotel penthouse suite from its most humble rooms or that make Park Avenue pricier hotel real estate than the Bronx. More fundamentally, this section explores the role that the hotel plays in architecting space broadly and often transnationally and in creating hierarchical economies of scale—in other words, the role that the hotel has in determining who has privileged access to the world's best places (aka: who is admitted to and permitted in which particular portions of the beachside resorts sprouting up along the world's most glamorous shorelines) and who inhabits its most uncomfortable and brutalizing spaces.

In our first section, we explored the various kinds of flexible private and public space that the hotel creates for those who walk through its doors and the kinds of individual exploration and development such mutable space enable. In this section we take space to scale, asking what kinds of multi- or extranational spaces the hotel creates and what differentially scaled access hotel life creates and sustains. At one end of the spectrum, global chains are reallocating space the world over, with all-inclusive logics that free guests from having to change currency, that enable them to amble unfettered along vast expanses of heavily curated terrain, and that thereby create a feeling, albeit temporary, of protection, vaccination, and dominion over the contagious and disadvantaged other. At the other end of the spectrum, hotels architect the absolute minimal conditions that separate temporary shelter from homelessness, offering hope in the guise of one-hundred-square-foot living coffins and human holding pens that the most disadvantaged feel relief verging on euphoria to obtain, even on the most tenuous terms. When viewed in this light, the kinds, quantities, and varied access to space that hotels dole out to different socioeconomic groups go far toward differentiating one life from another—toward creating contingencies of human value that are reflected seamlessly in how humans flow through hotel spaces, whether they linger aimlessly in plush lobby lounge chairs or busily sweep away sand from spa entry ways, whether they assume as their right unlimited comfort within the ample and heavily bejeweled arms of the Ritz Carlton or steel themselves for potential rebuff and rejection at the un-manicured hands of hotel managers looking only for guests willing to give them a cut of drug deals or prostitution done on the premises.

A substantial component of the hotel's allure, we suggest in this third section, is linked to its ability to temporarily offer guests the chance to reimagine their place within socioeconomic hierarchies and systems of meaning, whether by providing guests tantalizing, albeit temporary, positions of dominance within a global landscape of privilege or providing those vulnerable to global systems of capital the most minimal and threadbare respite in the form of a cot and sink. Regardless of whether the hotel temporarily confers dominant or marginal positions within global capitalism's pecking order, the hotel, as we will see in this and the following chapter, plays a substantive role in the logic of empire and the colonial thinking that naturalizes radically disproportionate scales of consumption and privilege through the quantity and quality of the space to which individuals have access. In this way, hotel life does not so much accommodate as perpetuate stark distinctions between rich and poor, the haves and have-nots, its imaginative fabric bound up in global systems of economic value that differentiate individuals and create social hierarchies that those checking in have both deeply internalized and desire to transgress.

Empire

It is tempting to imagine the hotel as one node in a larger network of places that travelers temporarily occupy as they wander the earth—to imagine the hotel, in short, as a part of the global "multiculture" so famously celebrated by travel writer Pico Iyer.[1] So viewed, a stay at the Caribe Hilton or at the Punta Cana resort becomes, much like a trip to the airport or shopping mall, a "mash-up" of old and new, First World and Third World, with all the modern conveniences and a dazzling array of languages, tastes, and sounds—a portal to scales of space and place ever more alluring to those on the move. People come from everywhere, they stay for a while, and they return or move on. These mixed-up sites are designed, Iyer believes, to be comfortable throughlines for the "spiritually homeless," for whom movement and circulation have replaced rest and stillness, and for whom the modern resort hotel is more akin to an airport or a shopping mall or a theme park than to the colonial outpost and imperial contact zone of the past.

But more than these other switching points, the resort hotel, as historian Christine Skwiot reminds us, has an extraordinary and protracted history of collaboration with the imperial interests of the nation-state. The resort hotel, her work reminds us, is saturated with empire, top to bottom. Its very existence is a reflection of a long history that cannot be so easily displaced or set aside. For centuries, occasional travel to warmer climates has been a mainstay of aristocratic and middle-class lives. The warm Caribbean breezes, the smell of salt water and sugar, and the rustle of palm fronds were necessary therapeutics, antidotes to the hustle of the steel and concrete world of modernity. Of course, the stay had to be brief, lest the traveler suffer from some form of "tropical neurasthenia" and devolve into an uncivilized state, an unnerving, medical consequence for the white, rich body of too much time in the global South. And, just as surely, while in the tropics, one needed the attentions of "the native"—brown, black, or yellow—to be fully restored to vigorous health. Across the nineteenth and twentieth centuries, there was, Skwiot tells us, an extraordinary continuity in the role of the hotel as an expression of the interests of the nation-state, as empire by other means.[2]

The modern hotel's function in this storyline has been to streamline and standardize the experience of imperial tourism, to make the sexuality and servility of the native employee predictable, accessible, and even affordable—and thus to make the space that guests occupy occur at the direct expense of local residents. We can see this feature of the hotel-as-empire clearly even in recent advertisements, which might have been ripped from an orientalist landscape of the nineteenth century, the prototype for so much hotel marketing. In one, a white man and woman, resting in intimate recline, smile benevolently at the dusky servant in front of them. On his knee, he, in turn, offers them a tall fluted glass of chilled champagne, which they have yet to accept. The trio's impending transaction is staged on a braided jute rug, laid down in a rain forest clearing and littered with the accoutrements of elite travel in foreign climes—picnic baskets, safari gear, binoculars, and, of course, the "native" informant. If the intruding foliage suggests that the group's control of this particular spot is short-lived, beyond the clearing there are miles of uninterrupted sandy beaches, and, running parallel, a slow-moving, winding river, twin tropes of the imperial fantasy of vast terrains there for the taking. "Where will you find your Shangri-La?" the ad asks, linking the couple's obvious, material satisfaction with nostalgia for dominion over Conrad's "white spaces" on the map of the world.

Such messaging is implicit in more nuanced hotel visuals, and the image that appears next attests to the portability and broad-scale relevance of this imperial narrative across hotel chains, continents, and geopolitical contexts. The glass of champagne can seamlessly be exchanged for a café au lait, the rain forest clearing gives way to a plush sitting room, the enticing urban landscape just discernible through hotel windows suggests guests' easy mastery of a vast, cosmopolitan urban space that is theirs for the taking. Hotel guests are implied rather than pictured in this particular mise-en-scène, and the "native" hotel waiter who serves them is positioned in such a way that he, in turn, serves all potential guests who happen to encounter this particular advertisement for Peninsula hotels.

As advertisement, the "Shangri-La" image draws upon this long-standing fantasy, the same one that the Peninsula Hotel chain markets so effectively. Both are compelling bits of high-end historical ephemera, but they also echo what we routinely see and hear elsewhere about the resort hotel and the kinds of privilege that it offers those who, in being rich enough to check in, suddenly acquire access to a spatial imaginary that reaches far beyond the hotel's finite geographic boundaries. We imagine the attractive, upwardly mobile young couple walking hand in hand along the hotel's private beachfront. We see them relaxing on a weekend morning in their room with cappuccino and newspaper strewn carelessly about—maybe even getting a his and hers massage while holding hands across their separate massage tables backlit by a spectacular sunset. In short, once the modern luxury hotel epitomized by Peninsula hotels is set apart from civilization, it offers overworked-dual-income-no-kid-couples the chance to "get away" from the sex-killing pressures of the job to "find each other" again not simply amid the hotel's sateen sheets but amid the expansive world that they are invited to temporarily occupy.

In these imaginings, the resort hotel is a monogamous heterotopia, a durable and expansive extension of the honeymoon trip proper, in which man and wife, surrounded by splendor and service, repeatedly reconstitute their relations against exotic, ever grander, and more expansive backgrounds. This envisioning offers up the hotel as a regenerative oasis from the very forces—and presumably plainer versions of the hotel—that fatigue and enervate the business traveler in the first place. In other words, even as the hotel becomes an overused and somewhat tired pitstop for constantly-on-the-road business travelers, hustling with ever more anxiety to meet clients and close the deals that will make the end-of-quarter numbers and therefore keep them employed for another fiscal year, the hotel, in its geographically expansive version, emerges as a hyperbolized neocolonial answer and alternative to the desire-killing phenomena to which it contributes.

As a flexible, shifting site of narrative making, the elite hotel for the rich and aspirant rich is a place where individuals seek alternatives to the domestic landscapes that confine them. It is a place literally offering

In this 2014 advertisement for the Peninsula Hotels chain (a match for the Shangri-La), we see the Shanghai skyline in the background, while a white-gloved, Asian attendant lays out high tea for guests. Such a scene—one of many "Peninsula Moments," the ad assures—suggests a world not all that different from the imperial past, a world defined by service in structures built to maintain the elite as they span the globe. (From the authors' collection)

new horizons that transform the public and private worlds they usually inhabit and thus providing them the alluring chance to see the world anew. In this particular iteration, the hotel offers a fantasy of renewal that has a distinctly territorial element, explicitly aligning fresh starts and self-discovery with the well-worn tropes of imperial exploration and discovery. As Edmundo O'Gorman has persuasively shown, discovery is a powerful node of imperial fantasy that goes back at least to 1492 and the "discovery" of America.[3] Of course, as O'Gorman cogently argued, America was an idea that was invented rather than discovered, created rather than found, and yet, ever since, this concept of discovery has been an enduring element of modernity—a key heuristic through which individuals create for themselves a sense of renewal and opportunity. The hotel, as we illustrate, institutionalizes and packages this habit of modern thought, making it portable and scalable to diverse landscapes and parts of the world.

This aspect of hotel life—its incipient capacity to package and enable guests' self-discovery—is dramatically expanded and altered when the hotel becomes a resort, when the hotel takes up more landmass and folds highly differentiated scales of space into its logos and topos. On the one hand, whereas the hotel-as-spa, as we have seen, offers guests an intimate clinical relation replete with technicians and support staff charged with the medical repair of tissue and soul, the resort hotel trades even more dramatically in the hotel's deep and abiding associations with such modern institutions of restraint as the clinic, asylum, compound, hospital, and prison. Dramatically refining and revising the notion of the domestic carceral, the modern resort hotel complexes that have sprung up along and beyond national and urban peripheries promise inmates "all-inclusive" experiences in which every aspect of human need and desire is legislated—in which human requirements and wants for food, alcohol, exercise, leisure, pleasure, and social distraction are absorbed within the overall logic of the resort and folded into its fee and organizational structure. Much like a hospital patient traverses the inner terrain of the clinic in hospital gown and wrist band, guests, upon registering at the resort hotel's front desk, have a plasticized identification tag affixed to their wrists that entitles them to the "run of the house" and all its privileges. The complimentary tropical drink or hot toddy presented to newcomers upon entry to the resort hotel makes immediately palpable and vividly present the benefits of temporarily ceding one's freedom of choice and movement to the compound's greater logos.

And yet, if the exclusive and isolated resort is a variation on the theme of the hotel-as-spa, it carries distinctive and unmistakable elements of imperial appeal. Synonymous with "refuge," and associated with the concepts of "repair" and "recourse," the resort quite literally offers its visitors the powerful opportunity to "re-sort" their own individual imaginings of their place within the world by inhabiting that world on an ever grander scale. Often perched at the outer edges of nations or natural wonders like mountains or oceans, the resort most often epitomizes the dramatic contact zone between human and nature—the place where human capacity to assert dominance over large-scale natural forces is most dramatically on display. These resorts, certainly, trade in the logic of the spa. The Broadmoor, for example, tucked up against the mountains in Colorado Springs, Colorado, recommends a "wine down," a full Chardonnay and sugar scrub, and a fitness evaluation by a specialist, but the central seduction is the "Lu'Lur," incorporating "Indonesian rituals" into its "flow of services," which, the resort suggests, have "been used for centuries by royalty" and "can make you feel like royalty—for a day." The Banff Springs Hotel in Alberta, defined as a mountain resort in the continental style, has "waterfall treatment whirlpools" along with an "indoor European mineral pool." The YHI Spa at the Paradisus Puntacana in the Dominican Republic offers its guests a menu of peelings, aromatherapies, and massages. There are yoga classes every day and meditation classes on the weekends, and, of course, the therapy provided by the warm waters and ocean breezes of the tropics. Most of these sites offer same-sex and co-ed divisions, couples rooms, and even vacation nannies. The emphasis, in every case, is on the opulence of physical isolation as much as the faux aristocracy that comes from the servile attentions of the institution.

Central to the resort's popularity and enduring fascination is the fantasy, and limited opportunity, it provides for individuals to literally and figuratively conquer the world. Whether it is in the sprawling resort's proximate location to high mountain peaks or whale- and dolphin-populated ocean waters, or the extensive and heavily constructed built outdoor environments of eighteen-hole golf courses and nature walks, the resort trades in the interplay of man and nature—of humans' capacity to organize a seemingly infinite expanse of world to suit their desires for play, leisure, exploration, and development of talents and skills unrelated to the workplace. As such, it is the ultimate human workshop, providing seemingly infinite new opportunities for reimagining the self in relation to the world—functioning as nothing less than a prime construction site for the architecture and refinement of the modern self. And it does so by gesturing outward to an imperial domain that includes ever more territory as it becomes ever larger in scale.

Within such environs, the resort often extends the idea that the grand expanse of terrain it carefully cultivates for its patrons is a playground for the most intimate, private needs and wants of the self—those parts of the self thus far undiscovered or long neglected. Often situated on a patch of ground wrestled from the tropics, the hotel offers a mix of sun, sex, and sand to the proverbial overworked, ground-down suburban housewife or the pasty, enervated midlevel banker. But if the hotel-as-spa offers an intimate, clinical relation with a technician charged with the intimate recalibration of the individual psyche and physique, the resort generally offers a form of restorative imperial remaking in which opulent class fantasies of those beleaguered or temporarily depleted by the demands of corporate capital have full run of the house. Tanning on the beach, sipping an El Presidente, and swimming in the warm, blue waters of the Caribbean are meant to offset the psychosis of too much civilization, too much modernity, too little space in which to move. Just as the lion, king of the forest, will not mate in captivity, so too do hotel patrons, once let loose from constraint, suddenly find themselves free to act out long-suppressed parts of their psyches with those brought or found on the premises. But such places are also protected by a *cordon sanitaire*—a distant remove or physical break—from too much closeness to subalterneity. In other words, the resort is meant to enable class privilege, so that every guest gets the right amount of therapeutic sun and surf but also has the chance to serve as imperial master of a domain built entirely for his pleasure and staged on irregular terrain, to ease his expression of authority. If the occasional trysting thrills of the Plaza Hotel are envisioned as a brief release from monogamy and the straight-and-narrow, as we saw in chapter 2, they are not staged in the great wide open, nor so recklessly or so imperiously as the sexual conquests at the resort. These are differences of kind as well as degree.

Such places are thus revealing signs of an increasingly stratified, neo-liberal global economy, in which "tourism" is both a consequence and a cause of difference. At its worst, the "industry" can foster greater socioeconomic distance, scar the geography of a country with class inflections, and restructure national economies in such a way that it becomes difficult to generate new revenue streams, pushing wages downward for larger and larger sections of the population. The creation of a tourist resort demands massive infrastructural investment. A resort has to be isolated, and far from civilization, and yet requires aggressive infrastructure construction for its support. New airports, bridges, and roads must be built, connecting the removed site to the world. New restaurants, markets, communications networks, and transit links must be fostered.

A vacation nanny, featured in an advertisement, with her client family at an FDR resort in Jamaica. Vacation nannies, the resort stresses in this advertisement, are assigned to guests with children and provide care from breakfast through dinner, allowing the guest to enjoy the all-you-can-eat buffet, the floating bar, or whatever luxury is nearby. (From the authors' collection)

A compound must be constructed, and reliable labor—both for construction and for the service needs to follow—must be discovered, controlled, and kept pliant. Security enhancements are needed at every step, to ensure the safety of the guest. And in the long term, the national context for the resort must increasingly be reoriented to a service economy model, building hotels and not factories, rerouting transportation away from natural resources and toward white sandy beaches, and posturing for a foreign clientele with interests and needs quite distinct from those of the local citizenry.

And so the tourist, as Jamaica Kincaid suggests, all too often sees the exotic ground with blinders on and only a sense of infinite possibility.[4] There must, of course, be palm trees and blue water and safe roads and isolation. And the bar must be fully stocked, and the restaurant must never run out of food. The food should seem local, or familiar, or both. The resort should be clean. The beaches must be free of what one normally finds on a beach—trash and broken glass and driftwood and old chicken bones. The pathways between buildings must be stone or concrete, not mud. The shrubs and plants should be suitably exotic and verdantly green, but also maintained and orderly. The roads to the resort must be smooth enough and gentle enough for rapid and forgettable entries and exits. There can be no patchwork tin roofs, or piecemeal concrete-block construction, or visible security fences. No discernible evidence, in short, of the deleterious effect of globalization, or of the absence of steady wage work. It takes a lot of work to foster this artificial authenticity.

Local culture is retained and present only to the extent that it can be comfortably consumed. Mariachis serenade guests as they enjoy "Mexican food night" at one of the all-inclusive hotels speckling Cancun or Cozumel beaches, or Hawaiian leys are draped around the necks of newcomers to Hawaii's resort hotel complexes by smiling women in grass skirts. Missing from these carefully crafted representations of local authenticity is the back-end labor that makes such seamless displays of local distinctiveness possible: the workers cutting fruit for tropical drinks, building and refurbishing elite recreational complexes, and endlessly laundering the resort hotels' opulent supply of beach towels. The economic imperatives implicit in providing First World comfort in Third World contexts are strategically erased—are written out of and purposefully excluded from the "all inclusive" experience, And yet they lurk as the dark underbelly of the resort experience, most evident at those times when guests segue from airport to resort and back again or temporarily leave the resort to do some local exploring. Confronted by clamoring taxi drivers and guides offering personalized local tours, special restaurant and shopping deals, and once-in-a-lifetime time-share opportunities, travelers just leaving airport immigration are overwhelmed by the cacophony of an alternately aspiring and despairing global southern capital. Indeed guests' transitory recognition of the ruptures and turbulence in the smooth operation of imperial resort recreation ultimately fuels the resort fantasy of protection from and dominance over desperate, potentially unruly subalterns.

The tropical resort, then, is a metaphor for the place of the wealthy and resource-rich First World in relation to the less moneyed "global South." A geopolitical concept coming to replace "Third World" after the collapse of the Soviet Union, the global South isn't so much a place as it is, among other things, a concept and an ever-shifting constellation of geopolitical locations characterized by conflicting struggles between modernity, modernization, and a logic of coloniality, on the one hand,

and resistance to these dominant and homogenizing forces, on the other. Formed in the friction between global domination and struggles to conceptualize new visions of the future that do not comply with modernity's logics, the global South carries a liberatory possibility that is almost irresistibly compelling to those disheartened by the totalizing logics of New World modernity. It offers itself up to the First World— its supposed antipode—as a not yet fully realized heterotopia, carrying the promise of alternatives to the logocentric master narrative of New World modernity with its mind-numbing apparatus of coloniality. If relatively poor in discretionary per capita income and liquid assets, the global South is, nonetheless, abundant in natural wonders, future possibility, and those intangible assets that make a world of difference—that give life meaning and value of a more substantive sort than that represented on a spread sheet. As a result, guests come from far and wide to resort hotels perched expansively upon the world's most lovely beaches and nature preserves. They come on missions of discovery, occupation, and exploration—through discovering the world anew, to discover the long-untended and ignored parts of themselves. In all senses of the word then, guests "occupy" the grandiose spaces the resort hotel provides: through their experience of occupation and invasion of an external but highly curated environment, they invent themselves anew, discovering and exploring the darkest recesses of their inner needs, wants, desires, and drives.

Discovery

Central to this process of occupation and discovery is the subjugation of those who inhabit these environments. As anthropologist Steven Gregory observes, the "practical application of increasingly global social hierarchies" is witnessed, most intimately, in the subjection of locals in places like Haiti, the Dominican Republic, Jamaica, Cuba, and elsewhere, to "fantasies of control and domination."[5] Such subjection, with its requisite fantasy of dominance, is nowhere more evident and heavily documented than in *Heading South*, the 2005 French film directed by Laurent Cantet, which contains a near-perfect expression of the fantasy of escape-into-domination provided to the affluent by the resort hotel. *Heading South* highlights what remains implicit and deeply embedded within tropical resort culture more generally, and so we explore it in detail in the following pages to delineate the shape and texture of the particular kinds of interaction between rich and poor that the hotel enables. We could just as easily have drawn from a different archive of textual materials, and so the story that *Heading South* tells has a familiar and naturalizing feel to it. This award-winning film is based on three short stories by the francophone Haitian and Canadian novelist and journalist Dany Laferrière and captures his sustained interest in interracial sex and sexual tourism.[6] But more fundamentally for our purposes, it explores how the resort becomes a privileged staging ground for interracial fantasies of personal and often explicitly sexual remaking—fantasies that trade in the economic and social pressures that we have been describing and that capitalize on the highly differentiated spatial scales of encounter that the hotel so carefully architects.

As the plot unfolds, three middle-aged white women are brought to a resort in Haiti that caters, it seems, to a cosmopolitan class of fairly ordinary people. The women—Ellen, a world-weary French professor at Wellesley; Brenda, the divorcee who pines for Legba, and who is haunted by her erotic memories of a previous sojourn in the same resort; and Sue, a quirky Canadian, enjoying the thrill of enhanced racial status in the Caribbean—are not, at first glance, members of the new master class. They spend the great bulk of their time at a commonplace resort, surrounded by black attendants, and enjoying the company of their sexual partners day and night. They exist, as far as we can tell, somewhere in the not-so-distant past or the temporally removed present. There are no cell phones, no televisions, and no signifiers of modernity. The story could be staged anywhere in the tropics or at any time in recent history. Such a plot is a counternarrative, of sorts, to the familiar story of imperial male predation, in which the male body—and usually the white male body—seeks sexual release and an authority denied to him elsewhere in the tropics.

Within the resort compound, each enjoys the pleasures of local black bodies, personified, in part, by Legba, the teenage lover preferred by many. Named for Papa Legba, the spiritual embodiment of the crossroads and the voice of God, the enigmatic young man at the heart of *Heading South* is both a national cipher for Haiti and an object of obsession for Brenda and Ellen. Habitually undressed and often asleep, Legba stands at the end of a continuum of desirable black male bodies—each a phallic icon—that can be traced back into the nineteenth century, and straight through Jean Le Nègre to Shaft and Mandingo. He is presented, through Ellen and Brenda, as every white woman's true fantasy. And

In this still image from *Heading South*, the 2005 French film directed by Laurent Cantet, Ellen, the aging French professor on holiday at a Haitian resort, enjoys some supposed intimacy with Legba, her lover. Of course, the intimacy has been purchased, and so, too, has the lover. (From the authors' collection)

we are shown, repeatedly, that there are many different Legbas. At one point, while he and Brenda dance, we see that the floor is filled with white women and their black partners, each dyadic couple swept up in the passion of their own engagements.

The resort's ability to accommodate the newly discovered intimate desires of its guests is enabled, strangely, by the ubiquity and utility of its servant class. Everywhere there are white bodies craving the attentions of black bodies. Everywhere there are black bodies, witnesses to the authority of the First World body. On the beach or at the restaurant, every drink is delivered graciously, every chair is opened courteously, and every request is received politely. When Albert initially refuses to serve Legba dinner at the restaurant, Brenda insists, invoking her colonial powers. "He is my guest," she says, incredulously. A simple plate of chicken is then prepared. In her cottage, after a night spent together, Ellen takes out her camera, and asks Legba to lie on his chest, and to close his eyes. "I want to see your face asleep, and your ass," she says. She seeks, there, to document his subservience, and to capture him after her discovery and conquest of his body. In this image, he will be perpetually conquered, exhausted, and submissive. As she insisted, he will be frozen in youth.

The setting for this set of dynamic relations is the Hotel Petit Anse ("the small cove"), at first glance, a rather uninspiring beachfront resort. Ellen describes it as "clean" and "quiet." It is well maintained but not luxurious, and, as such, it stands in for the broader range of resort possibilities in the tropics, from massive, elite preserves to off-of-the-beaten-path, "Rough Guide" retreats. The terrain is divided into two parts, with a moat or drainage ditch standing between the mainland and the beach. The main structures of the resort—the restaurant, the guesthouses—are enveloped by the foliage of the mainland and are attended to by the uniformed staff of the resort, by men and women like Albert and Denise. The wooden bridge across the moat leads to the beach, where the largely female clientele is serviced by groups of tall black men in bikini bathing suits, who share their food, apply their sun tan lotions, hold their hands, make polite and flattering chitchat, and swim with them in the bright blue sea. That structural divide marks more than the public and private domains of empire; it also denotes the distinction between the wage-earning employees of the resort itself and the unofficial servant class that frolics just across the bridge, hoping for access to wealth and privilege, and participating in a complex, off-the-books exchange that is irreducible to sex-for-money. It reminds us that the immediate shore-front is a borderland contact zone just barely under the nominal control of the resort and not a ruthlessly governed stronghold. On the beach, Legba and the men can eat, if their clients deign to buy them food; but the same is not true fifty yards inland at the restaurant.

In this colonial stronghold, sex seems to be the unofficial centerpiece of the resort's service economy and the way in which guests discover parts of themselves long forgotten or never before claimed. Providing the armature upon which guests' "discovery" of new expanses of themselves occurs with seemingly infinite novelty, sexual activity becomes a colonial act within the hotel. Over and over again, *Heading South* narrates the array of services and offers sex with boys and young men as a way to discover those parts of guests' interior landscapes unknown or long untended. But, much like the female sex workers whose lives were unearthed in anthropologist Kamala Kempadoo's work, Legba and his cohort of willing consorts aren't merely trading sex for cash.[7] Indeed, lounging in the sun, holding hands and caressing, dining on sandwiches and cold soda, they are enjoying—and enjoyment is the only word—the temporary perks of their modestly privileged positions. After a horseback ride to the beach, the troop of white women and black men share a joint or two, lounge peacefully together, and do not engage each other as if one were the master and the other were servant. Such subtle coercions—subtle in performance, not in material groundings—are what make the Hotel Petit Anse work as a sexual playground. Offsite, in Port-au-Prince, the food is scarce, the streets are littered with rubble, and the prospects for the young and the beautiful are grim. But at the Hotel Petit Anse, so long as they sleep peacefully on the thin strip of beachfront, and drape themselves on the arms of their white patrons, men like Legba can be well fed and comparatively safe.

Like the weather and the sand, then, Legba is a natural resource of the Caribbean. He is untransportable—taken away from his native soil, he would lose his virility. Unlike other resources that have historically been extracted from various parts of the colonial world, shipped to major cities in the metropole, and transformed, through production, manufacturing, and the factory system, into products, which are then shipped to consumer markets for purchase, Legba is a resource that cannot be relocated. To procure a desired experience—a warm ocean breeze in January, or the cool mist of a mountain lake in August, the well-off must travel to somewhere else. The resort hotel is the infrastructure that emerges to make that venture outside the metropole safe and standard, that ensures the appropriate result, and that regulates and standardizes pleasure. Hence, both Brenda and Ellen, creatures of the metropole, must travel to the terra firma of Haiti and troll the shore like beachcombers to find him. To stress the importance of his location, Ellen repeatedly makes a distinction between African Americans and black Haitians, concluding that the former are not an acceptable substitute for the latter. When Brenda dresses Legba up in a gold patterned shirt, Ellen disdainfully suggests that he looks like "a black guy from Harlem." The allure, then, is lost.

Sue, the relatively quiet and unassuming Canadian, best explains how the guests' "discovery" of their inner desires impacts and redefines their lives. Drawing a contrast between the life of a professor in New England— "a discreet woman, whose British accent makes her feel different"—and hotel life in the tropics, she declares that "here she is like a sun, a fixture of the landscape, whatever her mood, life revolves around her. All the boys are wild about her." For Sue, a clerk in a parts factory, the chance to be another "sun," another life-giving force in the universe of Haitian possibilities, is thrilling. "We all change when we get here," she continues. "Here, I feel like a butterfly—free, alive, and unattached." Of her beachside lover, Neptune, she confesses that she "loves him." Such a love, she adds, is only possible at the resort. "Here," she concludes, "we all become different." The Hotel Petit Anse is thus an escapist paradise, where comparatively ordinary people can become, by virtue of their relocation into a new political economy, goddesses, capable of bringing black statues to life, and imparting to them the capacity to love and fear "le blanc."

As we have seen, the resort hotel that is imagined by Laurent Cantet and a plethora of other writers, filmmakers, artists, and travelers embeds guests within a larger natural world with wonders that stimulate self-discovery and transformation through consumption of local resources both human and environmental. In such a context, the world both outside the hotel room window and inside guests' minds suddenly looks bigger, brighter, and better. *Heading South* is not unique in the story of hotel life that it tells. The textual record is peppered with accounts of how individuals world weary and woebegone occupy space with greater energy and optimism once they relocate beyond nation's edge to the soothing environs of the resort hotel. Terri McMillan's popular 1998 novel *How Stella Got Her Groove Back*, for example, tracks the affluent African American woman protagonist's transformative journey to a Jamaican resort hotel, and its title suggests how the abundance that Stella finds there restores that deep and abiding part of self long lost and lamented but not entirely forgotten.

These texts are part of a much larger corpus of archival material documenting how the affluent and rich consistently rely on the hotel and the particular kind of discovery that it provides guests to invent themselves anew amid the world's most lovely and carefully constructed environs by consuming local resources both corporeal and environmental. And as this record documents, this right is not only a heteronormative prerogative of the master class—the resort hotel does not only encourage a particular kind of heterosexual self-discovery. Geographically situated in the contact zone between global North and global South, the plethora of same-sex resorts that have cropped up in such places as Palm Springs and Key West add another dimension to the resort hotel's capacity to generate self-discovery and deep personal knowledge through immersion in the natural environments it provides.

These sites, like those described and imagined in the rest of the textual record, reflect the institution's deep saturation with empire. Palm Springs' Vista Grande Resorts, for example, offers male guests and visitors tantalizing views of each other in the natural landscape as well as of the homoerotic sculptures that are sprinkled throughout the property. Property pamphlets and advertising emphasize the integration of the gay male body into this eroticized landscape and foreground the ways in which the built environment of Vista Grande Resorts is a triumph of sexual will to power over undeveloped natural resources and terrain. Resort brochures visually reinforce the resort hotel's alignment of natural wonders with sexual exploration by depicting nude male bodies ripe for discovery sprinkled generously throughout the property's expansive acreage. Sculptures found on the property explicitly link the young nubile men posing naked below the sculptures to the natural world. Separated only by a rugged natural landscape of boulders and hot springs, these materials suggest the extent to which the resort hotel trades in the overwrought relations between the natural world and the world of men. A remarkable number of images of the resort's construction phase, replete with bulldozers, boulder movers, under-construction casitas, and tall cranes suggest the deep and abiding links between labor and leisure—between the wreaking of a heavily orchestrated and choreographed resort out of the raw material provided by the natural world and the languid, even sultry discovery and enjoyment of the fruits of such labor by men of means and compatible erotic inclinations.

If Vista Grande Resorts emphasizes the constructed nature of the resort as part of its advertising strategy and erotic allure, CCBC Resort Hotel, which identifies itself as the "largest clothing optional gay men's resort in southern California," trades even more emphatically in the resort hotel's seemingly effortless dominion over the natural world. Not only are the resort hotel room accommodations conducive to sexual discovery and exploration, but nature has been organized and embedded within the resort to maximize this discovery. Take, for example, the resort's legendary "Walk" that combines winding pathways, seductive alcoves, and lush foliage to enable guests to commune with nature. Inviting the wandering guest to "come upon a babbling brook, enjoy a seductive waterfall, or happen upon some of our 'wildlife,'" CCBC Resort Hotel insists on the interlocking nature of desire, design, and discovery. The resort's location at water's edge enables the creation of nude beaches and giant waterfalls with caves as well as nature paths, created specifically to optimize visitors' discovery. Danny's Nude Beach and the enticements that this artificially contrived natural environment affords is enhanced, and counterbalanced, by Danny Jail—a temporary holding pen for those whose forays into exploration run aground.

Once outside of the United States, though, the circuits of sex tourism join queer travels to the precisely same colonial atmospherics, often in exactly the same institutional settings. Sometimes, these relations take the form of an interest in the "native boy," a concept that can be traced directly back to the formal age of empires.[8] And sometimes, they emerge as a user's geography of the cities and spaces marked as queer-friendly, a guide for the traveler hoping for a one-night hookup with the darker-skinned locals, for whom access to the hotel is granted only conditionally, and for whom global travels are financially unimaginable. Puerto Vallarta, one *Lonely Planet* guide submitted, was the "gay capital" of Mexico, a confluence of local and global queer cultures washing over the cobblestone streets and kitschy "Aztec" décor of resort hotels. Still, despite its oft-cited and celebrated queerness, and the presumption of a natural counterculture, that color-coded, class-bound confluence is hardly innocent. Indeed, the *Lonely Planet* guide—along with the various "Best Gay Tourist Spots" featured in *Out*, or *The Advocate*, or other mainstream publications—is a form of colonial studies, written for a First World audience eager to dive deeply into the global south.

The Hotel Petit Anse, the CCBC Resort Hotel, the Punta Cana resort, and other parallel institutions reproduce a strange and often colonial version of intimate discovery in well-managed, if not thoroughly dominated, foreign territory. These resorts—real and imaginary—literally weave local cultures, economies, and logics into their design, a design meant to display the playful power of guests to exploit and deplete the sprawling resort environments in which they find themselves. Conspicuous and hedonistic consumption of bodies, natural resources, and precariously balanced human relations is the name of the imaginative and real game that the resort plays—a game both obscured and epitomized by opulently irrigated golf courses and nature preserves in arid wildernesses and by the carefully groomed bodies of those who tend to visitors and this built environment. And so, though the resort hotel presents itself innocently as an agent of self-empowerment through pleasure, or a way station for globetrotting cosmopolitans, it is, among other things, an imperial workshop, full of chances for us to learn a disturbing lesson about geopolitics, space, and First World power, and meant to reassure guests that they are the anointed and enabled overlords of the past, present, and future, ever able to occupy larger scales of space in a finite and increasingly populated world.

6

POOR

As we have seen, the resort hotel gives ever more space to its affluent guests, encouraging free-form and seemingly unscripted encounters with the wonders of the natural world—be it the pleasures of an eighteen-hole golf course or the breathtaking glimpse of an unexpected waterfall—as part of guests' discovery of inner worlds long forgotten, buried, or unacknowledged. Even as hotels for the wealthy invent ever grander scales of space for their guests' exploration, discovery, and pleasure, the plethora of hotels that have sprung up to accommodate the world's poor and indigent—the day laborers, retirees on fixed budgets, and working poor—create new ways to imagine the minimal amount of space that bodies can take up. Whether it is capsule hotels that offer guests minuscule enclosed sleeping spaces for thirty dollars a night or the modern equivalent of flophouses that provide those in search of shelter side-by-side cots and shared bathrooms, hotel life has historically reached down as well as up the socioeconomic food chain.

Of course, some hotels, like the Dutch-based Citizen M pod hotel chain, target the growing market that exists just between these two ends of the hotel spectrum. With its motto of "affordable luxury for the people," Citizen M offers guests, once they have self-registered via kiosk, 150 square feet of private space; but common areas including a 24/7 cafeteria, community dining table, living room, and den create a sense of whimsical community. Citizen M has the feel of a dormitory, a place at once offering minimal private comfort but also a local community comprised of those who "travel the world with wide eyes and big hearts," are "independent yet united in a desire for positive traveling," are "smarter than a dolphin with a university degree and realize you can have luxury for not too much cash." To this self-selecting group of "mobile citizens of the world," Citizen M promises a 150-square-foot room with a comfortable bed and communal spaces to get a cold drink no matter what time of day or night you jet in.

As Paul Groth reminds us, a "good hotel room of 150 square feet—dry space, perhaps with a bath or a room sink, cold and sometimes hot water, enough electric service to run a [light] bulb and a television, central heat, and access to telephones and other services—constitutes a living unit mechanically more luxuriant than those lived in by a third to a half of the population of the earth."[1] Along such a continuum, hotels have catered to those desiring dramatically more space, as we saw in the preceding chapter, but they have also accommodated and increasingly confined, within ever smaller and more restricted shelter, those who can only afford to take up radically less room. A 150-square-foot hotel room, for example, feels palatial to those used to staying in the cubicle-style hotels that offered cheap lodging to itinerant workers in the early twentieth century or to those who have inhabited the high-density hotels popular in Asia that provide sleeping capsules stacked in pairs and just big enough for a single mattress.

And just as the resort hotels that have sprung up to cater to the affluent have offered increasing amounts of space to their guests in the era of empire, so too have the hotels in which those of modest means congregate gradually diminished in number, size, and scale over the past century. The dramatic reallocation of space in which the hotel trades, in other words, seems to mirror and help to enforce the growing gap between rich and poor—the upper 1 percent versus the rapidly expanding rest. The number of cheap rooms for rent in the United States has decreased even as the number of working poor has dramatically increased, creating a low-income short-term housing shortage of unprecedented proportions. In Portland, Oregon, for example, the number of economy units has gone from 4,500 in 1994 to 3,200 in 2012, and these units have long waiting lists, according to Northwest Pilot Project, a short-term housing provider for seniors. The question of literally where to put all the aged, infirm, impoverished, and wanting bodies of the world's low-income and itinerant work force has, not surprisingly, created a pressing need for creative hotel solutions.

This hotel housing bubble does not, however, occur in a vacuum. Rather, it is the logical result of shifting perceptions of space that directly correlate to the changing socioeconomic climate of a robust imperial nation. Bunkhouses for day laborers, along with flophouses, residential

Flophouse on lower Douglas Street, Omaha, Nebraska, in 1938. Flophouses, which prioritized beds over privacy, were literal warehouses for the migrant poor or locally indigent and can be contrasted with the modern single-occupancy hotel, with its emphasis on the supposed dignity of an unshared domestic space. (Photo by John Vachon; Prints and Photographs Division, Library of Congress, Washington, D.C.)

hotels, working-class rooming houses, and other affordable short-term housing began to be gradually legislated out of existence in the United States beginning in the early twentieth century, and it was the rising affluence of the middle class that was largely responsible. Alan Durning observes that, as more space and increased amounts of privacy began to become the norm for the growing number of Americans of middle-class means, the low-income hotel, with its high-density populations of transients was increasingly seen as a threat and inhumane aberration.[2] State and local laws began creating legal disincentives for rooming houses, bunkhouses, and the like by legislating what constituted "decent" short-term housing along middle-class lines. Suddenly, health and fire code requirements that legislated minimal amounts of indoor space per person, along with requirements for private bathrooms and occupancy limits dramatically upset the business model of those hotels targeting the poor.

The standard sizes for hotel bathrooms, window areas per room, and minimal floor space that California set in the early twentieth century were based on an emerging middle-class standard and the optimistic belief that all people had a right to scales of space that reflected this emergent and seemingly inalienable human norm. But by insisting on larger amounts of space for all hotel guests regardless of hotel clientele, these codes had the opposite effect, dramatically reducing the number of hotels available to accommodate those of modest means. In regulating how space was architected within hotels, city, state, and federal leaders effectively deprived those living in cheap lodging of the already modest amounts of space they enjoyed, driving those marginally located in desirable neighborhoods and parts of the city further away from the most highly prized urban real estate.

The dramatic reduction of total space available to the impoverished traveler is witnessed most powerfully in the extinction of the most inexpensive temporary housing that had been so a popular and pervasive during the nineteenth century—the flophouse. Essentially a hall of bunks with community baths, the flophouse was, not too long ago, a familiar, even ubiquitous, feature of the urban landscape. The flophouse is now illegal because its rooms would be much too small to meet the minimal requirements of any state standard. Washington State, for example, has determined that a "habitable" room can be no smaller than seven feet by seven feet—this is the absolutely minimal amount of space that a living body can take up in a hotel. In such a framework, high-density hotels like flophouses, with their shared rooms, communal baths, and kitchen crawl spaces suddenly appear to be pernicious hotel aberrations, brokering in human rights violations.

Given the resulting erasure of low-income hotel options and the growing number of homeless people in search of temporary shelter, some developers are experimenting with new kinds of low-income hotel space and updated rooming houses reminiscent of last century's. One example is the aPodment, created by Seattle's Calhoun Properties and designed for exactly the demographic that has found the already modest space to which they can lay claim legislated away from them by laws, ironically, aimed at protecting their human right to space. At 150 square feet per unit, with shared kitchens and laundry facilities and a private bath, aPodment rooming houses have sprung up to meet a human need for short-term shelter in high-priced urban areas, with space scaled to price. They are being followed by similar experiments in short-term housing in Vancouver (British Columbia), San Francisco, and New York City but are, not surprisingly, encountering resistance from opponents who are concerned about the kinds of people who would be attracted to such modestly scaled facilities. Ranging from 150 to 300 square feet per unit, these microshelters are under threat and in danger of being shut down precisely because of the relatively small amount of space they dole out to their guests.

Single-Room Occupancy

Within the context of these large historiographical and geopolitical shifts—shifts characterized by the waxing and waning both of space within hotels and of total hotel real estate designated for those of lower income—the following pages focus on the single-room occupancy hotel (SRO), charting the lives that are variously enabled and frustrated within its walls. And they do so because, though the fortunes of SROs have risen and fallen alongside shifting long-tail attitudes about humans, space, and rented rooms, they have not entirely vanished from the hotel landscape. Indeed, SROs have continued to support hotel life with surprising durability, given the larger history of low-income hotels just outlined.

While the term originated in New York City in the 1930s, SROs date back at least fifty years earlier, and their existence was a marked and stark feature of the American urban landscape. From their emergence in the 1880s to a 1988 U.S. Department of Housing and Urban Development study and the 1987 Stewart B. McKinney Homeless Assistance Act, which aimed to ensure the SRO's continued presence by providing more than one thousand new SRO housing units for the homeless, most of these structures have been former residential hotels, though the odd mortuary, dry cleaner, nursing home, and school have also been repurposed. These former hotels have either deteriorated and inadvertently catered to the SRO clientele or have been specifically reconstituted to meet the requirements of the modern-day SRO—namely, a 140-square-foot private room for one person that has bed, chair, and space for clothing storage and, in their modern iterations, sometimes a desk, sink, small refrigerator, and microwave.[3]

We can begin to see in stark and protracted detail the SRO's particular power to confer class identity—to tell individuals exactly how much room they are entitled to take up within a hotel's walls and in life more generally—by turning to the pages of Theodore Dreiser's famous naturalist novel of American urban life, *Sister Carrie* (1900). Written as hotel life along the full spatial continuum was booming in big cities like Chicago and New York, Dreiser's landmark narrative of urban life features the hotel as a powerful workshop or laboratory in which characters test the quantity and quality of life that they can create for themselves. However, in *Sister Carrie*, it is not a single hotel's transition from bastion of luxurious transient living to last stop before life under a bridge that interests Dreiser but, rather, the power that different kinds and calibers of hotels have to confer new class positions through the quality and quantity of space they make available to those itinerant laborers who seek shelter in unfamiliar cities. As journalist, naturalist writer, and commentator on American urban life, Dreiser turned to the hotel as a key feature of the urban landscape and, in his most famous novel, sought to document both the range of hotels available to the isolated and transient urban dweller and the ways that these hotels confer and deny class identity and privilege to those seeking to make their way in the modern world. And in so doing, he inevitably attended to the violence as well as the respite that are endemic features of the SRO as a site of modern lodging.

We understand the role the SRO plays by charting how far beyond it the novel's protagonist, the initially impoverished and almost homeless Carrie Madenda, ultimately travels. Indeed, Carrie only begins to understand that she has "made it" as an actress in New York City when she is invited to relocate from the modest hotel room she shares with another chorus girl to the Wellington Hotel—a posh and conspicuously spacious new hotel on Broadway that seeks to attract a glamorous high-end clientele. Carrie receives a message from the Wellington Hotel manager, who tells her about some elegant rooms that he would like her to see and describes in detail the hot and cold water, private baths, special hall-service for every floor, elevators, spacious rooms, and other luxury accoutrements that make the Wellington a destination for the most discriminating customer. He does so in the hopes that she will be enticed to pay a visit to the hotel and consider residing there for the summer. As Mr. Withers puts it, "every hotel depends upon the repute of its patrons and a well-known actress" such as Carrie brings attention and good press to the hotel (316).

For that reason Mr. Withers tells Carrie that, though the grand accommodations he offers her would cost a hundred dollars a week normally, she can name her price or pay as little as three dollars a day, if she likes. With the three windows overlooking Broadway, two lovely bedrooms, replete with beautifully appointed furnishings, a parlor with piano, library table, and lovely chairs and tables, the hotel suite that Carrie enters seems as far away from an SRO as she could get for a few dollars more than an SRO costs. It is exactly "a place such as she had often dreamed of occupying" (318)—redefining her position within society upward even as it gains hard-won market share from her recently acquired popularity. In this negotiation—a negotiation directly correlating the hotel's grand and luxurious space to its guests' social value—each commodity sets its value in direct relation to the other. The "pre-money valuation," as it were, of the brand new Wellington Hotel is determined largely by the perceived "value" of its first guests, and so the aspiring hotel offers vast amounts of luxurious space at a bargain to promising rising social stock like Carrie, with the ultimate goal of securing the highest market value for a larger discriminating public that has money to spend and desire to be staying at the "right" hotel.

But if Carrie finds a grander, bigger, and better self at the Wellington for three dollars a day, the man with whom she had been living until his unemployment forced her to bunk up with another chorus girl finds his own downward mobility starkly marked by the ever seedier and smaller hotels to which he turns for increasingly insufficient refuge from a world that refuses to break his economic fall. From the vantage point of a third-rate Bleecker Street hotel and its "dingy, moth-eaten hotel lobby," the brooding Hurstwood reads of Carrie's success on the stage with a mixture of resentment and pride (314). But Hurstwood's deteriorating resources force him to seek refuge in ever dingier, smaller, and cheaper hotels—he goes from paying fifty cents a day to thirty-five cents a day—until his resources run out and he seeks work at the Broadway Central hotel where he sleeps in the attic at the roof of the hotel and eats what the cook gives him on the sly. This arrangement, tenuous as it is, fails when he gets pneumonia and is sent by the hotel physician to Bellevue to recover. From that point on Hurstwood seeks shelter in the homeless shelters and cheap lodging houses that are provided to those who can find the twelve cents to pay—that is until he remembers a hotel that has close, little rooms with gas jets in them that are, he thinks, "almost pre-arranged for what he wanted to do" (346). The impediment to Hurstwood's renting of such a room is economic, and he has to save up the fifteen cents that it will take to gas himself in this hotel.

The novel's final scenes mark the dramatically divergent scales of space that these two protagonists take up, and they do so through recourse to the hotels that each call temporary home. Carrie sits in her even more palatial suite of rooms at the newest hotel that has persuaded her to take up residence—none other than the iconic Waldorf—reading about class strife and suffering in *Père Goriot*, while a former lover sits in the Imperial Hotel lobby enjoying a good dinner as the snow falls. Against the relative sumptuousness of these two homes away from home, the readers' encounter with Hurstwood's hard-won hotel room—a "dingy affair, wooden, dusty, hard" with its "small gas-jet" (352)—highlights the radical economic disparities that make some people "larger than life" and others beneath notice. The suicide that Hurstwood stages in his unendurable rented space is a final gesture of despair and defiance against unrelenting economic forces that deprive him of the means to pay for even the most humble hotel room. Carefully tucking his ragged coat into the crack at the bottom of the door, taking off his shoes, and arranging his vest carefully before lying down for one last time, Hurstwood's final night of sleep in a hotel room registers the stark options that confront those who do not have the means to occupy any more space in the world. Choosing to leave the world rather than confront homelessness, indigence, and chronic want, Hurstwood represents that human residue that will not or cannot take up absolutely no space in the world. And the image of the black boat that silently leaves from the Twenty-Seventh Street Pier bearing Hurstwood's body along with many nameless others to Potter's Field is a dark and silent elegy to those for whom the SRO becomes the final resting place—a segue from haven to grave.

As Dreiser's novel makes abundantly clear, hotels allocate space based on class privilege, and if the grand rooms of a Waldorf Astoria mark one end of a fluid class continuum, the minuscule, dehumanizing, and dingy spaces of the SRO mark the other. Hotels register guests' shifting fortunes, functioning as a powerful diagnostic of guests' often rapidly evolving socioeconomic circumstances. But if the SRO is the inevitable hotel of the have-nots, it remains, nonetheless, a hotel of interest to the haves. In fact, those whose fortunes rise dramatically—those like Carrie Madenda, upon whom capitalism smiles because of talent, good looks, dumb luck, or great connections—often turn to the SRO as a powerful touchstone and reference point—to appease guilt, to "give back" to society, or to stay connected to their communities of origin.

Take the recent example of Beyoncé Knowles. In 2007 the Grammy winner, actress, and fashion designer turned developer, pledged $1 million to build a $4 million, forty-three unit SRO in her hometown of Houston. Located in the city downtown, the Knowles-Temenos Place Apartments were designed to provide, in the words of their creator, a "single room occupancy supportive housing facility for women and men who are taking significant steps in improving their lives after the traumatic effects of personal and natural disasters." In video clips Beyoncé speaks more particularly to the natural disaster that motivated her to build the SRO: it was the evacuees from Hurricane Katrina, who, newly homeless, relocated en masse to Houston, that, "still to this day," Beyoncé admits, caused her to take action and underwrite her own SRO. And she asks those interested in the Temenos project to engage with her in a thought experiment about how it would feel to be in the shoes of those in need of the SRO facilities that the Knowles-Temenos Place provides. She asks them to "picture" the "many of our brothers and sisters" who, without the SRO, would "be sleeping outside on the cold concrete or wet ground with no pillow on which to lay their head"—in other words, to picture people who, with their own shelters destroyed, literally, can find no temporary sheltering space. Then, much as Harriet Beecher Stowe famously asked the comfortably domiciled readers of *Uncle Tom's Cabin* to sympathize with the plight of the newly homeless slave mother Eliza Harris, Beyoncé asks those who are "resting in your bed, under a warm comfortable blanket" if they can "imagine sleeping outside in these elements." With this sharp comparison between the safely sheltered and the frightened homeless as a dramatic context, the SRO that Beyoncé funds emerges as a knight in shining armor: she asks us to "imagine a brand new four story apartment building, furnished with all the essentials to build the bridge from homelessness to a hopeful future." The scenario that Beyoncé describes is so effective that it becomes part of the SRO's official marketing and messaging campaign.[4]

Her identification with the plight of those itinerant and newly homeless because of natural disaster transforms singer into SRO developer and, in so doing, reinforces Beyoncé's own social value. Regardless of her quick rise to stardom, Beyoncé's pastor and supporter declares that her SRO work is proof of the "authentic humility" that has characterized her since childhood and that remains untempered by her stardom. Here the SRO becomes tangible proof of this star's ongoing connectedness to her community despite her dramatic socioeconomic rise above it. In other words, the SRO reassures fans that Beyoncé is still the same hometown girl, despite a meteoric career that is marked by the ever larger and more profuse temporary space that she occupies often at the expense of the less moneyed—most notably her recent million-dollar rental of an entire floor of bulletproof suites at New York City's Lenox Hill Hospital for the delivery of her child, an appropriation of space that summarily displaced other patients and refused parents of newborns access to their children in the neonatal intensive care unit.[5]

But more often than not, sharp increases in the numbers of people suddenly homeless and newly indigent because of unexpected disasters like Katrina, far from stimulating the expansion of SRO and other affordable hotel facilities, ultimately further constrict short-term hotel space designated for the poor. It is not only images of ruined, predominantly black families living on cots in the Houston super dome with no relief in sight that reveal quite starkly how little housing is actually available for the truly poor and disadvantaged. The FEMA trailers standing in lieu of hotels and flophouses raised the thorny question for the public of whether poor people deserved hotel service of any kind, ever. They stood in for the mixed-income, short-term housing that has gradually vanished over the past century, and they raised the question of whether the best we can do for those riddled with misfortune is to give them a trailer in the middle of a field and tell them to figure out their glide path to security.

Inconsistent as Beyoncé's investment in SRO housing may appear to those skeptical about stars' philanthropic pet projects, her support of an SRO to accommodate those displaced, homeless, and seeking temporary shelter because of natural disasters, acts of God, and large-scale game-changing forces beyond anyone's control reminds us of the larger threat that SROs experience when natural disaster does strike. On the margins and often collectively socially ostracized, SROs, as well as those in need of their modest rooms, become the unwitting most defenseless victims of disaster. Rather than proliferating to solve the short-term housing problems of displaced people, SROs all too often become, like their guests, casualties of these disasters, their total amount of space dramatically reduced in the wake of disaster. Take the case of the Loma Prieta earthquake that hit northern California in October 1989. Just as Hurricane Katrina's devastation of New Orleans held the world spellbound in horrified fascination with images of displaced persons in search of family members and pets, so too did the California earthquake tear through a highly prized region of the country, challenging the federal government and FEMA to respond humanely and quickly to what seemed like overwhelming human need.

And FEMA's response made dramatically clear how crisis could be turned into opportunity to reallocate space along bourgeois class lines.

FEMA was able to rebuild the iconic Bay Bridge within a month so that Silicon Valley executives could get to work again, but those who lived precariously in the region's SROs—the 1,300 residents of single-room occupancy hotels in Alameda County whose shelter was destroyed, for example, or the 500 occupants of SROs in Santa Cruz—found themselves chronically homeless and without recourse. After over a decade of slashed federal support for SROs, the effect of the natural disaster was particularly catastrophic, and a study of homelessness in the region found that between forty and fifty people were bunking up in shifts in three-bedroom apartments while waiting for SRO housing to be restored. FEMA's deprioritizing of SRO rebuilding in the region was compounded by rules that further disadvantaged SRO residents—for example, a stipulation that renters prove that they had lived in the same SRO building for thirty days, despite SRO owners' common practice of temporarily evicting occupants every twenty eight days to keep them from claiming permanent resident status. The amount and duration of aid further disadvantaged SRO occupants—those who could prove the thirty-day residence receiving only one month of assistance as opposed to homeowners' three months of support and renters receiving two months. FEMA's discrimination of SRO occupants resulted in more than half of those living in SROs not receiving any housing aid whatsoever. When the Homeless Advocacy Project in San Francisco brought FEMA to task, protesting its treatment of the SRO population, and then when nineteen community groups followed up with legal action, FEMA did agree to settle by providing funds to replace the SROs that were rendered uninhabitable by the earthquake. However, the sheer number of these units—more than two thousand buildings in all— made the task unfeasible.[6] As this illustrative case makes clear, rather than helping SROs, disasters all too often are used as the opportunity to further reduce the total amount of short-term housing space available to the poor and unfortunate.

And yet despite this larger refusal of space that SROs categorically have suffered, not all SROs are equal—not all confer the same kinds and quantities of space to residents. Within the large-scale context of SRO operation, there is a clear hierarchy of value, quality, and desire. Just like the hotel star system, where certain services, luxury, and amenities are directly correlated to the number of stars a hotel boasts, so too do different SROs register differently, conferring radically different spatial privileges to those in search of human possibility and regeneration. The

Knowles-Temenos project is the best of the bunch, its occupants proud of their environment and the particular kind of community and individual betterment that this SRO makes available to residents. Take, for example, Mr. Wes who has lived in Knowles-Temenos since its opening in 2009. Coming from an SRO in downtown Denver, he was impressed with what he can have at Knowles-Temenos for his $436 a month, all bills paid. A business center with internet and computers, a keycard front entry access for security, on-site case manager, and an aesthetically pleasing, brand-new room with bath, mini-fridge, two-burner stove top, and wall-mounted flat screen television: the Knowles-Temenos has the look and feel of new high-density residential apartment buildings that are springing up in Houston's downtown and midtown areas. Furthermore, its direct proximity to his church next door extends the SRO community beyond the SRO walls, enabling residents like Mr. Wes to imagine new beginnings and happier selves springing up in the larger spatial environment Knowles-Temenos creates for its guests.

Regardless of the relative perceived quality and quantity of SRO space, these hotels all operate on a shared assumption that the impoverished individual in need of shelter is an isolated and socially alienated figure—a modern self without a larger social network and support system. SRO space therefore reinforces social isolation. Mr. Wes can live in an SRO because he is single—children, families, or couples of any sort are not allowed he quickly points out. While hotel rooms cater to the couple, with a lesser number of suites to accommodate a nuclear family, SROs are premised upon the breakup of the family, their assumption that with poverty comes social fracture and isolation—a self that has reduced the social space it takes up through the human networks it forms. Their rooms operate much like a monastic cell, where isolated individuals are sequestered from the allure, messiness, and complicating dimensions of human coupling and family life, along with their spatial requirements. And so, SROs tend to be male dominated, with two men to every woman. Miss Mary, who lives on the second floor of Knowles-Temenos, is a benign matriarch, making sure that Mr. Wes is on time for choir practice, while the case manager Miss Ina plays tough cop, threatening and occasionally evicting those who don't play by Knowles-Temenos rules, and gatekeeper, for those trying to find a place at the inn. But these are isolated female figures who create social connection across the various spatial divides that carve up families and premise occupancy on isolation.

If Knowles-Temenos, like all SROs, upholds an idea of socioeconomic space that enforces human isolation for the world's unfortunates, the SRO is in other ways accommodating—taking in singles from eighteen years old as well as the disabled, mentally unstable, ill, and formerly imprisoned. Applications require those seeking shelter to provide information about criminal record and prior incarcerations, as well as employment history, banking information, and residential history. Those, like Miss Ina, who run SROs will generally help residents get a bank account if they do not already have one, as well as help them retrain and find work. Her own sense of social consciousness has caused Miss Ina to start a couple of women's groups focusing on sexual and substance abuse for the few women who do live at Knowles-Temenos. Success stories that Miss Ina shares include the story of a woman who, after living at Knowles-Temenos, began the process of moving to a home of her own, where she can have a pet, house plants, and room for family members.

But others—like Mr. Wes—architect human community out of the fractured lives and spaces around them. Described by Miss Ina and the other workers in the entry area as the unit's comedian, host, social conscience, and neighborhood watch, Mr. Wes has occupied more than his single room, becoming the face of Knowles-Temenos. He rushes into the street to wave in and guide the lost traveler safely to the front door. He is official greeter and brand rep. A faux concierge, Mr. Wes hooks people up. Saved by the lord, he does not facilitate the transfer of drugs, prostitution, or alcohol—instead he helps people find options, anything from the cheapest quart of milk to the next AA meeting. Saddened by the recent death of his own mother from breast cancer after a ten-year post-mastectomy remission, Mr. Wes is alert to those in need or trouble of any kind. He is about giving back to the world that has provided him a second chance and salvation when he least expected it, and he does so by reenvisioning, expanding, and reconstituting the kinds of space the SRO provides its guests.

Economies of Scale

The carefully parsed space that hotels for the poor allocate to their guests do not always enable life-giving strategies for their guests. More often than not, hotels for the poor continue to reduce and constrict the quantities and qualities of space to which occupants have access, ultimately creating crises that can result in despair, deterioration, and death. Once we approach the hotels provided for the poor with an eye to how they allocate space, we can see how the guests' stay takes on nothing less than life or death proportions. While guests, as we saw in the preceding section, turn to the hotel for either a new life or a final resting place, those already destitute who enter an SRO's lobby bring particular kinds of expectations and needs—needs that are either tersely ignored or unorthodoxly accommodated by the hotel.

We can see this particular feature of hotel life clearly in the case of the Ambassador Hotel in the Tenderloin section of San Francisco. Built in 1911, the Ambassador is a massive structure, decorated on the exterior in an ornate French Renaissance style. Indeed the building still seems out-sized, like a big six-story redbrick box, squatting on a street of two-story storefronts; its offerings of space to the naked eye appear to be expansive and potentially generous. Built in the optimism of the Progressive Era, the hotel, like so many that are now SROs, struggled to survive, and drifted, over the long decades of the Tenderloin's rich history, down-ward, catering less and less to the well-heeled traveler and more and more to the area's growing and increasingly disadvantaged underclass. By the 1970s, it had become the worst nightmare of hotel managers like Dreiser's fictional Mr. Withers, going from elitist preserve to economy lodge, and, finally, to no longer a functional hotel at all. And by the time the HIV/AIDS crisis hit in the 1980s, it had become a venue for local service providers, which is to say that it became something very different and, at once, very familiar. Like many old hotels in hardscrabble envi-ronments, the Ambassador survived in this latter period by serving as an SRO, offering a semipermanent address to those who could pay a small rental fee, typically with local, state, or federal assistance.

But it was in 1994 that the life- and death-giving properties of the Ambassador Hotel's spaces were thrown into dramatic relief. That was the year the local television station KRON issued a documentary that represented how the hotel managed its clientele. *Life and Death at the Ambassador Hotel* charted the real, on-the-ground workings of an SRO that catered to a clientele that was largely diseased, out of work, or ter-minally ill. For a "small fee" of $85.00 a month, or $97.50 if you wanted your own bathroom, guests got a very small room of their own, generally in decent repair, a bed on which to sleep, and a modicum of privacy. But most importantly, guests also gained immediate access to public health providers, who were then scrambling to address a gay community in the midst of a disaster. Though it was intended as a call to action in support of the city's unwell poor, *Life and Death* also became an archive of the haunting persistence and transformation of hotel life, even under the most deleterious circumstances, and the ways that its modest spaces could flex to accommodate the extreme needs of its occupants.

In an SRO like the Ambassador, the functions of the hotel are fundamentally diminished but still recognizable in the new kinds of hybrid and mixed-use spaces created within the hotel's dreary interior. The lobby becomes not only a great switching point but also a place to wait for the ambulance, or to meet your addiction counselor, or to laugh and sing. Room service is replaced by charitable meal delivery for the indigent, brought door-to-door and, in the documentary, delivered with a smile. And instead of the ring of coffee shops and clothiers that ribbon the high-end hotel, one finds HIV-AIDS outreach groups, nongovernmental organizations, and social services offices. In the hallways, as the camera roams, half of the doors are open during the day, to provide oversight and access to those in need. In short, the founding spatial logics of the hotel bend to meet dire human need and a clientele that periodically requires but cannot afford hospital as much as hotel space.

The heavily documented workings of its hybrid, multipurpose hotel spaces suggest that the Ambassador Hotel attempts to fashion a hotel life that does not assume the inevitable indigence and want that, all too often, lead guests like Hurstwood to despair and death. To an epidemic with no proven cure, the Ambassador responded with a kind of hotel life that reworked spaces in ways imaginative and born of human need, and it did so working within the reduced scale of space that, as we have seen, is available to those of the most modest means. Even as those watching the documentary hear a sense of optimism in the voices of the most positive residents of the Ambassador, it is clear that, all too often, these imaginatively reenvisioned hotel spaces are inadequate to provide what their rich counterparts do—the personal discovery and renewal that, as we saw in the preceding chapter, characterize the expansive spaces provided luxury hotel guests.

In its final minutes, *Life and Death* chronicles one particular story of hotel life that highlights the ultimate limits of the SRO to rework space in ways that ultimately sustain life for the indigent. We are drawn back to the lobby, where one of the managers is worriedly pacing. Malcolm, the hard luck case at the center of much of the documentary, is having chest pains and is next to the door, struggling to relax, and periodically grasping his heart. The men have been waiting for a taxicab for two

Photo of "Frank" looking out the lobby window of the Ambassador Hotel in 1993. This image—a part of a series by Paul Fusco—captures the unique geopolitics of the SRO, where a poor man, down on his luck, can sit in a hotel lobby and stare wistfully outside at the swirling social world on the street, a reversal of the way that hotels normally function. (Paul Fusco/Magnum Photos)

hours, with no luck. As the manager calls yet again, we learn that Malcolm insists on a taxi—and not on an ambulance. This insistence on the classic private transport—so ubiquitous in the modern cityscape—is an eloquent request for the dignity typically attached to a hotel, even as it is a pragmatic decision born of the need for lower-cost transport than a private ambulance. Malcolm wants to travel as a "guest" rather than a patient, clinging to hotel life even (or rather especially) on the verge of death. But the manager cannot get a cab to come to the Tenderloin, to an HIV/AIDS SRO, to take a terminally ill man where he needs to go. In desperation, he does what any good concierge would do: he walks out into the street and does the best he can, literally stopping traffic to get a car. And then he helps Malcolm into the cab, verifying that he has cab fare, making sure that the cabbie knows where he needs to go. "People are so quick to judge," he complains, watching the taxi drive away, "to paint with the broad brush, to talk about the drug addicts, the junkies, the faggots, the drag queens, the people with AIDS, the AIDS-infected whatevers. It's bullshit. We're all human beings." There is—or there should be, as Malcolm insists—a greater dignity in life at the Ambassador Hotel, the once-glamorous "almost home" to movie stars, artists, and novelists. But if Mr. Wes is able to find within the spaces offered by the SRO he occupies a future full of potential, those who occupy most SROs all too often do not discover new ways to occupy space and the world.

Malcolm returned to the Ambassador Hotel after his hospital trip, finding final rest within the hotel that tried but ultimately failed to keep him temporarily protected and safe. He returned to the SRO after the hospital trip he could not afford, only to die four days later, alone in his room. A resident assistant discovered him, naked and bloody and on the floor, with a slight smile on the corner of his mouth. He had fallen to the ground right next to his bed, looking, according to witnesses, "more peaceful in death than he did in life." Whereas Mr. Wes reaches creatively and proactively across the limited spaces that the Knowles-Temenos SRO provides its guests, Malcolm ultimately retreated into the most secluded chamber available to make his final peace. Against the backdrop of hotel walls and regularized, minimalist spaces, this particular guest seems to have clung to hotel life and the humble shelter it provides with a kind of ferocity until the final moment. Both men discover a powerful place of passing in the hotel and the modest space it provides to even the most impoverished guest—they find a place where the self that has suffered a lifetime full of affronts to basic human dignity, security, and acknowledgment discovers either a new chapter or a final end to the tragic book of life.

No Room at the Inn

Against the antipodal examples that the Knowles-Temenos and the Ambassador provide, we can begin to see the different kinds of life that the limited spaces constituting the SRO enable and support. If, at one end of the human spectrum, the SRO's modestly scaled spaces can be a rented venue for second chances and new life starts, as we saw was the case for Mr. Wes, it all too often seems to enable and support the misery, hopelessness, and despair so evident in Malcolm. In its starkest form, the space that the SRO provides guests is scaled inhumanely and in ways that do not support, even temporarily, the most basic human life.

The first four floors of the Sun Bright Hotel on Hester Street in New York's Chinatown, for instance, contain precious little "life" to counter an awful lot of "death." With the traditional boxy shape of a Gilded Age hotel, the Sun features a deliberately forgettable off-white color and exterior signs so small you can barely see anything but the word "hotel," printed in red letters and surrounded by Chinese characters. It hides in plain sight, seemingly wanting to deny that it takes up any space at all. Built in 1880, the building was an SRO in the 1950s and 1960s, when it was known as the Union Hotel. After its purchase by a Chinese businessman, it was transformed yet again into a veritable barracoon, warehousing and confining legions of immigrant workers, keeping them out of sight, off the streets, and readily available. These are not people who depend on public support, as do the residents of the Ambassador; instead, they cling to bare life, their fate lying beyond the power of the state, and their biological function hardly registering.

The fame of the Sun stems from a stretch of roughly two years—from 2004 to 2006—when more than a few of its tenants died tragically, when it was a scandalous feature of the nightly news, and when the space offered by the hotel came to the public's attention for being brutally intolerable and actively hostile to human life. If the Ambassador Hotel of the mid-1990s revised the script of the hotel as well as the modest space allocated for temporary use by the ailing poor, the Sun of the mid-2000s simply burned it up, refusing humans any room at all to sustain themselves. The Sun Bright has a lobby with no chairs. Access to the lobby comes only after the guest is buzzed through a locked metal door. Many of the floors prohibit women. Guests, if allowed, are few and far between. On the lower floors, where the sojourning and typically illegal immigrants congregated between shifts, there are only the most "bitter" atmospherics. "The truth is that we are slaves here," one unlucky soul confessed to an intrepid New York Times reporter; "We are the new blacks. Just like that."[7]

Above the grim barracks, the top few floors offer only dangerous, hostile, and depleted space for the most desperate sort of itinerant traveler. For European travelers trying to save a few bucks and American tourists, looking for a cheap place to stay on New Year's Eve, the fifteen-dollar-a-night charge at the Sun seems too good to pass up, regardless of what kind of space they are purchasing. But then they arrive at the corner of Bowery and Hester, enter the spare lobby, and trudge up five flights of stairs to their rooms. Amateur ethnographers, they all note in their upward passage the destitute human strata that dwell beneath their rooms. The first few floors," one anonymous traveler sums, "were basically extremely low income housing with cat urine and cats everywhere and people sitting in the hallways leering." Before you get to your room, another recalls, "you have to pass the other floors where a lot of Chinese people are staying. Or living actually." This dark transit through the netherworld where there is no difference between "living" and "staying" perverts the entire hotel, making it seem, even at the upper floors, like "more of a boarding house jail-like facility," or "more like a prison, a poultry farm or even a concentration camp."

Once above the modern detention camp, the typically sovereign guest finds his hard-won private space greatly compromised, as if, structurally, there was no difference between the hellish domain below and the hotel space above. The rooms—for men only—are closet-sized and without adornment or luxury. They lack ceilings and have, instead, a layer of chicken wire strung up at the top of every room. The result, drolly reported in the online testimonials of countless visitors, is "sorta private, but also not," an obliteration of the bright, mobile dividing lines that so repeatedly mark the presence of hotel life and carve out its disparate spaces. One denizen likened it to sleeping "in a beehive." Another, in an extended rant, concluded that the Sun "is not a hotel. It isn't even a hostel. It is a filthy storage facility with people crammed in it. If the plague were to spread throughout NYC, it wouldn't surprise me if it started in this dump. The 'rooms' are smaller than closets with chicken wire on top of make-shift walls. It is a horrible experience every second you are in that nightmare. You can hear every sound and smell every disgusting smell in all the dozens of rooms around you. You don't want to leave your belongings while you are around town. It is not safe. It is more of an insane asylum; it's beyond polite descriptions."[8] Pointing out the egregious lack of space allocated to human life in the Sun, these reviews make the tacit argument that the total quantity and quality of space designated for the poor should either be better or cease to exist entirely. But in so doing they raise the haunting question of how much space we are each entitled to occupy, regardless of the ability to pay.

AS WE HAVE SEEN in this third section, hotel life all too often grants the rich access to massive amounts of sumptuous space, thereby enabling imperial fantasies of discovery that encourage guests to explore their interior lives and inner selves. The poor, as the preceding pages have suggested, occupy increasingly minuscule scales of space that encroach on human life at the most basic level. Along the continuums of space provided by SROs, different iterations of the self become possible. Whereas residents of the relatively sumptuous Knowles-Temenos find within its comfortable if modest spaces the potential for reintegration into homes of their own or a renewed sense of self-worth and optimism, residents of the Ambassador Hotel seek within the hotel's caring if modest spaces the most slender reed of hope. For those who occupy "rooms" at the Sun, there is no hotel life to speak of—the space provided by this most extreme SRO is no real space at all: it fails to accommodate the most bare modicum of human need and so is nothing but a human warehouse. And, like their guests, all of these varied SRO hotels struggle for their own survival against a landscape that categorically and relentlessly deprioritizes space for the poor and indigent. Given this fact, it is not surprising that hotels like the Sun parse space as aggressively as they do. What is surprising is that some SROs like Knowles-Temenos and Ambassador Hotel continue to support human life and hope when, with every passing year, there is less and less "room at the inn" for the world's poor.

Affect

7

FORTUNE

The three previous sections have explored the various times, scales, and spaces that the modern hotel fashions for guests who are questing for profit, meaning, self-knowledge, sexual discovery, and, of course, a good night's sleep. In this final section, we turn to the range of dramatic feeling—ranging from intense sensations of fortune to failure—that hotel life supports and encourages. Those who are fortunate enough to occupy maximal scales of hotel space and to be able to hit the refresh button on their bodies, souls, and sexualities within the hotel's flexible spaces might be expected to feel fortunate indeed, whereas those cramped in the most inhospitable SROs, robbed of any modicum of privacy and human dignity might feel inclined to ending it all—to death dealing within and partly because of the hotel's hostile habitus.

But the feelings of fortune and failure that hotel life occasions are not so linear and self-apparent. As we will see in these last two chapters, those in deepest despair might turn to the promise of fortune like a moth to the flame, while the most pampered and privileged guests of five-star hotels can be particularly prone to being overwhelmed by despair when the facade that supports their brittle ego is shattered by the random sadistic hotelier or gross failure of service. In other words, fortune and failure develop unevenly and asynchronously in and because of hotel life. No one is sufficiently vaccinated by the Ritz-Carlton preferred customer account from reversals of fortune that lurk, always ready to strike, within the hotel's plush environs. Similarly, even the most downtrodden can win fortune's jackpot in the game that is hotel life. In sum, guests feel and they feel deeply in the worlds that hotels create for them, and this intense feeling forms a primal glue out of which modern subjectivity emerges, always in formation and development rather than in final form. Guests' feelings are as mobile and transient as are the tired bodies that they bring to the reception desk, and this fluidity forms the heartbeat of hotel life. This affective dimension of the modern subject's experience in hotels is also the hardest for global capital to harness, stream, direct, and exploit. In other words, affect is where the hotel's ability to work in the service of the larger corporate good can go, most unexpectedly, off the rails, and so it is with this volatile dimension of hotel life that we conclude our analysis.

Opportunity

Every hotel, of course, has a little bit of luck, or at least the chance of luck. Every random roadside motel, its illuminated sign beckoning to every driver, has the capacity to appear in the nick of time, just before exhaustion takes over. Every encounter in the lobby or the elevator is rich with the promise of connection, revealing in sideways glances, hesitant smiles, or surly disinterest. Every unexpected upgrade or suddenly available suite for no additional cost reinforces the random chance that guides the hotel receptionist's hands over the keyboard. When we walk through the doors of the hotel lobby, we want to be lucky. This sort of luck is advertised in a thousand different ways, broadcast as the reasonable truth to anyone who might have cause to rent a private bedroom from a strange corporation, trusting her privacy to a foreign agent. It makes the purchase of a hotel room for a day or two an ordinary thing. Luck, in short, is the reason we want to rent.

But sometimes the commonplace feeling of luck takes even more dramatic form. Sometimes the unquenchable desire for luck motivates travelers to pack their bags, get in their cars, and head across the desert to find within the welcoming arms of a temporary habitus new ways of experiencing the world and the hope that fortune will smile on them.

For hundreds of miles, respectful travelers, lured by rumors of its fortune-giving qualities, have followed Route 91 to the hotel hub of the southwest desert—Las Vegas. During the day, as they inch closer, weary travelers and hungry souls can see light reflecting off the glass, a twinkle on the horizon, a maker of the built environment rising up from the flat landscape. At night, the road is illuminated, its path guiding the eye to a distant pool of light, a faraway testament to the city's refusal to be bound by the dark, and a gesture to the unceasing illumination within each massive, gleaming resort. Moving closer, the names of the oasis's brilliant, magical structures grab your attention: the Palace,

AFFECT

the Cosmopolitan, the Aria, the Venetian, the Bellagio, or the Pallazo. Here, in the dry, arid wasteland of the American West, the tired vagabond has found in Las Vegas a version of ancient Rome, with all its vice and decadence, its dripping, neon splendor.

Within this gleaming oasis, fortune and luck are intertwined. Once a small town stuck in between bigger and better places, its rapid expansion and growth is connected to the story we have told here. The meteoric rise of Las Vegas is not merely the story of air-conditioning and interstate highways, or postwar car culture and mob intrigue. It is also the story, in the end, of declining wages and surging credit, of the diminishing middle class, of the greater and greater need for a radical transformation of the material circumstances of everyday life. Every building is a monument to hope—to the hope, more particularly, that a single game of chance, or a single day at the craps table, or a week at roulette, can change the course of a life for the better. The casino hotel is thus the apotheosis of the modern hotel, offering the illusion of control and choice over the future in a world that is increasingly without either.

In such a landscape, a seemingly innocent man can walk out of the desert and into a glamorous hotel—named, forbiddingly, the Bank, a reminder of the wealth buried deep within it. But the man's bad luck is rigged from the start. Patiently waiting to check in, he is pushed out of the way for a "V.I.P.," who is being ushered to the front of the line. The encounter leaves him gasping. "What does that make me," he wonders, "a 'V.U.P.'? A very unimportant person?" Without a valet to help him, he escorts himself upstairs. His room is unclean, even foul, suffused with a smell that knocks him over. He asks for a bigger room—a cleaner room— but is told that no such room is available. Leaving his room in search of fresh air, though, he sees the smiling V.I.P. from the lobby, being escorted to a different hotel space entirely of his choosing. In his quest for comfort, the guest goes to the hotel restaurant only to be told that, without a reservation, there is no available table. After an unhappy meal at the inferior restaurant recommended by the hotel, his body literally refuses the inferior nourishment, and he vomits. Ready for sleep, and checking his room for cleanliness, he finds bedbugs, thousands of them, crawling over his mattress. Within hours, he is sick and diseased, a blotchy, sputtering mess. In a final rebuke, he is forcibly evicted from the posh hotel, a consequence, we are told, of his supposedly dishygenic behaviors. Leaving through the lobby, he sarcastically thanks the owner for making him feel welcome. "Who are you?" he is asked. "Nobody," he replies, drolly, "I am nobody."

The unlucky guest at the Bank Hotel, in a scene from *Ocean's Thirteen*, the 2007 film directed by Steven Soderbergh. Within the film, he is a "Five Diamond" hotel reviewer, unwittingly transformed as a part of a major con into an ordinary guest, who then suffers a hellish ordeal in the Bank. (From the authors' collection).

The probability of such consistent, flagrant back luck seems highly unlikely. But as this subplot of the third and final installment of films about Las Vegas casino hotels—Stephen Soderbergh's *Ocean's Thirteen*—illustrates in glaring detail, luck and the hotel have a long and complex set of interconnections. We most often associate the casino hotel with luck —the allure of good luck enticing the guest to lay hands on slot machines and roulette tables. But in the case of *Ocean's Thirteen*, the "nobody's" bad luck is part of an elaborate ruse designed to ruin a casino hotel's good fortune and spotless reputation. He is not actually a nobody, of course. He is a reviewer sent to evaluate the hotel's amenities and services, to judge its eligibility for the "Five Diamond" award. Danny Ocean's team of gentlemanly con artists and thieves has marked him for bad luck, and they have gamed the entire system—hiring room attendants, slipping bad food on his dish, infesting the room with bedbugs, and even hiring the V.I.P—all to ensure that casino hotel that trades in luck, owned and operated by a dishonorable man, fails the test.

The rigging of this man's luck parallels the team members' creative scheme to fix the casino. To ruin the casino hotel's own long-standing winning streak on the strip, they need to arrange for everyone else in the hotel to win and win big. One of their group travels to Mexico, where the dice for the casino are made, to insert a new polymer technology, controllable by the flip of a cigarette lighter. Another cozies up to the hotel's chief of staff, plotting to get a magnetron placed within arm's reach of the casino's basement supercomputer, which ensures that no one is cheating and, therefore, that no one is winning. The group imports two massive tunnel borers to produce a faux earthquake, which, they hope, will trigger a panic after the big win and encourage the happy patrons to leave with their winnings before the system can reset. They do all of this—and more—because they earnestly believe that without a tipping of the scales, almost everyone will lose. And they, instead, want to game the system so that the guests' win becomes the hotel's loss.

This third and final installment of the *Ocean's* trilogy is, of course, the logical endpoint of Danny Ocean's longer game of chance with the casino hotel. In the original 1960 *Ocean's Eleven* (as well as its 2002 remake), Ocean's con artists look to win big from the casino hotel—to turn the game of chance decisively in their favor—and they do so by planning a New Year's Eve heist that involves rewiring all of the Vegas casinos' electrical systems and then demolishing the electrical transmission tower that powers all the casinos on the Strip. When Vegas goes dramatically dark at the stroke of midnight on New Year's Eve, the cashier cages open and Ocean's team collects everyone's winnings. Using the hotels' garbage bins as temporary storage for the loot, the con men collect their ill-got gains, only to have their luck turn dramatically bad when they subsequently hide the money in the coffin of one of their fallen team members. The widow decides not to ship the coffin to California as Danny suggested but rather to have the funeral in Vegas. In an evocative final image of the dramatically changing luck for which the Vegas casino hotel is legendary, the casket is cremated and the millions of dollars as well as the body literally go up in smoke.

While the original *Ocean's Eleven* was considered a success when it appeared in 1960, it was the 2001 remake that got really lucky—its story of big wins, big losses, and the vertiginous shifts of fortune experienced by the Ocean's team generating two sequels during the very period of time when the fortunes of moviegoers were dramatically oscillating because of 9/11, the global recession, and large-scale thefts on Wall Street. With a budget of $85 million, the 2001 *Ocean's Eleven* did remarkably well financially, grossing over $450 million, but it was the rave reviews that ensured the sequels. With *Entertainment Weekly* concluding that the movie's heist scene was the best robbery sequence of the decade and *Empire* magazine adding the movie to its "500 Greatest Movies of All Time" list, the Ocean's team seemed to be on a real winning streak with audiences that responded powerfully to the rapid, vertiginous oscillations in fortune that were so evocative of the early twenty-first-century moment. But, as is the case the longer a gambler stays at the table, *Ocean's Twelve* and *Ocean's Thirteen* did not fare as well at the box office or in the press as the first movie. Still, each film is a celebration of the casino hotel as a place where luck gets made, even if it also reminds us that every person marked as "lucky" has an "unlucky" opposite.

Ocean's Thirteen, as well as the original from which it derives, is stylish, an evocation of "Old Hollywood" glamour, but it is also a critique of luck and its opposite in the modern casino hotel. The parallel, if opposite, fates of the anonymous hotel reviewer and those winning "guests" remind us, rather boldly, that both luck and its opposite are engineered, and that the hotel is an excellent proving ground in which fortune, luck, and grace are produced, carefully, laboriously, and intentionally. In a casino hotel, each room is its own oasis of possibility, and every patron is an autonomous "guest," leading—the casino hotel suggests—a charmed life. Hundreds of workers toil deep in the bowels of the hotel to create this sense of luck. Suppressing it is hard. In such a context, it takes a skilled team of dozens, really, to make it possible for a single nobody to feel luck's absence. But it takes a work force of thousands, scattered across the globe, to make a single patron "feel" lucky.

Probability

Hotel casinos are, any statistician will tell you, actually rather unlucky places. Few win, and even fewer win big. The mathematical odds at any gaming table, or at any slot machine, are terrible. They are profitable for their owners, but not for the guests. They indiscriminately consume the personal savings of otherwise thrifty visitors and the disposable incomes of the truly rich, and, without much consideration, they transform one person's hope into another person's profit. Despite this rather obvious truth, they are also increasing in scale and number, growing more numerous and more gaudy. Indeed, as the apotheosis of this book, the casino hotel represents the most grotesque opulence amid the presence of decay, corruption, and exploitation.

Luck is, in this context, a structure of feeling attached to the very cables and girders, concrete and glass of the casino hotel. Luck is gold and neon, baroquely applied everywhere, a room, a street, a building literally dripping with colored signifiers of chance. But luck has a dark side, too. Its bright colors hide a dark, hidden history, a severely sloped backstage reality in which the costs of its production are shouldered by a dense body of ordinary people—unlucky nobodies, as John Bowe might call them—who labor ceaselessly on behalf of the casino hotel. Their purpose, in the great engine of capital reallocation, is to make you feel so well attended to—so lucky in the little things, even as you lose and lose and lose—that you will want to come back. They comp you a bigger room, fluff your pillows and clean your bathroom, bring you a free drink while you are parked at the slot machine, and stay smiling and silent in the background.

In order to maximize the casino hotel's good fortune, hotel managers give great care and calculation to the numbers of these employees—not only the total number needed to staff the casino hotel in ways that optimize its profitability but also to every quantifiable detail of their work flow. Computer systems, as the authors of *Casino Operations Management* make clear, are an integral part of all aspects of the casino hotel operation—to record revenue not only in gaming areas but also in hotel operations like payroll, accounting, and personnel. While computational assistance can aid hotel management in efficient operations, the human element proves trickiest for the manager to get right. Because understaffing can result in dramatic loss of revenue as customers interrupt their gambling to go in search of refreshment, the savvy hotel manager needs to calculate carefully exactly how many minutes out of each sixty-minute period are required for staff breaks. The rule of thumb for dealers on payroll is a twenty-minute break after sixty minutes of work in order to keep the dealer's attention at peak performance. Workers on the floor have somewhat different numbers to maintain optimal performance in the service of the casino hotel's good fortunes—a one-hour break and then two twenty-minute breaks every eight hours. In these careful calculations, exactly 74.67 employees are needed to staff a standard-size casino hotel optimally on a normal day, and eighty during peak days.[1]

Given the hotel's integral place in modern culture for people constantly on the move and in search of distraction, it makes intuitive sense that the casino and the hotel would align to create irresistible feelings of possibility of good fortune for those who walk in the door. Indeed, the hotel and casino blend so naturally as to create a hybrid sort of space—a space nominally referred to as the "hotel-casino" that blurs the boundaries between day and night, rest and activity, distracting consumption

The New York–New York casino in Las Vegas, Nevada, ca. 2000. Not merely a metaphorical wellspring of luck, the casino hotel is also a projection of some other place at some other time. Casino hotels often position themselves as dislocated from their temporal and spatial surroundings, either as ancient Roman palaces or as representations of other cityscapes, all of them associated—representationally or affectively—with the extremes of wealth and aristocracy. (Photo by Carol M. Highsmith, from the Carol M. Highsmith Archive, Prints and Photographs Division, Library of Congress, Washington, D.C.)

and moneymaking. In such an environment, oxygen is literally pumped into casino spaces to keep guests awake; room service extends to the casino public spaces a constant supply of food and drink to ensure that gamblers do not stop because of thirst or hunger; and light is kept uniform to obscure the passage of time over the course of a day. Guests move the short distance to their hotel rooms only for the most minimal and basic of human needs.

This constructed fabric of luck that the casino hotel creates draws the rapt attention of those who are interested in how modernity shapes built environments and vice versa, including architectural innovators such as Robert Venturi and Denise Scott Brown. Turning to the Vegas strip, replete with its glowing casino hotels and neon iconography, to contemplate architecture and urban sprawl more generally in modernity, the architect-authors' now iconic architectural treatise, *Learning from Las Vegas: The Forgotten Symbolism of Architectural Form*, finds in the sprawling, hybrid space that is the casino hotel an apt metaphor and instructional edifice for thinking more broadly about built environments in the modern and postmodern era. Passing through Las Vegas on Route 91—the archetype of the strip—reveals to Venturi the phenomenon that is Las Vegas "at its purest and most intense." According to the authors, "careful documentation and analysis of its physical form is as important to architects and urbanists today as were the studies of medieval Europe and ancient Rome and Greece to earlier generations."[2]

Through careful study of the modern-day casino hotel and the urban structures surrounding and enabling it, architects will be able to "define a new type of urban form emerging in America and Europe, radically different from that we have known" (xi). The architects' aim in studying Vegas's casino-hotel culture in detail is to understand the new form in an "open-minded and nonjudgmental" way and thereby "begin to evolve techniques for its handling" (xi). Of course, extended analysis of the hotel is integral to this process. If there is, as the authors contend, a "wealth of architectural information to be culled from Las Vegas," the casino hotels that are their signature piece and stock-in-trade—hotels like the Stardust Hotel, which the authors identify as "one of the finest on the Strip"—offer rich interpretive opportunities. Although the typical hotel-casino complex and, more particularly, its inevitable proximity to the highway foreground transience, impermanence, and shifting fortunes, these hotel-casino complexes are site specific: "A motel is a motel anywhere," in Venturi's estimation, but in Vegas motels are the "brightest thing in town" as a result of needing to compete with their surroundings (35). Las Vegas hotels have signs like no others, their architecture and signage both trading heavily in the art of persuasion and seduction.

In this iteration, the hotel is the casino's partner in crime, the enabler of irrational feelings of good fortune for gamblers and casino investors, and this has been the case since the beginning. Gambling has a long history, with the first recorded banning of card games going back to 1387 when John I, the King of Castile, prohibited card playing because members of his court were suffering acute financial losses. In Europe and the United States, gambling has alternately been encouraged and repressed, with greater tolerance generally a function of economic pressure and governmental need for revenue. Gambling is a remarkably lucky industry, producing consistently hefty revenue streams that appear to be largely recession resistant. When the Presidential Commission on the Review of the National Policy toward Gambling published its report in 1976, *Gambling in America*, readers were shocked to learn that $17.7 billion was gambled legally every year and that two-thirds of all Americans engaged in some kind of gambling. This pattern was not a recent phenomenon but goes back to the first year that a state in the nation (Nevada) levied a gaming tax. From 1946, when the total gaming revenues were $24.5 million, to the mid-1980s when that number exceeded $3 billion, the annual growth rate of the gambling industry has averaged 15 percent—a remarkably strong return on investment.[3]

The hotel is largely responsible for the persistent good luck of the casino industry as a whole. As Malcolm Greenless has observed, one primary reason for its resistance to economic downturn is the hotel casino's ability to provide a full array of services. Characterized by a very substantial physical plant, casinos have extensive overhead, with hotel room numbers ranging between five hundred and three thousand per business. Given that the income stream from these rooms consistently represents about 12–13 percent of the hotel casino's total gross revenue as opposed to the casino's 58–62 percent, the business model might seem, at first glance, to be in need of adjustment.[4] Yet the hotel dimension of these enterprises ensures that guests stay at tables and slot machines for hours on end, undistracted by logistics. As the illustrious German economic specialist in risk theory Hans-Werner Sinn has observed in *Casino Capitalism*, the longer that one gambles the more certain it becomes that the gambler will not get back his or her initial stakes.[5] Because there is an increased negative probability of winning over time and the good luck of the hotel casino is in direct inverse correlation to the good luck of the guest, the hotel ensures the long-term high profit margin for the industry.

Hotelier Thomas Hull recognized the immense good luck that the hotel could have for casinos as early as 1939 when he was driving through Las Vegas and had a flat tire south of town. As he was waiting for a mechanic to arrive, he noticed the massive number of people in cars flocking to the city to gamble. Putting their need for accommodation together with their desire to gamble, Hull opened his hotel casino in 1941 and was soon followed by others. Though there were earlier hotel casinos, most notably the Meadows Supper Club that opened in 1931 and had one hundred hotel rooms adjacent to its gaming spaces, Hull's was the first to enjoy the good luck with which the industry has become equated. The Meadows Supper Club was plagued with bad luck from the start and burned to the ground within a year of opening because firemen would not intervene given the business's location outside of city limits. But Hull was soon followed by businessmen like Bugsy Siegel who opened the first luxury hotel casino in 1941, by taking control of the Flamingo Hotel and Casino and renovating it to appeal to the affluent visitor in search of immediate and definitive evidence of his rapidly increasing good fortune. Though originally backed entirely by the risk capital of individual investors like Siegel and Hull, by the 1950s the hotel casino's success was attracting the attention of outside financiers, like Jimmy Hoffa, because of the high profit margins.

As investors like Hoffa suggest, the hotel casino has long been a highly profitable investment vehicle for those who tend to want to push their luck beyond the letters of the law. As early as 1932, the Carson City Prison inmates successfully lobbied to open the Bull Pen Casino. Operated and visited solely by inmates, the Bull Pen had a game boss who contributed a fixed amount of his proceeds to the Inmate Welfare Fund by way of a tax but otherwise kept his profits. The inmates who won at the blackjack, craps, roulette, and poker tables, likewise, attempted to turn the bad luck of a long prison sentence into good luck through gambling. The Bull Pen Casino's "hotel rooms" were actually prison cells, but the effect was essentially the same—with much time on their hands and total access to gaming tables, gamblers could focus on the game.

And as this example of the Bull Pen Casino suggests, the question of whether hotel casinos create good or back luck for those around them has been a topic of heated scholarly debate. In fact, so powerfully tethered has the hotel casino become to the concept of luck—both good and bad—that the eminent British economist responsible for macroeconomics, John Maynard Keynes, coined the term "by product of the casino" as early as 1936 to refer to a false state of confidence that individuals feel during times of acute doubt about the future. In his landmark *The General Theory of Employment, Interest, and Money*, Keynes describes in detail the large-scale impact on a nation and its capital development when too many individuals, made anxious by dubious future prospects, turn to irresponsible spending rather than conservative investment in secure assets. The spontaneous human "urge to action rather than inaction" when confronted with stress causes people to irrationally risk resources rather than objectively weigh the quantitative benefits and probabilities of secure investment.[6] For this reason, contemporary economists like Earl Grinols argue that national policy related to gaming is woefully irresponsible. The state and federal rationale for legalized hotel casinos—that they are a means of economic development for local communities—has not done objective cost-benefit analyses to substantiate the claim. Concluding that the costs exceed the benefits of hotel casinos by 3 to 1, Grinols builds social costs like crime, bankruptcy, suicide, illness, and regulatory and social service costs into his analyses to show the larger bad luck that hotel casinos create for everyone.[7]

This excess of feeling that the casino hotel carefully cultivates in its guests—the insatiable desire to risk it all, to throw security to the winds—is a primary reason that the very presence of the casino hotel creates powerful affective responses of irritation in some. The popularity of gambling, as historian Jackson Lears has noted, is often marked as a perversion of the public's historic morality. In this worldview, every casino is an outpost of corruption, and every tragic tale of loss is a fable of personal decline and national deterioration. This marking, though, is an anxious, official narrative, authored by a controlling, dominant culture aimed at a streamlined, machined, serious, and sober world. Pushing back, Lears reminds us that chance and luck, the intellectual raison d'être of chrome gambling machines and coruscating casino hotels, are a subversive, alternate tradition. Such a tradition celebrates the baroque pleasure of radical self-making, the carnivalesque of all that gold and chrome, all those neon lights and electronic beeps and bells. It envisions the casino hotel as a beacon of self-liberation.[8] For us, these two ways of seeing and thinking about the hotel are both suggestive of the work of the institution, producing in the guest the feeling of self-making but at great social and material cost. Hope is, after all, a rare and difficult thing to manufacture. The cost of its discovery and production is vast. And to sell it to the guest, that cost needs to be controlled, and the nature of that control kept hidden.

Chance

The Borgata Hotel Casino and Spa in Atlantic City is a prime example of this cost realized and in action. Clad in gold-toned glass, a wedge cleaving the skyline in two, the Borgata seems, like its alluring employees, to playfully tease its guests with the promise of "luck" broadly conceived. Every shower is built "for two," and no bed is smaller than king-sized or queen-sized. Pillows in the rooms once said "tonight" on one side and "not tonight" on the other. The implication is obvious: bring a lover to this golden palace (or find a new lover, perhaps) and get lucky twice over.

Inside and out, every surface is polished to a high sheen, and that includes the staff. The "Borgata babes," for instance, are "part fashion model, part beverage server, part charming host and hostess. All impossibly lovely." These Borgata babes, clad in short black dresses with recklessly plunging necklines, circulate like living totems of sex and luck. Famous enough to be featured in an old-school pin-up calendar, they are the public face of the Borgata, appearing to the outside world as envoys of the hotel's pitch-perfect confusion of sex and luck. Describing the babes as "costumed beverage servers," the hotel's "vice president of talent," Cassie Fireman, noted that the Borgata was a "fun, upscale, energetic, and sensual environment." But this perfection is a facade. Behind the scenes, the hotel mandates that women hired as Borgata babes maintain their "natural hourglass figures" and not gain more than 7 percent of their "base weight," defined at the point of the hiring. Their physical constraint—their maintenance of that high sheen through exercise, diet, and whatever is necessary—is an enforceable institutional mandate. Hired as sex objects, the courts have ruled, they can be fired if they become less sexy, less than perfect—if they do not addle male gamblers' brains, making the idea of "getting lucky" irresistible.

The gold wedge of the Borgata, Bryant Simon reminds us, is meant to be an oasis with walls, sealed off from the "everyday worries of work and family, crime and city streets." The Borgata is a "little village," a spa, a hotel, a casino, a clutch of restaurants, all bound together in a vast, gilded structure, set at the end of a tunnel that runs beneath Atlantic City. The destination is the Borgata, not Atlantic City, Simons notes, which means that the complex's impact on the dystopian local economy is limited to the creation of a few token jobs. In a world of hard bodies aimed at a wealthy—or would-be-wealthy—clientele, there is not much room to recruit the nearby poor and desperate populations, to train them to be smiling, congenial hosts, let alone to open the doors of the Borgata and develop the surrounding neighborhoods. The casino hotel might be a symbol of revolutionary self-making, but the miracle of reinvention is limited only to guests, to those who drive through the tunnel and park in the garage and enter the machine as paying customers. Anyone on the outside has to be contented with the warmth of the sun, reflected off the glass.[9]

The city around the casino hotel is a desolate, ruined place. This is true of the Borgata, but it is also true in fiction, in film, and in popular culture more generally. There are few manicured middle-class neighborhoods in the city that hosts the casino hotel. There are palaces and there are dumps. The original iteration of the serial crime drama, *CSI*, for instance, takes place in Las Vegas, and it moves, disorientingly, from the dizzying interior world of the casino to the disturbing working-class landscapes of the surrounding metropole. Moving back and forth from dark interiors to brightly illuminated exterior shots, *CSI* imagines an uneven world structured around the enterprise of luck and fortune, saturated with color, divided by class. Casino hotels are great generators of wealth, but they are not producers of broadcast economic prosperity. Indeed, as Simon and many others have shown, they are far better at creating class distance than at bridging class divides. More than 30 percent of Atlantic City residents live below the poverty line. In Las Vegas, neighborhoods near the strip often have poverty rates approaching 50 percent. These cityscapes are built to enable easy access to a solid gold interior, a corridor of arrivals and departures sealed off from the lowest forms of misery. A show like *CSI*—emblematic of a half-century's writing and thinking about Las Vegas and Atlantic City—is meant to shine a light on this class division, but it does little to break it down.

In such a larger urban context, reversals of fortune are immediate, dramatic, and unambiguous. They can happen, as did the one on the eve of the Borgata Hotel's tenth anniversary celebration, quickly and decisively. Three men, all clad unseasonably in heavy sweatshirts and jackets, walked into the Borgata, navigating their way through the lobby, until they arrived at the "Borgata Jewels" store. Video footage from security cameras shows them walking through brightly lit hallways, an oversized, overdressed trio moving swiftly past guests in light T-shirts. Then, in what was apparently a textbook "smash and grab," they broke into the glass-paneled display cases, grabbed handfuls of Rolex wristwatches, and hustled their way out of the place. A dark car was waiting out front. Laden down with glittering timepieces, the men sped away into the dark in a car without visible tags. Newspaper accounts noted that while petty thievery was common on the boardwalk, the Borgata was, by design, "a little ways away from where the danger tends to be."[10] *Forbes*, the media outlet of the ruling class, worried that "smash and grab" assaults along the class border were an indicator of the near future. And the president of the Jeweler's Security Alliance, using language that was coded racially and socioeconomically, suggested that these sorts of "three minute robberies," perpetrated by "large numbers of males," were more and more common along the East Coast.[11]

If casino hotels like the Borgata epitomize the hotel's seemingly infinite capacity to confer luck—to transform the modern individual's fortunes dramatically and irrevocably within seconds—they are not the end of fortune's story. Indeed, the casino hotel offers a broad and seemingly infinite spectrum of luck to both individuals and corporations— providing a cocoon-like haven and habitus in which fortunes can be made and venture capitalists can roll the dice on new ideas and inventions, regardless of whether the hotel is attached to a casino or not. Nowhere is this more evident than in the "Science Hotel" that anchors the Alexandria Innovation Center in Cambridge, Massachusetts. As one of four primary innovative proprietary products that the Alexandria Real Estate Equities Inc. offers the Life Science industry generally, its Science Hotel exploits the hotel's long-standing ability to offer new forms of sociability and imaginative opportunity. Offering early-stage life science company start-ups the much-needed laboratory space, office suites, and shared services and amenities for shorter lease terms than usual office buildings, the Science Hotel reduces the barriers and overhead that can encumber early-stage innovation.[12] As such, the Science Hotel temporarily provides shelter that sets up companies to win—and win big—in the life science innovation game.

As its Science Hotel might suggest, Alexandria does much more than provide real estate—it is nothing less than a "disciple of innovation," according to its founder Joel Marcus, operated on the founding belief that life-changing breakthroughs and discoveries are most achievable in built environments that blend world-renowned academic communities and medical institutions with sophisticated capital and savvy management. Alexandria creates a proven and unique ecosystem adjacent to leading universities like MIT and Columbia. This "cluster model" bundles science, talent, capital, and location into a dynamic whole that promises to accelerate discovery and commercialization. Alexandria creates space both real and imaginative that aims to incubate discovery and translate new knowledge into commercial success—in other words, to dramatically impact the fortunes of investors, investigators, and those in urgent need of new medical knowledge. And just as the casino hotel is integral to the fortunes of those at the gaming tables, so too is the

Science Hotel the anchor of the cluster model. Start-ups have to apply to enter the hotel, but once they are checked in, software systems order everything employees need to reduce distraction and optimize time spent on the task at hand. Much like gamblers at the casino are encouraged to remain in rapt attention at the craps table for as long as possible through the careful ministrations of beverage servers and waiters, everything is done to keep those hard at work in hot pursuit of the next big, time-sensitive medical breakthrough focused on the task at hand. Regardless of whether one is throwing the dice at the roulette table or taking major risks on the next big idea in the laboratory, the hotel enables and anchors the blended, hybrid worlds of risk, fortune, and, yes, luck, that have come to typify modern culture.

Much like the casino hotels that enable and sustain energetic gambling regardless of larger market fluctuations, the science hotel at the core of the cluster life-science-model concept has helped to shape the remarkably good fortunes of the Alexandria enterprise as well as its clients. Both the casino hotel and the science hotel have been remarkably profitable ventures for their backers. The "selfless and ego-less workers" that Alexandria has on its team are, according to Marcus, unique in the real estate industry and largely responsible for the company's remarkable, almost legendary success. With clusters on both coasts and in complex urban areas like Boston, New York City, and Mission Bay, Alexandria has a proven track record of dramatic success across regions, local cultures, and divergent economies. In fact, Marcus takes pride in the company's ability to move into an area and quickly create successful clusters out of whole cloth. In this way, these self-contained campuses feel much like the Bellagio or Paris Las Vegas—worlds unto themselves, impervious to outside influences, and creating embryonic environments in which opportunity is let loose to touch the lives of those lucky enough to find themselves temporarily ensconced within the hotel's sheltering arms. And like their casino-hotel counterparts, the numbers say it all: with more than 17 million square feet of space and 175 properties worldwide, Alexandria is a real dream for investors, trading briskly on the New York Stock Exchange, their fourth quarter 2013 numbers making them desirable by anyone's estimation.[13]

Grace

As Alexandria's Science Hotel makes all too apparent, outside of the desert—away from the oasis—luck is everywhere the hotel happens to be. It is marked by the door opened by the concierge just in time, or by the umbrella by the door on a rainy day, or by the fresh cookies or apples on the countertop when you register, just when you need a little something. Luck, after all, is merely an extension of grace, a sensibility made by human hands, crafted in the bowels of the hotel and in the broader world of commerce by a thousand servants, each earning minimum wage or less, producing it with the same efficiency as an auto-assembly work. A thousand sets of hands, tightening the corner on a set of sheets, wiping down the toilet, placing mints and shampoos, all so that we can feel lucky in *any* hotel, so that we can all feel a sense of grace.

THIS, IN THE END, is a part of the great work of the hotel: not merely the containment of the carnivalesque within a four-sided, steel-girdered, brick-and-glass structure, but also its reduction in scale. Philosophers as different as Jackson Lears and Michel Foucault remind us that the story of the modern world is one of rapid rationalization, as the contingent, magical, disorderly premodern is increasingly scanned, assessed, reorganized, and stripped clean of its earlier animated meanings. The hotel, we need to remember, is ancient as well as modern, old as well as ever new. So, too, is its role as a fateful crossroads. For this reason the hotel is such an effective and subtle manufacturer of affect—of irrational feelings of good fortune as well as despair.

And so we imaginatively imbue hotels everywhere with a rich arsenal of feelings and affect—with the pervasive conviction that they are sites of serendipity, magic, and, again, luck. More than anything, *this* is what we want to believe. In the forgettable 2001 film, *Serendipity*, a man initially encounters a woman not in a hotel but rather in a department store, and the universe provides them with a set of clues, reminders that they are destined for each other. Disbelieving, they stage a series of tests—she signs a five-dollar bill and turns it loose in the marketplace, and he signs a copy of *Love in the Time of Cholera*. But the initially powerful feeling that the department store unleashes is finalized by the hotel—the ride up a hotel elevator closing the deal on their mutual love. If they whimsically choose the same floor, the obvious truth—obvious to the viewer—will be revealed. Hijinks ensue, of course. A small boy, another guest in the hotel, intervenes, slowing the ascent of one car, and spoiling the final confirmation. And we spend much of the film watching the currency and the literature, searching for those other symbols of what Jackson Lears would call grace, luck, and fortune, that alternative tradition of the carnivalesque. But in the end, the all-knowing hotel brings them back together. Years later, a chance meeting of two minor supporting characters at the Waldorf Astoria begins a chain of events and, ultimately, completes the cycle. And she, our female lead, staying at the hotel, is given a sign that her true love waits for her nearby. The venerable Waldorf, a wellspring of good fortune, is, indeed, a lucky place.

Serendipity might just be a trivial, inconsequential film, having little cinematic or financial distinction. But, as an expression of the classical cultural history of the hotel—with its chance encounters and its fortunate intersections—it is linked to the blockbuster *Ocean's Thirteen*. Both remind us—as do literally thousands of other short stories, first-hand memories, TripAdvisor comments, novels, and movies—that the hotel has a certain kind of magic attached to it. Rather than romanticize that magic, we might ask ourselves what sort of history it reflects, what sort of apparatus promotes it, and why we want to believe, so desperately, that such a place continues to exist.

8

FAILURE

As we saw in the preceding chapter, the hotel is, among other things, a place where fortunes are made and undone between check-in and check-out, and therefore a place richly steeped in intense feelings of hope, desire, and optimism as well as despair. The hotel, we suggested, offers those who are in search of dramatic upward mobility the fantasy of alternative, infinitely more lucrative social welfare than the state could ever provide. The casino hotel and hotels like the science hotel create economic ecosystems in which guests attempt to radically redefine their relation to capitalism as well as their relative place in the socioeconomic order and, indeed, the world.

Dramatic upticks in guests' feelings of good fortune, however, are only one part of the larger story of affect and the hotel. Because the hotel can and does create equally dramatic and immediate negative feelings in guests' sense of their socioeconomic place and privileges in the world, this final chapter explicitly attends to the hotel's failures of service—to what happens when the hotel cannot or will not deliver on its promise of rest, restoration, and refreshment and when it seems to purposefully and maliciously withhold luck. This countercurrent, we suggest, is an often-overlooked but essential dimension of the hotel's emergence as a global industry. The hotel as a hell, this final chapter illustrates, is as imaginatively important to its modern emergence as are its increasingly luxurious accommodations and the fantasies of betterment that it provides. Indeed, in this dialectic between a heavenly and a hellish place, part of the hotel's enduring fascination and vitality lies.

At its metaphorical worst, the hotel can be a hell. The spare website for the Hotel Carter, for instance, presents a modest hotel in a big city, a stopping point for thrifty visitors to New York City. "The pleasures

The faded exterior of the Hotel Carter, suggesting a very basic warehousing of human bodies and hinting at the troublesome interior workings. (Jim Henderson/ Wikicommons)

of budgeting" is the slogan of the day. Offering "warm hospitality and service," the site generously describes an overnight stay at the modernist structure as "a unique, inviting departure from traditional hotels in Manhattan."[1] The few dark, amateurish pictures of available rooms suggest a plain, Spartan interior, with a tiny DIY snack bar and a soda machine in the lobby instead of room service, and a boxy, smallish television pressed up against the bed instead of a giant flat screen. On the website, the only representations of the exterior of the hotel are an old print taken from an antique postcard and a more recent aerial view. Images of the interior spaces are—comparatively speaking—lackluster and tired.

Regularly ranked as one of the worst hotels on earth, the Hotel Carter is a study in contrast. A midrange hotel in the middle of New York's theater district, its tan brick facade attracts and holds the city's dirt as if it were a disguise. Deteriorating window air conditioners suggest interior conditions that are less than idyllic. The exterior aesthetic of the structure is simplest and plainest near the street level, which makes the building easily forgettable. And the once outsized architecture of the whole, with a few minor art deco flourishes in the upper half, is now eclipsed by neighboring skyscrapers, too removed to be seen and too minuscule to be appreciated. Old and getting older, the Hotel Carter looks blank rather than dramatic, boring and sad rather than creepy or shifting or absurd. But there, seducing tourists in search of a cheap rate in the middle of the street-level scrum, is the one glittering bauble meant to catch the public's eye: the neon overhang, offering flashing red an invitation to enter. "Hotel Carter," it reads, in regal cursive, "Welcome to Times Square!"

The gruesome reputation of the interior life of the Hotel Carter is widely circulated as fact, with abundant accompanying testimonials. Populist demagogue Glen Beck singled out the hotel on his radio program. TripAdvisor, the online hotel review site, routinely puts it at the top of its list of the "10 Dirtiest Hotels in the U.S." Some recall that it was once used as lower-income housing, that it is perennially in financial distress, that its early history was pockmarked with suicides, and that it seems, by and large, to provide more service to local prostitutes than to guests in search of a retreat from the noise of traffic and construction. "Only stay in this hotel if you are a biologist looking for new diseases," one report begins. "The lobby of the Carter," another concludes, "is festooned with mirrors and strings of red lights that remind you of a terrible 1970s disco palace where you half-expect to see a man in a white suit and medallion to saunter across the lobby singing 'you can tell by the way I walk that I'm a woman's man.'" Reviewers regularly report televisions that are antiquated, the finding of dead mice and cockroaches, confrontations with staff that are unruly or downright unhelpful, the rental of rooms without towels, without clean sheets, without anything. Even those who recommend the hotel do so with gritted teeth, suggesting that a cheap rate is more important than a clean room, and urging their fellow travelers to simply shut their eyes tightly, stay on the bed, and get out quickly. "Preparing for a stay in such circumstances requires planning," one intrepid *USA Today* reporter indicated in a January 2009 profile, "Silk sleeping bag liner to help thwart bed bugs? Check. Bottled water and towel brought from home? Check. Pajamas? Uh, no. At the Hotel Carter, where reports of vermin and questionable characters are legion, it's probably best to sleep in your clothes in case a quick exit is required."[2] Brave sojourners to the Hotel Carter describe a hell on earth, where their petitions for clean towels and the absence of vermin are regularly refused.

Of course, the Hotel Carter is not a one-off, the inevitable outcome of Gotham's darker sides. On the West Coast, the Ford Hotel has earned the dubious title "hotel hell" for an entirely different set of reasons. Originally built in 1925, this Los Angeles hotel was long the worst drug-trafficking spot in the city and home to off-their-meds psychiatric patients, addicts, gang members, and domestic abusers before being purchased in 2008 by SRO Housing Corp as part of a larger plan to redevelop the neighborhood and offer affordable housing to people with mental health issues. So legendary had the Ford become that its legal history has been described as reading like a skid-row crack dealer's rap sheet.

Recollections of life in the Ford Hotel by two nineteen-year-old former residents, one of whom raised himself in the hotel, include eerily nostalgic tales of bloodshed, violence, and suicide. The two swap stories about life in the Ford that include seeing a woman who was like a mother to the orphaned boy stabbed to death and hearing the commotion caused by a woman who killed her abusive husband by chopping off his genitals. Seeing a balcony reminds them of the woman who dropped her nine-month-old daughter off the sixth floor balcony before jumping to her death and another man who jumped out of an adjoining window only to get caught in barbed wire halfway to the ground. Finally, a walk up to his old room reminds one visitor of the man next door who blew his brains out only to remain undiscovered for a week, until bodily fluids

AFFECT

The men of the Mayflower Hotel's barbershop, ready and alert, a pitch-perfect expression of the hotel in perfect operation, as opposed to the hellish structure described in this chapter, in which everything is mixed up and nothing is working as it should. (Photo by Theodore Horydczak; Theodor Horydczak Collection, Prints and Photographs Division, Library of Congress, Washington, D.C.)

from the corpse leaked out from under the hotel room door and those who opened the door almost stepped in brains, blood, maggots, and a decomposing body.[3] This hellish rap sheet finally motivated the city to take action against the hotel owner, a Beverly Hills slumlord—action that resulted in transforming the "hotel hell," as it was commonly called, into a newly renovated, orderly, and highly sanitized haven for those down on their luck but suddenly rendered optimistic about their futures by the orderliness of the Ford's new environs. When one of the boys visits his newly renovated former room, he registers the magnitude of the transformation, declaring that "it's like heaven." After asking about how much a room at the Ford now costs, he begins to plan a future for himself—one in which he is "gonna get a job," either as a mechanic, chef, artist, or martial artist.[4]

In its utopian guise, the hotel presents itself as a rationally organized space, designed for maximum comfort and profit, attentive and nurturing. Such a presentation depends on the containment of the unusual, the unexpected, and even the frightening. This containment manifests itself through efficiency studies, employee time clocks, hospitality best practices, and the rituals of cleaning, laundering, and room service. It is coded in the very language of hospitality studies, now an academic discipline, and in the fables of excess and satisfaction that structure the advertisement and consumption of the building itself. It is personified by the overbearing concierge, the surveilling security staff, the snore patrol, the roving eyes of the cleaning staff, and the nosy neighbor, who enlists these forces in the service of much-desired private comfort. But this effort at containment is always on the very edge of spectacular failure.

The utopian hotel is always on the threshold of becoming something different and always haunted by its past as a reckless, ungoverned association of travelers and ne'er-do-wells. When that failure happens, and when its once-upon past and inevitable future rips through the scripted presentation of order, the hotel, as the Hotel Carter and Ford Hotel suggest, can become hell on earth.

At its very worst, the hellish hotel is a playful reversal of the sovereign reign of rationality and order, a carnivalesque reimagining, to borrow from Mikhail Bakhtin, of what is normal and expected. Rooms that are meant to be clean become dirty, foul, unholy. Safe spaces become dangerous, even murderous. The rational architecture of the space becomes, sometimes literally, a house of horrors. In these moments of carnivalesque absurdity and breathtakingly complete reversal, we enter a threatening landscape that might have been drawn by Hieronymus Bosch. When seen in this light, the repeated protests of the once entitled and typically cherished guest are not merely the outraged expressions of a privileged class suddenly bereft of its "rights," as its members understand them, but also evidence of a subterranean history, long repressed but never erased, in which the hotel functioned as an anarchic, lawless structure, full of danger, humor, ribaldry, and a startling panoply of voices and possibilities. In this seeming chaos, as Bakhtin, noted, there is evidence of another, alternative universe of meanings and valuations. The hotel-as-hell, then, is thus a principal expression of the world turned suddenly and seemingly irreversibly upside down. The rational, or "sane" guest, stands as the active agent of modernity, dialogically engaged with his or her opposite, and straining to maintain composure in the face of perdition.

Horror films and certain narrative genres like the murder mystery, cop show, or spy thriller trade in the hotel's precarious teetering between order and disorder—its seemingly infinite capacity to offer both solace and a safe haven for the fugitive from justice and a rich field for sadistic experimentation to those seemingly upstanding citizens who register at the front desk. In the hands of the deranged, desperate, or depraved, the hotel can quickly become reenvisioned as a playground for nefarious practices that need to be hidden from the more licit public and private spaces graphing contemporary life. The hotel room as scene of unexpected bloody carnage has therefore become a stock-in-trade for popular novels and movies, and these moments of horrific disclosure are meant to jolt the witness into an altered relationship to his or her

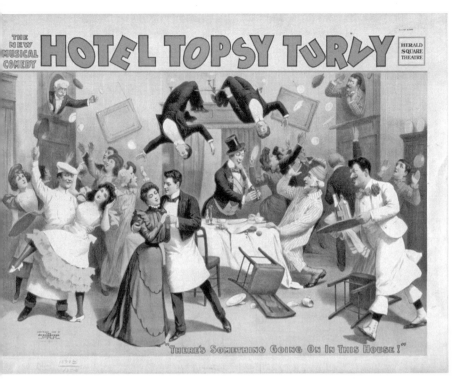

THE NEW MUSICAL COMEDY · HOTEL TOPSY TURVY · HERALD SQUARE THEATRE

"THERE'S SOMETHING GOING ON IN THIS HOUSE!"

The idea that the hotel could serve as the backdrop for a tragic farce, or for a world-gone-mad storyline, has a long history. *Hotel Topsy Turvy*, a turn-of-the-century play, chronicles the experiences of guests in a building managed a bit haphazardly by a circus troupe. A mix of vaudeville and melodrama, it foreshadowed the campy visions of the "hotel hell" of the contemporary moment. ("Hotel Topsy Turvy," a color lithograph, printed by the Strobridge Lithography Co., ca. 1899, from the Prints and Photographs Division, Library of Congress, Washington, D.C.)

surroundings—to highlight, in a heartbeat, the capacity of the world as we know it to fall apart. The elevator that suddenly stops midfloor, the chase scenes up and down emergency staircases, and the ominous click of a closing hotel room door are all part and parcel of this narrative arc, leading the witness from order to disorder and, usually, back to the world as we like to know it.

But these abrupt tears in the social fabric that the modern subject depends on and takes for granted in order to move seamlessly through the urban landscape are not solely the stuff of fiction. In the same fashion, the low-intensity carnage of the Carter highlights a similar set of disruptions: the brown water in the bathroom sink, the mysterious stains on the mattresses and the walls, and the constant sound of rats in the walls, clawing and scratching; the bedbugs and cockroaches; the broken phones, the absent room service, and the cold showers. In these manifestations of daily combat, too, we see the hotel rising up in arms against the bourgeois guest, laying waste to the rights of the typically pampered patron. In the myriad lamentations of the anonymous traveler, we find the shock of recognition, and the discomforting awareness that there are places—awful places—where we should fear to go. Places, again, where a disruptive, alternate array of possibilities is likely to emerge.

Dramatic as these magisterial revelatory moments are, they are usually part of a larger narrative in which the forces of good and evil battle it out for dominance. If the hotel operates as a privileged stage for this drama, it does so because of its seeming infinite malleability—its ability to transform, with unparalleled ease and facility, from a space built explicitly for the apparatus of the civilian state to that of its doppelganger and evil twin—the state of exception in which human rights are up for grabs and civil liberties a quaint throwback to an earlier, more innocent era. At one end of the spectrum the hotel functions as oasis and at the other as that place where actions are too unspeakable to see the light of day. The ultimate asylum in both senses of the word, the hotel can be heaven or hell, depending. And it is this depending—the constant variability, changeability, and suggestibility—to which we attend in the following pages.

Chaos

At its most grotesque, the hellish hotel is produced through horror films, which offer it up as a natural site for the unnerving carnivalesque. In the now iconic illustration of hotel hell *Psycho* (1960), a wayward traveler, on the run from danger, holes up in a desolate "Bates Motel" and drifts into the orbit of a tortured, psychotic hotelier. In *The Shining* (1980), a caretaking family assigned to watch over a resort hotel during the lonely winter descends, slowly, into a madness that cannot be explained. Despite its campy, grindhouse vibe, *Motel Hell* (1980) is suffused with an air of menace that surrounds the structure, and imagines the rural hotel as a predatory space, a human trap if you will, for the literal cultivation of human flesh. Likewise, in *Hostel* (2005), a trio of comely young lads on a hedonistic European tour fall victim to a gruesome market, in which their bodies will be offered for torture. These are genre pieces, emphasizing a nightmarish experience that cannot be traced merely to incompetence or mismanagement or to the sad realities of urban poverty. In doing so, they transform, or confine, the carnivalesque, partially evacuating its revolutionary politics and turning it into a disembodied product of the unexplained and incomprehensible.

These popular portraits of the weird and bloody hotel often focus our attention on the dialectical relation of control and release, turning the struggle between good and evil in the "haunted" hotel into a metaphor for the war between the superego and the id. In *1408* (2007), Mike Enslin, a cynical writer who trades in portraits of spooked rooms and attics, has lost his faith in the supernatural. Without explanation, he receives an unsigned postcard with an image of the Dolphin Hotel—a rival to the Plaza and the Carlisle, we are told—on the front. The simple message, scrawled in an obscure handwriting, reads, "Don't Enter 1408." Intrigued, Enslin investigates the room from afar, and learns of a succession of suicides and unexplained deaths, all connected to one room—the randomly numbered room 1408. The rest of the hotel, it seems, is a perfectly normal, or rational, space. After being confronted by the hotel manager, Gerald Olin, and informed that fifty-six people have died in room 1408, Enslin is given a skeleton key to the room. (Electronic entry cards, we are told, do not work.) Once settled in, he begins to take notes, investigating the room's little details and caustically commenting on the clichéd artwork and dated furnishings. Slowly and inexorably, the room's malevolence reveals itself. An alarm clock misbehaves. A mischievous window falls on his hand. A scalding hot sink burns him. Things get worse, not better. And within an hour, Enslin is battered, bloody, and nearly dead. But he is also a believer, once again, in the supernatural.

Before his faith is restored, Olin confronts Enslin—a caricature of the rumpled, boozing snoop—in the glamorous lobby of the Dolphin. The well-manicured Olin—dressed impeccably and speaking French, so that we can read him as a citizen of the world—initially refuses to allow Enslin to assume occupancy of room 1408, imploring him to choose a different room, to take the word (or accept the authority) of hotel management that it is "an evil fucking room." "I don't want to clean up the mess," says Olin. "Hotels are all about presentation and fertile creature comforts," he continues, "my training is as a manager and not a coroner."[5] With a somber gravitas, Olin (played by veteran actor Samuel L. Jackson) recounts that after four deaths on his watch, he has reclassified room 1408 as uninhabitable, as an ungovernable space increasingly at odds with the smooth and professional orchestration of life everywhere else in the Hotel Dolphin—an orchestration that he so perfectly embodies. If Olin is, in the end, unpersuasive, he still manages to perfectly express the official will of the hotel as a modern institution. But his concern is also proof that official will is not enough. There is still a bit of madness built into the place. Based on a Steven King short story, *1408* is a cultural critique masquerading as a classic set piece, a sober-eyed expression of our lingering suspicion that the hotel, despite its rational, controlled public image, is not that far removed from its earlier, wilder, dangerous histories.

But such narratives are not the privileged domain of the horror film with its choreographed and heavily orchestrated representational distance from its alternately enraptured and repulsed viewers. Indeed, hotels like the Maribel Caves Hotel in Maribel, Wisconsin, literally live in communities, occupying a tenuous and terrifying meridian between the world of the rational and irrational, order and chaos. Popularly known to residents as "hotel hell," the Maribel is the physical site of a series of data defying happenings that include but are not limited to multiple unexplained fires occurring over numerous decades but always on the same date; a mass murder of hotel guests; and a horde of evil spirits unleashed by witches who visited the hotel to put to rest the lingering ghosts of burned and murdered guests but instead opened a portal to hell through the old fountain by the front door from which demons emerged to terrorize the town—that is, until a white witch sealed the portal thereby containing the demons to the burned-out remains of the hotel and the yard surrounding it. With its weird, eerie, and ultimately inexplicable history, the Maribel is relegated to the dubious category of "unexplained research" on the website that features its untoward history—the gaps between local lore and scientific observation getting ever wider with every passing year and unexplained event.[6]

Indeed, scientific method is brought to bear on the Maribel with unusual force and urgency, and the fraught relations between rumor and innuendo, on the one hand, and rigorous objective analysis, on the other, are built into the very fabric of the representational architecture of the Maribel website as well as the architectural ruins that are featured prominently on its homepage. With sections devoted to investigations that supposedly confirm or discredit "the reputed history" and "the reputed phenomena" that have built up around the Maribel, the website offers tenuous and fleeting reassurance to the wary visitor that the scientific method has been brought to bear on this hotel hell, creating a coherent account of seemingly bizarre and indescribable events. If the white and black witch episode is recounted with the dispassion of a psychoanalytic therapist diagnosing the twisted reasoning of a serial killer, the annotated catalog of the investigation into the allegations is one that is both meant to reassure the hapless wanderer into the hotel hell's environs and to reinforce the bizarre other-worldliness of the place. Thus the investigation "reassures" the viewer with reports of those who spent the night in the hotel and with photos of the possible "ecto-mist" that they saw as well as the voices and footsteps that they heard, even as it suggests, ultimately, that the hotel needs an exorcist as much as an anthropologist and physicist to contain the terror it occasions in local residents.[7]

But not all hotel hells are the product of evil forces unleashed by witches from the dark beyond and let loose to wreak disaster in lobbies and hallways—most, if not all in fact, are the result of human error, neglect, stupidity, and occasionally malfeasance. These built environments are, in many ways, the most terrifying, because they suggest the deep and depraved indifference of which humans are capable when it comes to the task of caring for others. Whether it is plumbing systems that cause urine from upper floor toilets to leak from bathroom light fixtures onto the heads of unsuspecting guests at Las Vegas's Plaza Hotel and Casino or the chronically broken elevators that force guests to drag their luggage up and down exterior staircases at the Los Angeles Radisson adjacent to the University of Southern California campus, gross negligence is built into the very fabric of the hotel experience.[8] The logic governing these hotel hells is not one of malevolent extraterrestrial interference but rather of all-too-human lack of concern—the kind of refusal to intervene that results in human beings catching diseases, breaking bones, and getting bugs. In these dystopias, well-heeled guests, expecting posh therapy, are confronted, unhappily, with an experience that does not live up to their class-bound expectations, an experience that all too often has a human face.

And such disinterest in the well-being of others is not always a result of the hotel's deterioration over time. Often hotels are constructed, from the start, in ways that antagonize, torture, and humiliate their customers. Witness the hotel constructed with a footprint that ensures that a maximum number of rooms front one of the busiest and noisiest freeways in America—the westernmost segment of Interstate 10, otherwise known as the Santa Monica Freeway and notable for its fourteen-lane width and four-level interchange with Interstate 405. This segment of highway does not just produce typical city noise; it is one of the busiest freeways in the world, notorious for the number of cars it handles and consistently ranked one of the ten most congested spots in the United States. High traffic volume on this stretch of I-10 generates so many car accidents that special accident investigation sites have been constructed along the freeway, separated by fences, so that California Highway Patrol can quickly clear vehicular carnage from through traffic lanes and reduce the rubbernecking that only further clogs the already congested freeway.

Forced by the act of checking in to be both witness and victim of this scene of urban noise and devastation, bleary-eyed, sleep-deprived guests at such a hotel literally have nowhere to go but curbside. Unlike those who man the special accident investigation sites peppering the off-ramps, hotel guests have not knowingly signed on for the mobile triage and trauma center activity that they are forced to witness. If they are not kept awake throughout the night by the sheer volume of traffic noise, punctuated by the blare of a horn or skid of wheels as cars crash into each other, they are all too often standing rapt at poorly insulated windows in mesmerized horror at the vehicular carnage unfolding in front of them. In this iteration, the hotel in its very architectural design goes from being a basic service provider of rooms conducive to sleep to being a trauma center, much like the ones to which the broken bodies and the mangled cars that contain them are brought by vulture-like tow trucks that idle along the highway's shoulder in order to swoop in quickly on the road kill. And it does so not because of physical plant deterioration that hotel managers and workers are loath to correct, but because of the hotel's very conceptual design and execution.

These disparate representations of hell-on-earth-and-right-next-to-the-freeway are proof that despite decades of careful image making, the hotel is not a perfect substitute for the supposed sanctity of the home, that "haven in the heartless world." Whatever solace it provides is temporary, ephemeral, uncertain, and contingent. In the blink of an eye, everything might change. Indeed, the idea that every room has some infinite capacity—that each space could be a supernaturally infested nightmare, or a technological disaster, or a lover's nest, or a clinic, or all of the above—seems to be a part of the problem with the hotel. Unlike the scripted performance of the home, the hotel has infinite capacity, the chance to be anything at any moment, depending on the luck of the draw. Its potential manifestations of the carnivalesque—the room inhabited by spirits, or the hotel up in arms against the guest—are buried just below the surface, fostering unease and concern, regardless of socioeconomics. Drawn to it by necessity and hoping for a utopia, we want a space with fixed meaning and function, and when we get something else, something wild or weird, we see it as utter pandemonium.

Order

In the face of such chaos, guests react in various ways—capitulation being one option, as we have seen, but individual and systematic attempts at resistance and even restoration are also creative responses to the hotel's humiliating and demoralizing failures. Individuals might attempt to warn others through social media sites or file complaints with the better business bureau in order to pressure owners into doing the right thing; and angry letters and refusing to pay the bill are intimate acts of resistance to the hotel's malicious authority. Such efforts can make incremental differences—small dents in the hotel's self-protective armor. In such an environment the crowd-sourced rating system of TripAdvisor or Angie's List prove powerful market drivers, even as those hotels that are truly uncommitted to guest services and indifferent to the environment they create may be well beyond such rating systems' rational reach.

These often heroic attempts to fight back against the hotel's worst acts of depraved indifference are, however, most palpable and evident in the public work of Rosanne Haggerty—later a winner of the MacArthur "genius" award—who in the 1990s formed Common Ground, a non-profit advocacy organization aimed at the restoration of historic buildings and the provision of livable domestic spaces for the homeless and other downtrodden populations. Common Ground made its strongest claim to fame by restoring the historic—and decrepit—Times Square Hotel, which now provides both employment and fair housing and shared public space for a population that might otherwise have been left behind or extinguished. That restoration, coming in the midst of the large cleanup of the Times Square neighborhood, was a metaphor for the city's attempt to plot a way forward after the disastrous 1970s and 1980s. Common Ground, in turn, has gone on to use the Times

Square "model" in other cities and in other hotels, making parallel ventures—like the West Coast restoration of the Ford Hotel—possible. What might once have been yet another version of the Hotel Carter (a dystopian, dreary hotel in the extreme) is now a socially committed, feel-good domestic imaginarium. And Times Square itself—once exclusively home to a beggar's landscape of seedy pawnshops, strip clubs, and thieves—is now a Disney-esque tourist paradise.

The opportunity to "make things right and people whole again" at hotels gone so terribly wrong is one that alternately allures and daunts those who undertake the perilous task of attempting to transform hotels that exhibit depraved indifference to the social fabric of which they are a part into something different—something new and better. And so it should come as no real surprise that the ultimate bad boy of the kitchen—none other than Gordon Ramsay—has undertaken a fourth reality TV deal with Fox to do just that. *Hotel Hell*, as his new show is called, is vintage Ramsay—calling on all his legendary skills as an obscenity-shouting disciplinarian and enraged petty tyrant to right hotels seriously and seemingly irrevocably run aground on the four horsemen of the hotelier's apocalypse: sloth, greed, wrath, and gluttony. In Ramsay's alternately creative and abusive hands, these dens of iniquity are transformed into havens of order and sanctuaries of solace. Ramsay and his swat team of hotel gurus tour the United States looking for the worst offenders—those hotels that not even the desperate would want to frequent—and he brings the flamboyantly punitive disciplinary regime that has guided his *Hell's Kitchen* and *Kitchen Nightmares* to the top of prime-time TV charts to bear on that ultimate challenge—the hotel. Advance billing for Ramsay's *Hotel Hell* reassured the wary viewer that Ramsay has training in the hotel business—that he even went to hotel school, studying hotel management and working in hotel restaurants—before becoming that infamous chef that we love to watch scream, bully, and fume his way through the kitchen and its staff's equanimity to ensure the best possible dishes emerge with the Ramsay "Order Up" seal of approval.

The hotel hells that Ramsay takes on for reclamation cover the gamut from the bug-infested River Rock Inn, which desperately needs cleaning, to the converted sixteen-room former schoolhouse turned hotel, which is run by a manager who is more interested in dressing up like Sherlock Holmes to play mystery games than in helping guests. Part of the amazing success of Ramsay's *Hotel Hell* and its popularity with

He's checking in to work out the bugs.

GORDON RAMSAY'S

HOTEL HELL

MON JUN4
8PM FOX 11

A promotional still for Gordon Ramsay's *Hotel Hell*, an effort to define the ideal function of the hotel through the repair of something terribly broken, warped, or dangerous. (From the authors' collection)

viewers has to do with the creative scope and range of hotel error that Ramsay uncovers. But Ramsay's reactions reassure viewers that there is no hotel beyond reclamation. No matter how hellish the environs, Ramsay's righteous indignation and industry savvy can set things right ultimately, transforming guests' and employee's intense feelings of despair and frustration into solace.

Some failures have, not surprisingly, to do with financial mismanagement. Take, for example, Vermont's Juniper Hill Inn. Despite the fact that the locals complain that the elite hotel's owners make them feel inferior, Ramsay quickly sees that the owners' delusions of grandeur are the source of the hotel's deep failure for clientele and employees. Ramsay's sumptuous room is marred by the unmistakable smell of raw sewage. The restaurant both overcharges for improperly cooked food and does not pay its staff. The hotel's owner brings friends to eat for free and then shamelessly pockets the waiters' tips. The "priceless" antiques that the owner shows Ramsay are, upon assessment by the outside appraiser that Ramsay hires, fakes. In order to puncture the owners' delusions of superiority and the fantasy world of wealth that is their protective shield, Ramsay's team brings in former hotel guests and employees to stage an intervention. Here the psychology of management is the disease troubling Juniper Hill Inn, and once addressed, the symptoms are treatable. Plumbing problems are fixed, and the staff receives timely payment.

As this episode illustrates, the hotel's grotesque failures of service and the subsequent intensely negative affect these failures create are often the direct result of hotel owners' perverse thinking and resistance to approaching hotel operation rationally as a business, and this facet of hotel hell holds viewers of Ramsay's show particularly spellbound. The owner of San Diego's Keating Hotel charges more than $800 per night for rooms in his plush concept hotel, and at first glance the guest who checks in would not sense trouble in such luxury environs. Yet, because the former-Ferrari-dealer-turned-owner has taken his personal enthusiasms and idiosyncrasies into his business model, the kitchen staff is compelled to serve skeptical guests chocolate-bacon-strawberry pizzas and deliver room service in plastic containers and cardboard boxes.

And the Keating Hotel is not unique: the Roosevelt Hotel is owned and operated by a former student of Roosevelt Elementary, and his purchase of the repurposed building largely motivated by nostalgic memories of his own days as student at the school. But the owner's interest in using the hotel as staging ground for monthly mystery games in which he plays Sherlock Holmes means that the linens are filthy, the kitchen inadequate, and the décor hopelessly out of date. As both the Keating and Roosevelt make clear, hotels that are held hostage to owners' eccentricities are on the road to inevitable disaster, harming staff and guests through depraved indifference to the well-being of either. Though Ramsay's skill and energy appear to be inexhaustible, some hotels are beyond even his saving reach; the Cambridge Hotel, for example, closed owing to mismanagement before he could sufficiently work his magic.

These experiments in reclamation are as far a cry from the touchy-feely intervention of Common Ground as you can get—they are nothing less than a tough-love hall of famer bitch-slapping recalcitrant, slothful, and nefarious hotel management into shape. Ramsay endeavors to get even the most egregious outliers of the hotel world to shout with military speed and precision "Yes, Chef!" or mentally capitulate to

Ramsay's rugged truth telling as they ponder the error of their ways. His confrontation with the Juniper Hill Inn owners was considered by thousands of viewers to be "the best ever Gordon rant!," sprinkled as it was with accusations that the hotel was a "living nightmare" and the owner a "disrespectful, disgusting man."[9] Inevitably, this desirable image of the tow-headed, rugby-playing, hard-nosed Englishman, manfully beating back the madness of the carnivalesque, works well to burnish Ramsay's celebrity mystique. Indeed, the triple punch of shame, blame, and fame that Ramsay brings to the kitchen packs a sufficient wallop to right the worst offenders of the hotel world, and this fantasy of an almost infinitely powerful force of correction holds such seductive allure for the viewer.

Yes, many of us have had bad hotel experiences and can swap stories about all the flagrant fouls we have seen in the hotel hard ball game we all play. But, more fundamentally, hotels function as a kind of "third place"—the arena that Ray Oldenburg has argued so persuasively was crucially important for civil society, civic engagement, and most integrally for establishing a deep and abiding sense of place.[10] If the first place is the home and the second place is the workplace, this third place functions as the anchor of community life, fostering more creative interactions and providing a sort of living canvas upon which modern selves play, self-fashion, and self-soothe. That such a canvas when it features the hotel as the leading lady of this third space can depict a pungently dark and evocative picture of human depravity born of entropy, psychosis, and inattention, by now, is abundantly clear. What Ramsay's ultimately palliative version of *Hotel Hell* provides is the reparative thrust also implicit in the hotel as third space—the redemptive arc of hotel dystopia no more and utopia, tenuously but triumphantly, regained.

It is this final and most seductive twist in the hotel life plot—the veering away from certain despair to unexpected euphoria—that master showmen like Ramsay bank on to hook viewers, visitors, and rubberneckers on the hotel highway. We all want to end up in a better place, even as we fear that we may find ourselves in perilously permeable and fungible spaces that erode our inevitably tenuous sense of self-worth and social value. That such hotel spaces might be able to be remade in our desired image is seduction indeed. Thus hotel and guest are engaged in a delicate dance of wish fulfillment, with beauty as our desired partner whirling us around a lovely dance floor and the beast always lurking on the sidelines, ready to tap our partner on the shoulder and cut in on the final waltz.

CODA

—————

"Boutique hotels," *New York Times* columnist David Brooks opined, are "kind of ridiculous." Sketching out a simple history of the hotel, Brooks suggested that "mass boutique" followed midcentury bland business hotels, which had themselves replaced "luxury hotels" that "mimicked European palaces." Focusing on the contemporary moment, Brooks looked around his boutique hotel room and found much to dislike. It is "too dark," he complained, "which makes it hard to read. The bed is often too low. The bathroom door is sometimes a flimsy, sliding shutter, sacrificing privacy for style." The list went on. There were no more closets, and the lobbies were filled with dozens of guests, each hunched over a tablet or a laptop. Still, despite these complaints, Brooks acknowledged that a night in such a hotel created "emotional arousal," with guests drawn into an intimate relation with structure and form, a relation formed around "psychographic profiles," and aimed at producing "unusual products and distinctive experiences." The end result? A richer, happier, more enjoyable experience. "We are significantly better off," he concluded confidently.[1]

Hotel life—the object of Brooks's trademark armchair social commentary—is a big, complex, bewildering thing. It ranges the gamut from beginnings to endings, from rich to poor, from fortune to failure, and from the most intimate privacy to the startling glare of public encounter. In doing all of this, hotel life thrives in a contemporary, hyper-commercialized culture and the messy social mix that is its ever-present hum. As the desired loci for modern selves on the move and in search of new forms of comfort, security, affirmation, and experience, hotels have become experimental spaces that draw increasingly large numbers of guests because of the new kinds of encounters and personal evolutions that they promise. What Brooks saw as a single trend, then, was actually a script—and one of many.

These intersections and revolutions, as we have seen, take place within and because of the various feelings, spaces, scales, and temporalities that the hotel creates for guests. As a built environment, the hotel is always dynamically calibrating and recalibrating these four crucial features—sentiment, space, scale, and time—of its habitus.

If careful calibrations of encounter and change have been key to the hotel's successful evolution in the modern era, one wonders, what will the hotel of the future look like? What is it becoming and what kinds of new realities and selves will it help to script into existence?

Not surprisingly, such questions have been the focus of energetic and intense debate, study, collaboration, and experimentation among architects, hoteliers, and those in the service industry. Commissioned by the premier global travel distribution firm Amadeus, the think tank Fast Future published an exhaustive report, "Hotels 2020—Beyond Segmentation," concluding unequivocally that hotels will need to become "living innovation laboratories" that "embrace extreme personalization" to thrive in the turbulent coming decades, which will be characterized by more numerous, entitled, knowledgeable, and discriminating guests. Embracing rather than rejecting the innovations of new social media, the most successful hoteliers, the study concludes, will "reap the benefits of developing a vibrant online and offline personality, while gradually defining and managing a new notion of privacy for the twenty-first century."[2]

Just as hotels of the late eighteenth and nineteenth centuries helped shape new notions of privacy and possibility for individuals, so too will the hotel of the twenty-first century focus on the self. Personalization, says Fast Future's CEO Rohit Talwar, is going to be the key to customer satisfaction. By utilizing technology to integrate various networks, hoteliers will be able to make the room that a guest inhabits for a few hours "customizable"—replicating the familiar comforts of home, with temperature, entertainment, and lighting options mirroring the domestic setup. Hotel guests will expect their stay to be personalized around choices they make ahead of time—types of pillows, mattress firmness, audiovisual facilities—and hotels will need to develop strong social media "listening skills" to hear these evolving customer "needs." In theory, such sensitivity does more than ensure good ratings; it also drills down deep into the self and unearths the core soul of every customer, revealing it as an object of study and celebration.

As the owner of Seattle's Hotel 1000 observes, the hotel will need to continue what we have shown to be its long-standing delicate balance between personal attention and strategic indifference, and it will need to do so in a networked and digital age that will pose increasing challenges. As Chuck Marratt, vice president of IT at MTM Luxury Lodging, Hotel 1000's parent company, puts its: "Our mantra is, don't be creepy. In the past, hotels have been sensitive to customers' wishes for privacy, even sometimes anonymity," and maintaining that delicate balance between attentiveness to the highly individualized requirements of their guests and their need for anonymity will be an exponentially increasing challenge as technology accumulates data on guests' most personal habits, behaviors, and inclinations.[3] To what uses ultimately will the Polish boutique hotel Blow Up Hall 5050 ultimately put all of the data it inevitably aggregates from the smartphones, preloaded with a virtual concierge app, that are given to each guest at check in? Conversely, as the hotels of the future become awash with information, not only about their guests but also about their own operation, hotels will suddenly have the data analytics to lay bare every aspect of their inner workings to the scrutiny of ecosensitive guests. The next iteration of the hotel, then, promises to be a veritable big-data mine for anyone interested in the care of the self.

Many hotels are already moving in the direction of conspicuous personalization as a proactive business strategy. Take, for example, the St. Regis Hotel in Orange Country that offers guests a surf butler who will measure your wetsuit, monitor surf conditions for you, and wax your board. Or the personal sessions with a pet psychic that Portland Oregon's Kimpton Hotel Monaco makes available to its pooch-porting guests. Not to be outdone, the Hotel DeLuxe in Portland has begun to offer a spiritual menu to guests that not only coincides with each guest's religious preferences but also provides spiritual offerings for pets. The Ink and Stay special at Venice Beach's Hotel Irwin, not surprisingly, includes a one-hundred-dollar tattoo coupon for guests who stay three nights or more, making the sleep concierge at New York City's Benjamin hotel or the expert bath-ologist who comes to Chicago Fairmont Hotel guests' rooms with personalized aromatherapy oils, lotions, and soaps seem like the antiques of yesterday.

Hotel researchers, hoteliers, and technologists are conceptualizing the future anew around the hotel. So too are architects, experimenting with the cement and steel, the form and function, and the founding spatial assumptions of the hotel. The world renowned founders of the German Laboratory for Visionary Architecture (LAVA), Tobias Wallisser,

Chris Bosse, and Alexander Rieck, for example, recently undertook a research collaboration focused on the future hotel with Franhofer IAO (Institute for Work Organization) in order to investigate the interfaces between architecture, technology, and the human body. LAVA designed the Future Hotel Showcase Room as a demonstration project space that applied parametric design methods and semiautomated production to create in-time realization of the original design.[4] In other words, the methods that the collaborators used to conceptualize the future hotel demo closed the traditional architectural gap between digital modeling and built showcase, leading to an instantaneous and identical realization of the design.

But their vision was not only pioneering in method and approach. It did nothing less than blur the distinctions between technology, interior space, and a highly individualized guest, creating a symphony of technologically calibrated cocoon-like hotel rooms that responded instantaneously to the bodily needs of the weary traveler. With their anti-jet-lag lights, intelligent mirror, active comfort bed, personal spa area, and integrated media and room service capabilities, the hotel rooms envisioned by Future Hotel are human travel pods— quasi-amniotic sacs in which guests have their every need and want anticipated in ways reminiscent of the fetus. And Future Hotel is not the only architectural envisioning of a future hotel in which the individual reigns supreme—in which human comfort takes on utopic proportions and technology is pressed into the service of personal betterment. Commenting on the seven most stunning hotel architectural wonders being designed and built in the coming decade—hotels like Bucharest's Dorobanti Tower, São Paolo's sustainable luxury Hotel Aliah, Dubai's solar-powered hotel and residential Vertical Village, and Singapore's sixteen-story business hotel PARKROYAL on Pickering—design curator Donald Albrecht concludes that "one of the ur-building types of tourism and globalization—the hotel—is alive and well and remains on the cutting-edge of architectural trends."[5]

These new visions of hotel life conceive of ever more attentiveness to the individual person. They also enable "unbundlings" of service, disconnections that compel those economically strapped to make decisions about what constitutes a livable short-term habitus that often cuts too close to the bone. Looking ever more like an umbilical cord to those sources of comfort that meet our deepest human needs, the hotel of the future carries a dystopic as well as utopic message. Low-budget versions of future hotels are already springing up across Southeast Asia—the

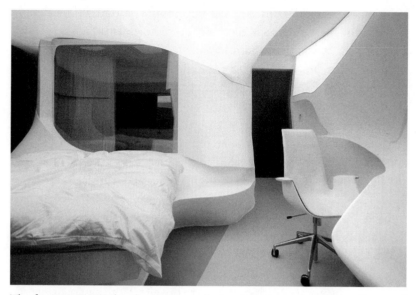

The futuristic LAVA hotel room, part of a brochure representing the architectural firm's ambitions to revolutionize hotel design. The undulating, "free form" exterior wall is meant to mimic human skin. (http://www.l-a-v-a.net/projects/future-hotel/; accessed June 5, 2014)

first Tune Hotel is already open in Kuala Lumpur, and construction is underway for thirty more sites in Southeast Asia with the goal of one hundred hotels in Asia in the next few years. With hotel rooms as low as three U.S. dollars a night, the allure of Tune Hotels is obvious.

But the pay-for-what-you-use logic of Tune Hotels means that guests are constantly asking dehumanizing questions about what they can do without—as opposed to what they want or desire. On the lower frequencies, austerity itself can be personalized. With towels, A/C, toiletries, and hair dryers all considered nonessential items and thus carrying additional charges, the budget hotel's future as Tune envisions it looks stark indeed—it is a future in which the bright colors of the billboard-like Tune Hotel facade will welcome the weary traveler into a world of radically diminished expectations. It is a world in which the growing socioeconomic gap between rich and poor is registered with the withholding of a bar of soap, the refusal of toilet paper, and the terrifying inner calculation economically down on their luck guests will no doubt have to make about what they can do without. With every tissue carrying a fee that guests may not be able to pay, the low-budget hotel of the future seems to deny human need with a whole new level of calculation, premeditation, and parsimony. Reminiscent of Oliver Twist's baleful plea "Please sir I want some more," this vision of the hotel of the future has as its CEO a Dickensian capitalist outraged at human want and need that cannot pay for its rudimentary comfort.

And if these two visions of the hotel of the future seem radically disconnected—the luxury cocoon worlds apart from the dehumanizing way station—it is nonetheless the case that both will be run by the same corporate entity. This is the case because, as "Hotels 2020—Beyond Segmentation" predicts, economic segmentation will only superficially appear to be greater across the hotel spectrum in twenty-first century. In fact, the hotel business model of the future is one in which global hotel groups will increasingly seek to cover the full range of hotels from budget through luxury to heritage properties—they will, in short, move beyond segmentation to capitalize on human want and need at every economic register. A resounding 81 percent of those consulted for the study see a future in which hotels will experiment with a range of business models, and full-spectrum hotel chains will deliver one-star budget to six-star luxury properties as part of their business plan. In such a dramatically and vertically integrated model, class stratification will be reinforced and the temporary respites that the hotel can and often does currently offer from life's economic grind will be harder to come by.

If these industry projections of the hotel's future uphold a global capitalism from which there appears to be increasingly little respite, the hotel, nonetheless, continues to be a powerfully imaginative place both real and invented, evoking alternative realities and possibilities for modern selves. Take, for example, the case of New York City's McKittrick Hotel. Completed in 1939 and located at 530 West 27th Street, the McKittrick was supposed to be the city's most decadent luxury hotel offering more intimate luxury than the Waldorf Astoria or the Plaza. Initially attracting visitors like Alfred Hitchcock, who named the hotel in *Vertigo* after the McKittrick, the hotel fell on hard times after the outbreak of World War II and was closed and condemned within the year. Left locked, the McKittrick remained closed to the public, a hotel never realized, until 2008 when the space became the site for an interactive play.

A collaboration between London's award-winning Punchdrunk and Emursive, *Sleep No More* reconceives the McKittrick as the staging ground for an adaptation of Shakespeare's *Macbeth*, reinterpreted through the lens of art deco and film noir. Every evening, numerous audiences move freely through more than one hundred rooms of this newly constituted hotel space, choosing their path through the play and following the different story strands that the various characters represent. In this interactive model, every individual's experience of the play is unique and self-fashioning, and there is no standard "play" experience. The play becomes, in short, play, and, the flexible and fluid reclaimed hotel space—Koolhaas's idea of "junkspace" par excellence—enables highly personalized, discrete "stories" or plays to emerge synthetically and in the interplay between characters, sets, and audience members. In other words, this iteration of the hotel creates a sensory experience unlike that generated by other art forms or cultural endeavors. Not only do viewers/guests create their own discrete story line by how they choose to move through the hotel, but each hotel space offers viewer/guests an immersive multisensory environment of their own making, utilizing but reconstituting the basic building blocks of the hotel. So reenvisioned, the McKittrick Hotel becomes the site of the most unique theatrical experience in the history of New York and a collaborative endeavor creating alternative realities out of the imaginative raw materials of drama, hotel space, creativity, and invention.

But the case of the McKittrick Hotel's transformation from luxury hotel to experimental, interactive three-dimensional stage is far from unique. Hotels have long been multiform sites of innovation, invention, and transformation, pushing those who imagine walking through their doors into new relations with their surroundings and generating new kinds of creativity, experimentation, and healing. One hundred years before the McKittrick Hotel reopened as an interactive theater space, the Catalan sculptor and architect Antoni Gaudí was asked by two American businessmen to design a grand hotel for the site that would later become the World Trade Center. Gaudí proposed, instead, to build a futuristic skyscraper hotel that would, at 360 meters, rival the Empire State Building in height and that, when Gaudí proposed it in 1908, was probably unfeasible. The backers had envisioned something like Henry Hardenbergh's Waldorf-Astoria, which epitomized modern luxury at the time, but Gaudí designed instead a gigantic cluster of towers rising as high as the Eiffel Tower, surrounded by glass, tile, alabaster, and other decorative materials. Hotel Attraction would have at its summit a sun-shaped observatory that Gaudí dubbed "The Sphere of All Space." With its theaters, lecture rooms, galleries, and central hall with sculptures of all the U.S. presidents, not to mention the monstrous series of dining rooms replete with murals and room for a full symphony orchestra to serenade guests while they ate, the Hotel Attraction was a modern phe-nomenon of epic proportions. The project's initial concept drawings show a hotel space unlike any other then in existence—they are a vision of new scales, modes, and spaces of encounter and exchange. It is possi-bly because of this very revolutionary feel that the Hotel Attraction pro-ject was inexplicably and abruptly halted, and Gaudí's vision was soon forgotten, relegated to the dust heap of ideas too radical for their time.

That is, until 2002 when U.S. architect Paul Laffoley spearheaded an effort, along with art historians, architects, and Gaudí enthusiasts, to enter Gaudí's original Hotel Attraction designs in the competition for redesigns of the former World Trade Center site. Originally conceived for the World Trade Center site, Hotel Attraction, many believed, would resolve the dispute between developers and family of those who died in the 9/11 attack about how to treat the trauma site and would allow every-one, in the words of one enthusiastic supporter, to "dream again."[6] The cathedral-style space that was originally designed to honor the presidents could be reenvisioned as a memorial site. With its historic and inter-national points of origin, Hotel Attraction gave everyone the chance, according to its advocates, to be involved in a historical project from around the world and to resolve the polarizing effect that discussions about rebuilding the World Trade Center site was having on the city.

The euphoric vision of global healing that Hotel Attraction made tangible to a grieving international population was powerful. As one proponent of the Gaudí project summarized, "Gaudí designed the building ninety-five years ago for the future. Well, that 'future' is now here. Let us seize the moment."[7] Within the context of the 2002 Gaudí International Year, the "Hotel Attraction Project" resuscitated Gaudí's original plans, re-created them virtually and within the context of an early twenty-first-century New York, making use of innovative tech-nologies to illustrate the power of the project for the current time. The work of Marc Mascort/Boix under the advice of the curator of the Bar-celona Gaudí royal chair, Joan Bassegoda Nonell, the "Hotel Attraction Project" asked the provocative question: Why not carry out Gaudí's project in the city for which it was conceived?

And this was a question that immediately went viral on a global scale, generating international buzz and speculation about Hotel Attraction as a site of healing and hope. As Laffoley put it, "Ground Zero is a gaping wound on the body of New York City and on the soul of America" and "anything placed there to begin the healing process cannot proceed from

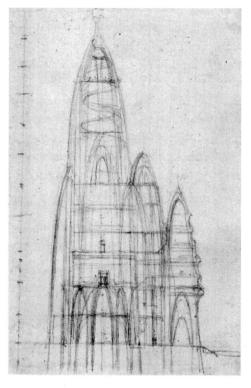

A pencil sketch of the exterior and interior of Hotel Attraction, produced by Gaudí in 1908. (commons. wikimedia.org)

the same living-ego impulse" that animated the World Trade Center architects or those who destroyed it.[8] The YouTube video "Gaudí's New York City Vision,"[9] provides a powerful visualization of the hotel's capacity to create hope out of despair, a future out of a shattered present. "Gaudí's New York City Vision" creates an arresting counterfactual past in which Gaudí's project looms over the city's skyline by way of brokering a new post 9/11 reality of healing and hope. Hotel Attraction becomes the "what could have been" hotel, creating a narrative arc that seamlessly aligns the New York City of 1908 with the New York City of 2008. As we watch the skyline move from how it would have looked in 1908 with the Gaudí hotel through the fin de siècle twin tower skyline to a 2008 skyline in which the Gaudí Freedom Tower marries past and present, futurism with nostalgia, we see sketched through the brushstrokes of the hotel an urban history that looks brighter, more resilient, and whole. The greatest hotel story never told is—like the interactive multimodal endeavor that is *Sleep No More*—told not only via building specs and images but through multiple sensory modalities. The May 30, 2002, release of "Hotel Attraction: Gaudí's Project for New York" is a compilation of thirteen acoustic musical interpretations of Gaudí's hotel by musicians like Peter Schirmann, John Sutil, Organic Dream, and Bluprint to name a few, and it is intended to add substance and heft to the visuals that the "Hotel Attraction Project" provides, hence the haunting use of key songs from the album in the YouTube video.

From the immanent new reality that documents like "Hotels 2020— Beyond Segmentation" foretell and LAVA's "Future Hotel Showcase Room" fabricates to thought experiments like "Hotel Attraction Project" and *Sleep No More*, the hotel of the future looks to be the habitus for new kinds of reality and new forms of awareness. Hotel life is thus a dynamic and durable thing—a thing that morphs and changes but that also stays weirdly the same. For those who range across its premises, the hotel reveals new worlds and protects endangered ones, and this irresistible promise to do both continues to appeal to us, becoming the subject of recent popular films, from Wes Anderson's *Grand Budapest Hotel* (2014) to Paul Haggis's *Third Person* (2013). With their attention to the hotel as a locus for risk and protection, nostalgia and new beginnings, remaking and unmaking, kindness and exploitation, these new iterations of hotel life form part of a longer story, the next chapter of an unfolding tale. As they continue to remind us, Kant's Enlightenment notion that all modern subjects have the inalienable "right to visit" and that hospitality is necessary to bring together those the world over into peaceable exchange with each other yields spatial realities as diverse, ever-changing, and mutable as the various hotel forms that the preceding pages have touched upon.

None of this would surprise Monsieur Gustave H., the precise, charismatic head concierge at the "picturesque and elaborate" Grand Budapest. For Gustave, hotel life, in all its splendor, is both his charge and his mission. A skillful orchestrator of the abundant staff, and sometime lover of the hotel's older female guests, Gustave brilliantly employs the hotel as if it were a collection of revolving set pieces for his romantic partnerships, his poetic, prescriptive speeches, and—above all else—his cultured, "liberally perfumed" management of so many rapidly shifting interior landscapes. Along with his protégé, Zero Moustafa, Gustave embodies the totality of the Grand Budapest and of the promise of the hotel more generally.

We learn about Gustave from the Author, to whom Zero has told the story decades later. For the Author—who will someday write up his reminiscence of the tale of Gustave H. after recovering from a protracted

A doorman's jacket, worn
in the early 1900s at the
Willard Hotel, Washington,
D.C. (Photo taken by Carol
Highsmith, between 1980
and 2006; Photographs in the
Carol M. Highsmith Archive,
Prints and Photographs
Division, Library of Congress,
Washington, D.C.)

bout of "scribe's fever" and thanks to his conversation with the aged
Zero—the Grand Budapest is not a busy, swirling orchestration but a
place of quiet, solitary contemplation. Surrounded by a small handful
of guests—drifters in the off-season—the Author notices Zero in the
lobby of the declining Grand Budapest and sees not merely that he is
"alone" but also that he is "lonely," a distinction that readers of *Hotel Life*
will, we hope, better understand. The two men, the Author and Zero,
share each other's company in the many and varied public spaces of the
hotel, retreating periodically to their respective rooms.

What makes this evocative film, released as we were finishing this
book, such a closing touchstone for what we have called "hotel life" is its
clever, provocative play with space and time. Anderson's colorful portrait
of Gustave, his "vocation," and the "costly, unprofitable, doomed hotel" he

A still image of Gustave H., the earnestly seductive concierge, from the 2014 Wes Anderson film *Grand Budapest Hotel*, a prolonged, nostalgic meditation on the function of the classic hotel, in the abstract, as a transformative, self-making space. (From the authors' collection).

so perfectly embodied, captures all of the tones and emotions and themes of the great, complex, and bewildering structure we set out to examine in these pages. Deftly managed by Gustave, the Grand Budapest is a kaleidoscope of places and times and affects and themes and experiences. It is everything to its guests, even as it is set in its own time and space, and even as it is reproduced elsewhere as a perfect copy. Its curator and protector, Gustave, was, as Zero tells the Author, a man whose singular gift was the ability to extend into the present that which had vanished long before he was born—the hotel life that those aged patrons who entered the Grand Budapest's environs believed in and sought out year after year, regardless of war, changes in personal fortune, and the inevitable vicissitudes of aging and infirmity. And yet, in the end, Monsieur Gustave is not unique, but a type, a member of the "Society of Crossed Keys," a brotherhood of concierges, all managing other versions of the Grand Budapest, each perfectly capable of getting whatever the guest wants or needs.

HOTEL SPACE, AS the preceding pages remind us, is at once flexible and firm—junkspace and, as the Anderson film makes all too palpable, inevitably fetishized. It can, on the one hand, enable imaginative leaps unprecedented in individual guests' lived experiences and, on the other hand, deliver predigested temporary spaces both mind-numbingly canned and familiar. It can, too, make it impossible to tell the difference. In any case, it delivers life form and experience that is fluid and ever changing and that feels, at times, shockingly new. It wants to be marketed, to be rated, to be celebrated as restorative, as healing, and as restful. But it surely does not want to be understood in all of its big, bewildering complexity. Doing that—the task of *Hotel Life*—would demystify the supposed charm of submitting oneself to the authority of the glass and steel boxes that surround us and would reveal that what we have assumed was a matter of simple self-making—a need to be "alone," or to recover from "scribe's fever," or to find romance—is, in the end, something far less innocent.

Notes

INTRODUCTION

1. Norman Hayner, *Hotel Life* (Chapel Hill: University of North Carolina Press, 1936), 182.

2. Rebecca Onion, "How Grand Hotels Shaped Modern Life (and Not Just Wes Anderson's Film)," *Boston Globe*, March 9, 2014, and Molly Berger, *Hotel Dreams: Technology, Luxury, and Urban Ambition in America, 1829–1929* (Baltimore: Johns Hopkins University Press, 2011).

3. http://upload.wikimedia.org/wikipedia/commons/a/af/Tremont_House_IV.JPG or http://upload.wikimedia.org/wikipedia/en/8/83/Tremont_House,_Boston.jpg.

4. Sinclair Lewis, *Work of Art* (New York: Jonathan Cape, 1934), 259.

5. Immanuel Kant, *Toward Perpetual Peace*, in *Immanuel Kant: Practical Philosophy*, ed. and trans. Mary J. Gregor (Cambridge: MIT Press, 1996), 328–31.

6. A. K. Sandoval-Strausz, *Hotel: An American History* (New Haven: Yale University Press, 2007), 9.

7. Hiram Hitchcock, "The Hotels of America," in *One Hundred Years of American Commerce*, ed. Chauncey Depew (New York: D. O. Haynes & Co., 1895), 1:156.

8. *New York Mirror*, June 25, 1836, quoted in Carolyn R. Brucken, "Consuming Luxury: Luxury Hotels in Antebellum America, 1825–1860" (Ph.D. diss., George Washington University, 1997), 173.

9. "16 Firms Face NAACP Picketing," *Atlanta Journal*, July 3, 1962; Luke 2:7.

10. *Congressional Globe*, 42nd Cong., 2nd sess., December 20, 1871, 242; December 21, 1871, 280; and January 15, 1872, 381–83.

11. *Congressional Globe*, 42nd Cong., 2nd sess., appendix part 6, January 25, 1872, February 4 and 6, 1872, 28–29.

12. http://4.bp.blogspot.com/-BWE1zljgO6M/TxCUlvx5KoI/AAAAAAAARPQ/8ElB3Lk8fiU/s1600/htheresabus.jpg.

13. Sondra Kathryn Wilson, *Meet Me at the Theresa: The Story of Harlem's Most Famous Hotel* (New York: Atria Books, 2004).

14. For work that addresses the production of modern space and capitalism, see, for example, Neil Smith, *Uneven Development: Nature, Capital, and the Production of Space* (Athens: University of Georgia Press, 2008); Ali Madanipour, *Public and Private Spaces of the City* (New York: Routledge, 2003); Mark Kingwell and Patrick Turmel, eds., *Rites of Way: The Politics and Poetics of Public Space* (Toronto: Wilfrid Laurier University Press, 2009); Sarah Edwards and Jonathan Charley, eds., *Writing the Modern City: Literature, Architecture, Modernity* (New York: Routledge, 2012); Łukask Stanek, *Henri Lefebvre on Space: Architecture, Urban Research, and the Production of Theory* (Minneapolis: University of Minnesota Press, 2011); and David Crouch, *Flirting with Space: Journeys and Creativity* (Surrey: Ashgate, 2010). For foundational theories of space, language, and capitalism,

see Henri Lefebvre, *The Production of Space*, trans. Donald Nicholson-Smith (Oxford: Blackwell, 1991), and Gaston Bachelard, *The Poetics of Space*, trans. Maria Jolas (New York: Orion, 1964).

15. For work that considers the role of hotels in the global economy, see Rachel Sherman, *Class Acts: Service and Inequality in Luxury Hotels* (Berkeley: University of California Press, 2007); Toby Shelley, *Exploited: Migrant Labour in the New Global Economy* (London: Zed Books, 2007); Luis L. M. Aguiar and Andrew Herod, eds., *The Dirty Work of Neoliberalism: Cleaners in the Global Economy* (London: Wiley-Blackwell, 2006).

16. Jacob Tomsky, *Heads in Beds: A Reckless Memoir of Hotels, Hustles, and So-Called Hospitality* (New York: Anchor Books, 2012).

17. See, for example, Carolyn Steedman, *Dust: The Archive and Cultural History* (New Brunswick: Rutgers University Press, 2002); Jacques Derrida, *Archive Fever: A Freudian Impression* (Chicago: University of Chicago Press, 1998); and Rodrigo Lazo, "Migrant Archives," in Russ Castronovo and Susan Gillman, eds., *States of Emergency: The Object of American Studies* (Chapel Hill: University of North Carolina Press, 2009), 36–54.

CHAPTER 1

1. Christopher Alexander, *A Pattern Language: Towns, Buildings, Construction* (New York: Oxford, 1977).

2. Elizabeth Grosz, *Architecture from the Outside: Essays on Virtual and Real Space* (Cambridge, Mass.: MIT Press, 2001). See also O. F. Bollnow, *Human Space*, trans. Christine Shuttleworth (London: Hyphen Press, 2011).

3. Fredric Jameson, *Postmodernism, or the Cultural Logic of Late Capitalism* (Durham: Duke University Press, 1991), 39.

4. In *Race Matters* (Boston: Beacon Press, 1993), Cornel West invokes Henry James's observation that American civilization is just like a hotel in that it is obsessed with comfort, convenience, and contentment. It is for this reason that, West concludes, it is such a challenge to engage "in a serious discussion about race in a hotel civilization" (x).

5. http://en.wikipedia.org/wiki/Grand_Hotel_(film).

6. Siegfried Kracauer, *The Mass Ornament: Weimar Essays* (Cambridge, Mass.: Harvard University Press, 1995), 53.

7. Ratha Tep, "Coolest Hotel Lobbies," *Travel and Leisure*, February 2011.

8. Cajunmama, "Hilton Hotels & Resorts Introduce New Lobby Design," TravelingMamas .com, http://travelingmamas.com/hilton-hotels-resorts-introduce-new-lobby-design/.

9. "Your New Workplace Is Waiting. . . . in the Lobby," *360*, October 2007.

10. Bryant Simon, *Everything But Coffee: Learning about America from Starbucks* (Berkeley: University of California Press, 2011).

11. Will Self, "Room with a Purview," *New York Times Magazine*, December 4, 2011.

12. http://www.eloisewebsite.com/eloise_at_the_plaza.htm.

13. Ibid.

14. http://abcnews.go.com/GMA/Parenting/tour-eloise-shop/story?id=9218964.

15. http://www.nytimes.com/2010/02/21/arts/design/21maltzan.html?pagewanted=all.

16. http://www.skidrow.org/wwa_or.html.

CHAPTER 2

1. "Capri Anderson Breaks Her Silence," http://abcnews.go.com/GMA/Entertainment/video/capri-anderson-breaks-silence-charlie-sheen-incident-12210384, accessed August 26, 2011; "Capri Anderson, Charlie Sheen's Escort during Drunk Plaza Hotel Rampage, Hid Porn Job from Folks," http://www.nydailynews.com/gossip/2010/10/28/2010-10-28_capri_anderson_charlie_sheens_escort_during_drunk_plaza_hotel_rampage_hid_porn_s.html, accessed August 26, 2011; "Charlie Sheen spent $12K on wine with Capri Anderson at Daniel Restaurant Prior to Hotel Breakdown," http://articles.nydailynews.com/2010-10-30/gossip/27079613_1_french-wine-cocaine-overdose-charlie-sheen, accessed, August 26, 2011.

2. Alain de Botton, *How to Think More about Sex* (London: Picador, 2012), 97ff.

3. A. K. Sandoval-Strausz, *Hotel: An American History* (New Haven: Yale University Press, 2007), 203–4.

4. The letter was posted on July 12, 2012, at http://www.thepublicdiscourse.com/2012/07/5815/, accessed June 20, 2013.

5. David Collins, *New Hotel: Architecture and Design* (London: Conran Octopus, 2001), 92.

6. "Woman Recounts Quarrel Leading to Agent Scandal," *New York Times*, April 18, 2012.

7. http://www.libraryhotel.com/offers.html, accessed February 1, 2013.

8. Rachel Kramer Bussel, *Do Not Disturb: Hotel Sex Stories* (San Francisco: Cleis Press, 2009), 5, 1.

9. http://www.hotelsexguide.com/, accessed February 1, 2013.

10. *Men's Health*, May 27, 2009.

11. http://www.sandiegoreader.com/news/2002/jun/06/hotel-porn; Egan, "EROTICA INC.—A Special Report; Technology Sent Wall Street into Market for Pornography," *New York Times*, October 23, 2000.

12. John Eligon, "What Happened in Room 2806: Three Possibilities," *New York Times*, July 8, 2011.

13. Curt Donovan, *Hotel Widow* (Boston: Beacon Books, 1965).

14. Karen Karbo, "Heartbreak Hotels," *New York Times*, June 13, 1999, http://www.nytimes.com/books/99/06/13/reviews/990613.13karbot.html.

15. Lisa Zeidner, *Layover* (New York: Random House, 1999), 240.

16. July 26, 2011, cover story in *US Weekly*, titled "Denise Richards Finally Opens Up about Charlie Sheen's Hotel Meltdown"; Denise Richards, *The Real Girl Next Door* (New York: Gallery, 2011).

17. Richards, *Real Girl Next Door*, 254–56.

18. "Meet Denise Richards' Baby Girl Eloise Joni!," *US Weekly*, July 20, 2011.

CHAPTER 3

1. http://www.nytimes.com/2012/03/15/opinion/hospitals-must-first-hurt-to-heal.html.

2. http://www.time.com/time/magazine/article/0,9171,729723,00.html.

3. http://www.nytimes.com/2007/02/13/nyregion/13ink.html.

4. John Martin Smith, *French Lick and West Baden Springs* (Mount Pleasant, S.C.: Arcadia Publishing, 2007); the postcard is reprinted on p. 19. Also see Greg Gatsos, *History of the West Baden Springs Hotel* (Springs Valley Herald, 1985).

5. http://www.crescentcourt.com/services_such/spa/.

6. http://www.nytimes.com/2011/08/30/business/companies-tiptoe-back-to-luxury-hotels.html.

7. Michel Foucault, *The Birth of the Clinic: An Archaeology of Medical Perception* (New York: Vintage Books, 1994), ix.

8. http://www.aetna.com/voluntary/hospital.html.

9. http://www.canyonranch.com/tucson/.

CHAPTER 4

1. http://hospitalityandtravelnews.weebly.com/celebrity-hotel-deaths.html.

2. http://www.dailymail.co.uk/news/article-1334120/Police-mistake-movie-set-murder-scene-grisly-murder-35-years.html.

3. http://www.telegraph.co.uk/health/healthnews/10011431/Hospital-hotels-for-30000-elderly-patients.html.

4. Nick Seddon, "Could State-Funded Patient Hotels be the Future?," *The Guardian*, March 26, 2013, http://www.theguardian.com/healthcare-network/2013/mar/26/state-funded-patient-hotels-future.

5. Siegfried Kracauer, "The Hotel Lobby," reprinted in *The Mass Ornament: Weimar Essays*, ed. Thomas Y. Levin (Cambridge, Mass.: Harvard University Press, 1995), 179.

6. http://query.nytimes.com/gst/abstract.html?res=F10A15F73F5F12738DDDA80894D1405B808DF1D3.

7. Paul Erling Groth, *Living Downtown: The History of Residential Hotels in the United States* (Berkeley: University of California Press, 1994), 222.

8. Simon Brett, *The Hanging in the Hotel* (New York: Berkley, 2004), 35.

9. http://www.cbsnews.com/2100-204_162-599070.html.

10. http://bjs.ojp.usdoj.gov/content/pub/pdf/shsplj.pdf.

11. http://eresearch.qmu.ac.uk/2199/.

12. Richard Harding Davis, "The Last Days of the Fair," *Harper's Weekly*, October 21, 1893, 1003.

13. For more information on Dr. Holmes's confession and hotel murders, see Judy Snavely, *Devil's Disciple: The Deadly Dr. H. H. Holmes* (Bloomington, Ind.: Authorhouse, 2006).

14. Erik Larson, *The Devil in the White City: Murder, Magic, and Madness at the Fair that Changed America* (New York: Vintage, 2004).

15. http://www.mirror.co.uk/news/uk-news/down-hall-country-house-hotel-1859016.

16. http://www.dailymail.co.uk/news/article-1334120/Police-mistake-movie-set-murder-scene-grisly-murder-35-years.html.

17. http://usnews.nbcnews.com/_news/2013/02/21/17043914-la-hotel-where-body-was-found-in-water-tank-has-chilling-history?lite.

CHAPTER 5

1. Pico Iyer, *The Global Soul: Jet Lag, Shopping Malls, and the Search for Home* (New York: Vintage, 2011).

2. Christine Skwiot, *The Purposes of Paradise: U.S. Tourism and Empire in Cuba and Hawai'i* (Philadelphia: University of Pennsylvania Press, 2010).

3. Edmundo O'Gorman, *The Invention of America: An Inquiry into the Historical Nature of the New World and the Meaning of Its History* (Westport, Conn.: Greenwood Press, 1972).

4. Jamaica Kincaid, *A Small Place* (New York: Farrar, Straus and Giroux, 2000).

5. Steven Gregory, *The Devil behind the Mirror: Globalization and Politics in the Dominican Republic* (Berkeley: University of California, 2006).

6. Dany Laferrière, *Heading South*, trans. Wayne Grady (Vancouver: Douglas & McIntyre, 2009).

7. Kamala Kempadoo, *Sun, Sex, and Gold: Tourism and Sex Work in the Caribbean* (London: Rowman & Littlefield, 1999).

8. E. A. DeMoya and R. Garcia, "Three Decades of Male Sex Work in Santo Domingo," in *Men Who Sell Sex: International Perspectives on Male Prostitution and HIV/AIDS*, ed. P. Aggleton (Philadelphia: Temple University Press, 1999), 127–40.

CHAPTER 6

1. Paul Groth, *Living Downtown: A History of Residential Hotels in the United States* (Berkeley: University of California Press, 1994).

2. Alan Burning, "Bring Back Flophouses, Rooming Houses, and Microapartments," *Slate*, July 17, 2013, http://www.slate.com/articles/business/moneybox/2013/07/sros_flophouses_microapartments_smart_cities_are_finally_allowing_the_right.html.

3. http://www.huduser.org/portal/publications/homeless/mckin/sro.html.

4. Bread of Life, Inc. website, http://s119575209.onlinehome.us/legacy_Structure.html, accessed September 12, 2014.

5. http://musicworldent.com/philanthropy.

6. Ted Steinberg, *Acts of God: The Unnatural History of Natural Disaster in America* (Oxford: Oxford University Press, 2006).

7. Richard Morgan, "Bleak House," *New York Times*, February 19, 2006.

8. http://www.indypressny.org/nycma/voices/192/news/news_3/; http://www.tripadvisor.com/Hotel_Review-g60763-d673661-Reviews-Sun_Bright_Hotel-New_York_City_New_York.html; http://www.hotels.com/ho375716/sun-bright-hotel-new-york-united-states/#reviews.

CHAPTER 7

1. Jim Kilby, Jim Fox, and Anthony Lucas, *Casino Operations Management* (New York: John Wiley & Sons, 2005), 49–59.

2. Robert Venturi, Denise Scott Brown, and Steven Izenour, *Learning from Las Vegas: The Forgotten Symbolism of Architectural Form* (Cambridge, Mass.: MIT Press, 1977), xi.

3. For more information on the history of gambling and the hotel casino, see, for example, Joseph Mazur, *What's Luck Got to Do with It? The History, Mathematics, and Psychology of the Gambler's Illusion* (Princeton: Princeton University Press, 2013); Herbert Ashbury, *Sucker's Progress: An Informal History of Gambling in America* (New York: Thunder's Mouth Press, 2003); and William Thompson, *Gambling in America: An Encyclopedia of History, Issues, and Society* (New York: ABC-CLIO, 2001).

4. E. Malcolm Greenless, *Casino Accounting and Financial Management* (Reno: University of Nevada Press, 1988).

5. Hans-Werner Sinn, *Casino Capitalism: How the Financial Crisis Came About and What Needs to Be Done Now* (New York: Oxford University Press, 2010).

6. John Maynard Keynes, *The General Theory of Employment, Interest, and Money* (London: Macmillan and Cambridge University Press, 1936), 142.

7. Earl Grinols, *Gambling in America: Costs and Benefits* (Champaign-Urbana: University of Illinois Press, 2004). For more regarding the social and economic impact of gambling, see, for example, Cathy Hsu, ed., *Legalized Casino Gaming in the United States: The Economic and Social Impact* (New York: Haworth Hospitality Press, 1999), and Robert Goodman, *The Luck Business: The Devastating Consequences and Broken Promises of America's Gambling Explosion* (New York: Free Press, 1995).

8. Jackson Lears, *Something for Nothing: Luck in America* (New York: Viking, 2003).

9. Bryant Simon, *Boardwalk of Dreams: Atlantic City and the Fate of Urban America* (New York: Oxford University Press, 2006), 221–22.

10. http://www.examiner.com/article/borgata-robbery-500-000-jewelry-stolen-from-borgata-casino-store.

11. http://www.forbes.com/sites/anthonydemarco/2013/07/02/smash-and-grab-borgata-theft-is-a-common-form-of-jewelry-store-burglaries/.

12. http://www.are.com/life-science-expertise.html.

13. http://investor.are.com/CorporateProfile.aspx?iid=111908.

CHAPTER 8

1. http://www.hotelcarter.com, accessed June 13, 2014.

2. "Carter Wears Smudged Crown as USA's 'Dirtiest Hotel,'" January 29, 2009, http://usatoday30.usatoday.com/travel/hotels/2009-01-29-carter-dirtiest-hotel_n.htm.

3. http://blogs.laweekly.com/informer/2011/10/hotel_hell_the_ford_hotel_is_g.php.

4. http://www.puretravel.com/blog/2009/04/15/7-worst-hotels-in-the-world/.

5. *1408*, dir. Mikael Håfström (2007).

6. http://www.wisconsinsickness.com/death-trip/maribel-caves-hotel-hell/.

7. http://www.unexplainedresearch.com/files_spectrology/maribel_hotel_hell.html.

8. http://www.puretravel.com/blog/2009/04/15/7-worst-hotels-in-the-world/.

9. http://www.youtube.com/watch?v=F3xO9IjckmU.

10. Ray Oldenburg, *The Great Good Place: Cafes, Coffee Shops, Community Centers, Beauty Parlors, General Stores, Bars, Hangouts, and How They Get You Through the Day* (New York: Paragon House, 1989).

CODA

1. David Brooks, "The Edamame Economy," *New York Times*, January 6, 2014.

2. http://www.boutiquehotelnews.com/home/blog/2012/12/18/boutique-hotel-future-trends-2013/.

3. http://eandt.theiet.org/magazine/2011/07/hotels-of-the-future.cfm.

4. http://www.l-a-v-a.net/projects/future-hotel/?locale=en_US.

5. http://www.forbes.com/sites/bethgreenfield/2012/04/20/hotels-of-the-future-7-architectural-stunners-on-the-horizon/.

6. http://www.sinehead.com/Gaudi1.html.

7. "Gaudí Design Proposed for World Trade Centre," *BBC News*, January 23, 2003.

8. http://www.sinehead.com/Gaudi2.html.

9. http://www.youtube.com/watch?v=wDof_56hSTc.

Index